W9-AWF-652

THE BOOK OF **UNDERSTANDING**

More OSHO Books

INSIGHTS FOR A NEW WAY OF LIVING SERIES

Awareness
Courage
Creativity
Freedom
Intelligence
Intimacy
Intuition
Joy
Maturity

OTHER BOOKS

Autobiography of a Spiritually Incorrect Mystic
The Book of Secrets
Pharmacy for the Soul
Love, Freedom, Aloneness
Meditation: The First and Last Freedom
Sex Matters
Your Answers Questioned
Osho Transformation Tarot
Osho Zen Tarot
Tao: The Pathless Path
Zen: The Path of Paradox
Yoga: The Science of the Soul
Tarot in the Spirit of Zen
Meditation for Busy People
Body Mind Balancing
The ABC of Enlightenment

AUDIO

Book of Secrets: Keys to Love and Meditation
Osho *Meditations on Buddhism*
Osho *Meditations on Sufism*
Osho *Meditations on Tantra*
Osho *Meditations on Tao*
Osho *Meditations on Yoga*
Osho *Meditations on Zen*

Creating
your own path
to freedom

OSHO

THE BOOK OF UNDERSTANDING

Harmony Books
New York

Published in the United States by Harmony Books, an imprint of the Crown Publishing Group, a division of Random House, Inc., New York.
www.crownpublishing.com

The material in this book is selected from various discourses by Osho given to a live audience. All of the Osho discourses have been published in full as books and are also available as original audio recordings. Audio recordings and the complete text archive can be found via the online OSHO Library at www.osho.com.

Library of Congress Cataloging-in-Publication Data
Osho, 1931–1990.
The book of understanding: creating your own path to freedom / Osho.—1st ed.
1. Spiritual life—Osho International Foundation. I. Title.
BP605.R34B678 2006
299'.93—dc22 2005023978

ISBN-13: 978-0-307-33694-1
ISBN-10: 0-307-33694-8

Printed in the United States of America

DESIGN BY BARBARA STURMAN

10 9 8 7 6 5 4 3 2 1

First Edition

I do not believe in believing. My approach is to know, and knowing is a totally different dimension. It starts from doubt, it does not start from believing. The moment you believe in something, you have stopped inquiring. Belief is one of the most poisonous things to destroy human intelligence.

All the religions are based on belief; only science is based on doubt. And I would like the religious inquiry also to be scientific, based on doubt, so that we need not believe but we can come to know someday the truth of our being, and the truth of the whole universe.

CONTENTS

THE BOOK OF **UNDERSTANDING**

PREFACE

A New Spirituality for the 21st Century

Not a political revolution but an individual rebellion

A revolutionary is part of the political world; his approach is through politics. His understanding is that changing the social structure is enough to change the human being.

A rebel, as I use the term, is a spiritual phenomenon. His approach is absolutely individual. His vision is that if we want to change the society, we have to change the individual. Society in itself does not exist; it is only a word, like "crowd"—if you go to find it, you will not find it anywhere. Wherever you encounter someone, you will encounter an individual. "Society" is only a collective name—just a name, not a reality—with no substance.

The individual has a soul, has a possibility of evolution, of change, of transformation. Hence, the difference is tremendous.

The rebel is the very essence of religion. He brings into the world a change of consciousness—and if the consciousness changes, then the structure of the society is bound to follow it. But vice versa is not the case, and it has been proved by all the revolutions because they have all failed.

No revolution has yet succeeded in changing human beings; but it seems we are not aware of the fact. We still go on thinking in terms of revolution, of changing society, of changing the government, of changing the bureaucracy, of changing laws, political systems. Feudalism, capitalism, communism, socialism, fascism—

they were all in their own way revolutionary. They all have failed, and failed utterly, because man has remained the same.

A Gautam Buddha, a Zarathustra, a Jesus—these people are rebels. Their trust is in the individual. They have not succeeded either, but their failure is totally different than the failure of the revolutionary. Revolutionaries have tried their methodology in many countries, in many ways, and have failed. But the approach of a Gautam Buddha has not succeeded because it has not been tried. A Jesus has not succeeded because the Jews crucified him and the Christians buried him. He has not been tried—he has not even been given a chance. The rebel is still an unexplored dimension.

We have to be rebels, not revolutionaries. The revolutionary belongs to a very mundane sphere; the rebel and his rebelliousness are sacred. The revolutionary cannot stand alone; he needs a crowd, a political party, a government. He needs power—and power corrupts, and absolute power corrupts absolutely.

All the revolutionaries who have succeeded in capturing power have been corrupted by the power. They could not change the nature of power and its institutions; the power changed them and their minds, and corrupted them. Only names became different, but the society continued to be the same.

Human consciousness has not grown for centuries. Only once in a while someone blossoms—but in millions of people, the blossoming of one person is not a rule, it is the exception. And because that person is alone, the crowd cannot tolerate him. His existence becomes a kind of humiliation; his very presence feels insulting because he opens your eyes, makes you aware of your potential and your future. And it hurts your ego that you have done nothing to grow, to be more conscious, to be more loving, more ecstatic, more creative, more silent—to create a beautiful world around you. You have not contributed to the world; your existence has not been a blessing here but a curse. You introduce into the world your anger, your violence, your jealousy, your competitiveness, your lust for power. You make the world a battlefield; you are bloodthirsty, and you make others bloodthirsty. You deprive humanity of its humanness. You help man to fall below humanity, even sometimes below animals.

Hence a Gautam Buddha or a Chuang Tzu hurts you because they have blossomed and you are just standing there. Springs come and go, and nothing blossoms in you. No birds come and make their nests near you and sing their songs around you. It is better to crucify a Jesus and poison a Socrates—just to remove them, so that you need not feel in any way spiritually inferior.

The world has known only very few rebels. But now is the time: if humanity proves incapable of producing a large number of rebels, a rebellious spirit, then our days on the earth are numbered. Then the coming decades may become our graveyard. We are coming very close to that point.

We have to change our consciousness, create more meditative energy in the world, create more lovingness. We have to destroy the old—its ugliness, its rotten ideologies, its stupid discriminations, idiotic superstitions—and create a new human being with fresh eyes, with new values. A discontinuity with the past—that's the meaning of rebelliousness.

These three words will help you to understand: reform, revolution, and rebellion.

Reform means a modification. The old remains and you give it a new form, a new shape—it is a kind of renovation to an old building. The original structure remains; you whitewash it, you clean it, you create a few windows, a few new doors.

Revolution goes deeper than reform. The old remains, but more changes are introduced, changes even in its basic structure. You are not only changing its color and opening a few new windows and doors, but perhaps building new stories, taking it higher into the sky. But the old is not destroyed, it remains hidden behind the new; in fact, it remains the very foundation of the new. Revolution is a continuity with the old.

Rebellion is a discontinuity. It is not reform, it is not revolution; it is simply disconnecting yourself from all that is old. The old religions, the old political ideologies, the old human being—all that is old, you disconnect yourself from it. You start life afresh, from scratch.

The revolutionary tries to change the old; the rebel simply comes out of the old, just as the snake slips out of the old skin and never looks back.

Unless we create such rebellious people around the earth, humanity has no future. The old man has brought us to our ultimate death. It is the old mind, the old ideologies, the old religions—they have all combined together to bring about this situation of global suicide. Only a new human being can save humanity and this planet, and the beautiful life of this planet.

I teach rebellion, not revolution. To me, rebelliousness is the essential quality of a religious person. It is spirituality in its absolute purity.

The days of revolution are over. The French revolution failed, the Russian revolution failed, the Chinese revolution failed. In India, even the Gandhian revolution failed, and it failed in front of Gandhi's own eyes. He was teaching nonviolence his whole life, and in front of his own eyes the country was divided; millions of people were killed, burned alive; millions of women were raped. Gandhi himself was shot dead. That is a strange end for a nonviolent saint.

And in the process, he himself forgot all his teachings. Before his revolution was secured, Gandhi was asked by an American thinker, Louis Fischer, "What are you going to do with the arms, armies, and all the different weapons, when India becomes an independent country?"

Gandhi said, "I'm going to throw all the arms into the ocean and send all the armies to work in the fields and in the gardens."

And Louis Fischer asked, "But have you forgotten? Somebody can invade your country."

Gandhi said, "We will welcome them. If somebody invades us, we will accept him as a guest and tell him, 'You can also live here, just the way we are living. There is no need to fight.'"

But he completely forgot all his philosophy—that's how revolutions fail. It is very beautiful to talk about these things, but when power comes into your hands . . . First, Mahatma Gandhi did not accept any post in the government. It was out of fear, because how was he going to answer the whole world if they asked about throwing the weapons into the ocean? What about sending the armies to work in the fields? He escaped from the responsibility for which he had been fighting his whole life, seeing that it was going to create tremendous trouble for him. If he had accepted a position in the government, he would have had to contradict his own philosophy.

But the government was made up of his disciples, people chosen by him. He did not ask them to dissolve the armies; when Pakistan attacked India, he did not say to the Indian government, "Now go to the borders and welcome the invaders as guests." Instead, he blessed the first three airplanes that were going to bomb Pakistan. Those airplanes flew over the villa where he was staying in New Delhi, and he came out into the garden to bless them. With his blessings they went ahead to destroy his own people, who just a few days before were "our brothers and our sisters." Unashamedly, without ever seeing the contradiction . . .

The Russian revolution failed in front of Lenin's eyes. He was preaching according to Karl Marx, that "when the revolution comes, we will dissolve marriage, because marriage is part of private property. As private property disappears, marriage will also disappear. People can be lovers, can live together; children will be taken care of by the society." But when it came about that the power was in the hands of the Communist Party and Lenin was the leader, everything changed. Once power comes into their hands, people start thinking differently. Now Lenin's thinking was that to make people so independent of responsibilities could be dangerous—they could become too individualistic. So let them be burdened with a family—he forgot all about dissolving families.

It is strange how revolutions have failed, failed at the hands of the revolutionaries themselves, because once the power comes into their hands they start thinking in different ways. Then they become too attached to their power. Then their whole effort is in how to keep the power forever in their hands, and how to keep the people under control.

The future needs no more revolutions. The future needs a new experiment, which has not been tried yet. Although for thousands of years there have been rebels, they remained alone—individuals. Perhaps the time was not ripe for them. But now the time is not only ripe . . . if you don't hurry, the time has come to an end. In the coming decades, either mankind will disappear or a new human being with a new vision will appear on the earth. That new human being will be a rebel.

WORLDLY VS. OTHERWORLDLY

Understanding the Great Divide

I propose a new religiousness. It will not be Christianity and it will not be Judaism and it will not be Hinduism; this religiousness will not have any adjective to it. It will be purely a quality of being whole.

Religion has failed. Science has failed. The East has failed, and the West has failed. Something of a higher synthesis is needed in which East and West can have a meeting, in which religion and science can have a meeting.

The human being is like a tree, with its roots in the earth and the potential to flower. Religion has failed because it was talking only of the flowers—and those flowers remain philosophical, abstract; they never materialize. They could not materialize because they were not supported by the earth. And science has failed because it has cared only about the roots. The roots are ugly, and there seems to be no flowering. Religion has failed because it was otherworldly and it neglected this world. And you cannot neglect this world—to neglect this world is to neglect your own roots. Science has failed because it neglected the other world, the inner, and you cannot neglect the flowers. Once you neglect the flowers, the innermost core of being, life loses all meaning.

Just as the tree needs roots, so does the human being need roots—and the roots can only be in the earth. The tree needs an open sky to grow into, to come to great foliage and to have thousands of flowers. Then only is the tree fulfilled; then only does the tree feel significance and meaning, and life becomes relevant.

The West is suffering from too much science, and the East has suffered from too much religion. Now we need a new humanity in which religion and science become two aspects of one humanity. And once we have brought this new humanity into existence, the earth can become for the first time what it is meant to become. It can become a paradise: this very body the Buddha, this very earth the paradise.

Zorba the Buddha: A meeting of earth and sky

My concept of a new human being is one that will be Zorba the Greek and will also be Gautam the Buddha: the new human being will be "Zorba the Buddha"—sensuous and spiritual. Physical, utterly physical—in the body, in the senses, enjoying the body and all that the body makes possible—and still a great consciousness, a great witnessing will be there. Zorba the Buddha—it has never happened before.

That's what I'm talking about when I talk about a meeting of the East and the West, the meeting of materialism and spirituality. That's my idea of Zorba the Buddha: heaven and earth are united.

I want there to be no schizophrenia, no split between matter and spirit, between the mundane and the sacred, between this-worldly and that-worldly. I don't want any split, because every split is a split in you. And any person, any humanity that is divided against itself is going to be crazy and insane. We are living in a crazy and insane world. It can be sane only if this split can be bridged.

Mankind has lived believing either in the reality of the soul and the illusoriness of matter, or in the reality of matter and the illusoriness of the soul. You can divide the humanity of the past into those who are spiritual and those who are materialists. But nobody has bothered to look at the reality of the human being. We are both together. We are neither just spirituality—not just consciousness—nor are we just matter. We are a tremendous harmony between matter and consciousness. Or perhaps matter and consciousness are not two things but only two aspects of one reality: Matter is the outside of consciousness, and consciousness is the interiority of matter. But there has not been a single philosopher, sage, or religious mystic in the past who has declared this unity; they were all in favor of dividing the human being, calling one side real and the other side unreal. This has created an atmosphere of schizophrenia all over the earth.

You cannot live just as a body. That's what Jesus means when he says, "Man cannot live by bread alone"—but this is only half the truth. You need consciousness, you cannot live by bread alone, true—but you cannot live without bread, either. You have both dimensions to your being, and both dimensions have to be fulfilled, to be given equal opportunity for growth. But the past has been either in favor of one and against the other, or in favor of the other and against the first. Man as a totality has not been accepted.

This has created misery, anguish, and a tremendous darkness; a night that has lasted for thousands of years and seems to have no end. If you only listen to the body, you condemn yourself to a meaningless existence. And if you don't listen to the body, you suffer—you are hungry, you are poor, you are thirsty. If you listen only to consciousness, your growth will be lopsided. Your consciousness will grow, but your body will shrink and the balance will be lost. And in the balance is your health, in the balance is your wholeness, in the balance is your joy, your song, your dance.

The materialist has chosen to listen to the body and has become completely deaf as far as the reality of consciousness is concerned. The ultimate result is great science, great technology—an affluent society, a richness of things that are mundane, worldly. And amidst all this abundance there is a poor human being without a soul, completely lost—not knowing who he is, not knowing why he is, feeling almost like an accident or a freak of nature.

Unless consciousness grows along with the richness of the material world, the body becomes too heavy and the soul becomes too weak. You are burdened by your own inventions, your own discoveries. Rather than creating a beautiful life for you, they create a life that is felt by intelligent people to be not worth living.

The East in the past has chosen consciousness and has condemned matter and everything material, the body included, as *maya*. They have called it illusory, a mirage in a desert that only appears to exist but has no reality in itself. The East has created a Gautam Buddha, a Mahavira, a Patanjali, a Kabir, a Farid, a Raidas—a long line of people with great consciousness, with great awareness. But it has also created millions of poor people, hungry, starving, dying like dogs—with not enough food, no pure water to drink, not enough clothes, not enough shelter.

A strange situation. . . . In the developed countries every six months they have to drown millions and millions of dollars' worth of foodstuffs in the ocean, because it is surplus. They don't want to overload their warehouses, they don't want to lower their prices and destroy their economic structure. On the one hand, in Ethiopia a thousand people are dying every day, and on the other hand the European Common Market is destroying so much food that the cost of destroying it is in the millions of dollars. That is not the cost of the food; it is the cost of taking it and throwing it into the ocean. Who is responsible for this situation?

The richest man in the West is searching for his soul and finding himself hollow—without any love, only lust; without any prayer, only parrotlike words that he has been taught in the Sunday schools. He has no sense of spirituality, no feeling for other human beings, no reverence for life, for birds, for trees, for animals. Destruction is so easy—Hiroshima and Nagasaki would never have happened if people were not thought to be just things. So many nuclear weapons would not have been piled up if the human being had been considered to be a hidden god, a hidden splendor—not to be destroyed but to be discovered, not to be destroyed but to be brought into the light, with the body as a temple for the spirit. But if a human being is just matter—just chemistry, physics, a skeleton covered with skin—then with death everything dies, nothing remains. That's why it becomes possible for an Adolf Hitler to kill six million people—if people are just matter, there is no question of even thinking twice.

The West, in its pursuit of material abundance, lost its soul, its interiority. Surrounded by meaninglessness, boredom, anguish, it cannot find its own humanity. All the success of science proves to be of no use—because the house is full of things, but the master of the house is missing. In the East, the end result of centuries of considering matter to be illusory and only consciousness to be real has been that the master is alive but the house is empty. It is difficult to rejoice with hungry stomachs, with sick bodies, with death surrounding you; it is impossible to meditate. So, unnecessarily, they have been losers.

All the saints and all the philosophers—the spiritual and the materialist both—are responsible for this immense crime against humanity.

Zorba the Buddha is the answer. It is the synthesis of matter and soul. It is a declaration that there is no conflict between matter and consciousness, that we can be rich on both sides. We can have everything that the world can provide, everything that science and technology can produce, and we can still have everything that a Buddha, a Kabir, a Nanak finds in his inner being—the flowers of ecstasy, the fragrance of godliness, the wings of ultimate freedom.

Zorba the Buddha is the new human being, is the rebel. The rebellion consists of destroying the schizophrenia of humanity, destroying the dividedness—destroying the idea that spirituality is against materialism and materialism is against spirituality. It is a manifesto that body and soul are together. Existence is full of spirituality—even mountains are alive, even trees are sensitive. It is a declaration that the whole of existence is both material and spiritual—or perhaps just one energy expressing itself in two ways, as matter and as consciousness. When energy is purified, it expresses itself as consciousness; when energy is crude, unpurified, dense, it appears as matter. But the whole of existence is nothing but an energy field. This is my experience, it is not my philosophy. And it is supported by modern physics and its research: Existence is energy.

We can allow ourselves to have both the worlds together. We need not renounce this world to get the other world; neither have we to deny the other world to enjoy this world. In fact, to have only one world while you are capable of having both is to be unnecessarily poor.

Zorba the Buddha is the richest possibility. We will live our nature to its utmost and we will sing songs of this earth. We will not betray the earth, and we will not betray the sky either. We will claim all that this earth has—all the flowers, all the pleasures—and we will also claim all the stars of the sky. We will claim the whole existence as our home.

All that existence contains is for us, and we have to use it in every possible way—without any guilt, without any conflict, without any choice. Choicelessly enjoy all that matter is capable of, and rejoice in all that consciousness is capable of.

There is an ancient story. . . .

In a forest near a city there lived two beggars. Naturally they were enemies to each other, as all professionals are—two doctors, two professors, two saints. One beggar was blind and one was lame, and they were very competitive; the whole day they were competing with each other in the city.

But one night their huts caught fire, because the whole forest was on fire. The blind man could run out, but he could not see where to go. He could not see the places where the fire had not yet spread. The lame man could see where there were still possibilities of escaping from the fire, but he could not run. The fire was spreading fast, so the lame man could only see his death coming.

They realized that they needed each other. The lame man had a sudden realization: "The other man can run, the blind man can run and I can see." They forgot all their competition. In such a critical moment, when both were facing death, each necessarily forgot all stupid enmities. They created a great synthesis; they agreed that the blind man would carry the lame man on his shoulders and they would function as one person—the lame man could see, and the blind man could run, and in this way they saved their lives. And because they saved each other's lives they became friends; for the first time they dropped their antagonism.

Zorba is blind—he cannot see, but he can dance, he can sing, he can rejoice. The Buddha can see, but he can *only* see. He is pure eyes, just clarity and perception—but he cannot dance. He is crippled, he cannot sing, he cannot rejoice.

It is time. The world is on fire and everybody's life is in danger. The meeting of Zorba and Buddha can save the whole of humanity. Their meeting is the only hope. Buddha can contribute consciousness, clarity, the eyes to see beyond, the eyes to see that which is almost invisible. Zorba can give his whole being to Buddha's vision—and his participation will make sure that it does not remain just a dry vision but a dancing, rejoicing, ecstatic way of life.

? **Is the meeting of Zorba and the Buddha really possible? If it is, then why have other religious leaders never thought about it?**

The first thing to be understood: I am not a religious leader. A religious leader cannot think of things, cannot see things the way I can, for the simple reason that he has an immense investment in religion; I have none.

Religions are necessarily splitting people, creating a duality in the human mind. That is their way of exploiting you. If you are whole, you are beyond their control. If you are cut in fragments, then all your strength is destroyed, all your power, your dignity abolished. Then you can be a Christian, a Hindu, a Mohammedan. If you are left just the way you are born—natural, without any interference from the so-called religious leaders, you will have freedom, independence, integrity. You cannot be enslaved. And all your old religions are doing nothing but enslaving you.

To enslave you, they have to create a conflict within you so you start fighting with yourself. When you are fighting with yourself, two things are bound to happen. First, you will be miserable, because no part of you can ever be victorious, you will be always defeated. Second, a feeling of guilt is produced in you that you are not worthy to be called a real, authentic human individual. This is what the religious leaders want. A deep feeling of unworthiness within you makes them leaders. You cannot depend on yourself because you know you cannot do anything. You cannot do what your nature wants, because your religions prevent it; you cannot do what your religions want, because your nature is against it. You find yourself in a situation where you cannot do anything; somebody else is needed to take responsibility for you.

Your physical age goes on growing, but your mental age remains retarded, just around thirteen. Such retarded people are in great need of somebody to guide them, somebody to lead them to the goal of life, to the meaning of life. They themselves are incapable. Religious leaders could not have thought of the meeting of Zorba and Buddha because that would have been the end of their leadership and the end of their so-called religions.

Zorba the Buddha is the end of all religions. It is the beginning of a new kind of religiousness that needs no labels—no Christianity, Judaism, Buddhism. One is simply enjoying oneself, enjoying this immense universe, dancing with the trees, playing on the beach with the waves, collecting seashells for no other purpose than just for the sheer joy of it. The salty air, the cool sand, the sun rising, a good jog—what more do you want? To me, this is religion—enjoying the air, enjoying the sea, enjoying the sand, enjoying the sun—because there is no other God than existence itself.

Zorba the Buddha, on the one hand, is the end of the old humanity—the old religions, politics, nations, racial discriminations, and all kinds of stupidities. On the other hand, Zorba the Buddha is the beginning of a new humanity—totally free to be ourselves, allowing our nature to blossom.

There is no conflict between Zorba and Buddha. The conflict has been created by the so-called religions. Is there any conflict between your body and your soul? Is there any conflict between your life and your consciousness? Is there any conflict between your right hand and your left hand? They are all one, in an organic unity.

Your body is not something to be condemned but something to be grateful for, because it is the greatest thing in existence, the most miraculous; its workings are just unbelievable. All the parts of your body are functioning like an orchestra. Your eyes, your hands, your legs are in some inner communion. It is not that your eyes want to go towards the east and your legs are going towards the west, that you are hungry but your mouth refuses to eat. "Hunger is in your stomach, what has it to do with the mouth?"—the mouth is on strike. No, your body has no conflict. It moves in some inner synchronicity, always together. And your soul is not something opposed to your body. If your body is the house, the soul is your guest, and there is no need for the guest and the host to continuously fight. But the religions could not exist without you fighting with yourself.

My insistence on your organic unity, so that your materialism is no longer opposed to spirituality, is basically to demolish all these organized religions from the earth. Once your body and soul start moving hand in hand, dancing together, you have become Zorba the Buddha. Then you can enjoy everything of this life, everything that is outside you, and you can also enjoy everything that is within you.

In fact, the within and without operate in totally different dimensions; they never come in conflict. But thousands of years of conditioning—that if you want the inner you have to renounce the outer—has taken deep roots in you. Otherwise, it is such an absurd idea. . . . You are allowed to enjoy the inner—what is the problem in enjoying the outer? The enjoyment is the same; that enjoyment is the joining link between the inner and the outer.

Listening to beautiful music, or looking at a great painting, or seeing a dancer like Nijinsky—it is outside you, but it is in no way a hindrance to your inner rejoicing. On the contrary, it is a great help. The dance of Nijinsky may bring out the dormant quality of your soul so that it can also dance. The music of a Ravi Shankar may start playing on the strings of your heart. The outer and inner are not divided. It is one energy, two aspects of one existence.

Zorba can become Buddha more easily than any pope. There is no possibility for a pope, no possibility for your so-called saints to become really spiritual. They don't know even the joys of the body—how can you think they will be able to know the subtle joys of the spirit? The body is the school where you learn, in shallow water, to swim. And once you have learned swimming, then it does not matter how deep the water is. Then you can go to the deepest part of the lake; it is all the same to you.

You have to be reminded about Buddha's life. Up to his twenty-ninth year, he was a pure Zorba. He had the most beautiful young girls available in his kingdom, by the dozen. His whole palace was full of music and dance. He had the best food, best clothes, beautiful palaces to live in, great gardens. He lived more deeply than poor Zorba the Greek.

Zorba the Greek had only one girlfriend—an old, faded woman, a prostitute who had lost all her customers. She had false teeth, false hair—and Zorba was her customer only because he could not afford to pay anybody else. You call him a materialist, a hedonist, and you forget completely the first twenty-nine years of Buddha's life, which were far richer. Day in, day out, this prince called Siddhartha was simply living in luxury, surrounded by everything that he could imagine. He was living in a dreamland. It was this experience that turned him into a Buddha.

It has not usually been analyzed this way. Nobody bothers

about the first part of his life—which is the very foundation. He became fed up. He tasted every joy of the outside; now he wanted something more, something deeper, which was not available in the outside world. For the deeper you have to jump in. At the age of twenty-nine he left the palace in the middle of the night, in search of the inner. He was a Zorba going in search of the Buddha.

Zorba the Greek never became a buddha for the simple reason that his Zorba-hood was incomplete. He was a beautiful man, full of zest, but poor. He wanted to live life in its intensity, but he had no opportunity to live it. He danced, he sang, but he did not know the higher nuances of music. He did not know the dance where the dancer disappears.

The Zorba in Buddha knew the highest and the deepest of the outside world. Knowing it all, now he was ready to go on an inner search. The world was good, but not good enough; something more was needed. It gave momentary glimpses, and the Buddha wanted something eternal. All these joys would be finished by death, and he wanted to know something that would not be finished by death.

If I were to write Gautam Buddha's life, I would start it from Zorba. When he is completely acquainted with the outer and whatever the outside can give, and still finds the meaning missing, he goes in search—because that is the only direction that he has not explored. He never looks back—there is no reason to look back, he has lived it all! He is not just a "religious seeker" who has not known the outer at all. He is a Zorba—and he goes towards the inner with the same zest, with the same strength, the same power. And, obviously, he finds in his innermost being the contentment, the fulfillment, the meaning, the benediction that he has been seeking.

It is possible you can be a Zorba and stop there. It is possible that you may not be a Zorba and start looking for the Buddha—

you will not find him. Only a Zorba can find the Buddha; otherwise, you don't have the strength: you have not lived in the outside world, you have avoided it. You are an escapist.

To me, to be a Zorba is the beginning of the journey, and to become a buddha is reaching the goal. And it can happen in the same individual—it can *only* happen in the same individual. That's why I am insisting continually: Don't create any split in your life, don't condemn anything of the body. Live it—not unwillingly—live it totally, intensely. That very living will make you capable of another search. You don't have to be ascetics, you don't have to leave your wives, your husbands, your children. All that nonsense has been taught for centuries, and how many people—out of millions of monks and nuns—how many people have blossomed? Not one.

Live life undivided. And first comes the body, first comes your outer world. The moment the child is born he opens his eyes, and the first thing he sees is the whole panorama of existence around him. He sees everything except himself—that is for more experienced people. That is for those who have seen everything of the outside, lived it, and are freed from it.

Freedom from the outside does not come by escaping. Freedom from the outside comes by living it totally, and then there is nowhere else to go. Only one dimension remains, and it is natural that you would like to search in that remaining dimension. And there is your buddhahood, your enlightenment.

You are asking, "Is it possible that Zorba and Buddha can meet?" That is the only possibility. Without Zorba there is no Buddha. Zorba, of course, is not the end. He is the preparation for the Buddha. He is the roots; Buddha is the flowering. Don't destroy the roots; otherwise there is not going to be any flowering. Those roots continuously supply the juice to the flowers. All the color in the flowers comes from the roots, and all the fragrance in the flowers comes from the roots. All the dance of the flowers in the wind comes from the roots.

Do not divide. Roots and flowers are two ends of one phenomenon.

? **It seems so difficult to bring these two aspects of life together, because it goes against our whole conditioning. Where do we start?**

Do things with your whole heart, with as much intensity as you are capable of.

Anything done halfheartedly never brings joy to life. It only brings misery, anxiety, torture, and tension, because whenever you do anything halfheartedly you are dividing yourself into two parts, and that is one of the greatest calamities that has happened to human beings—they are all split. The misery in the world is not surprising; it is a natural outcome of living halfheartedly, doing everything only with one part of our being while the other part is resisting, opposing, fighting.

And whatever you do with half of your being is going to bring you repentance, misery, and a feeling that perhaps the other part that was not participating was right—because following this part, you have attained nothing but a miserable state. But I say to you: If you had followed the other part, the result would have been the same. It is not a question of which part you follow, it is a question of whether you go totally into it or not. To be total in your action brings joy. Even an ordinary, trivial action done with total intensity brings a glow to your being, a fulfillment, a fullness, a deep contentment. And anything done halfheartedly, however good the thing may be, is going to bring misery.

Misery does not come from your actions, neither does joy come from your actions. Joy comes when you are total. It does not matter what action you are involved in, misery is the outcome when you are partial. And living a halfhearted life is creating a hell for yourself every moment—and this hell goes on becoming bigger and bigger.

People ask, is there a hell somewhere, or is there a heaven somewhere?—because all the religions have been talking about hell and heaven as if they are part of the geography of the universe. They are not geographical phenomena, they are in your psychology.

When your mind, when your heart, when your being is pulled in two directions simultaneously, you are creating hell. And when you are total, one, an organic unity . . . in that very organic unity, the flowers of heaven start blossoming in you.

People have remained concerned about their acts: Which act is right and which act is wrong? What is good and what is evil? My own understanding is that it is not a question of any particular act. The question is about your psychology.

When you are total, it is good; and when you are divided, it is evil. Divided you suffer; united, you dance, you sing, you celebrate.

Can you say more about the art of balancing these opposites? My life is often an experience of extremes, and the middle way seems difficult to maintain for any length of time.

Life consists of extremes. Life is a tension between the opposites. To be exactly in the middle forever means to be dead. The middle is only a theoretical possibility; only once in a while are you in the middle, as a passing phase. It is like walking on a tightrope; you can never be exactly in the middle for any length of time. If you try, you will fall.

To be in the middle is not a static state, it is a dynamic phenomenon. Balance is not a noun, it is a verb; it is *balancing*. The tightrope-walker continuously moves from the left to the right, from the right to the left. When he feels now he has moved too much to one side and there is a danger of falling, he immediately balances himself by moving to the opposite side. In passing from the left to the right, yes, there is a moment when the tightrope-walker is in the middle. And again, when he has moved too much to the right and there is a fear of falling, he is losing balance, he starts moving to the left and again passes through the middle for a moment.

This is what I mean when I say balance is not a noun but a verb—it is balancing, it is a dynamic process. You cannot just be in the middle. You can go on moving from left to right and right to left; this is the only way to remain in the middle.

Don't avoid the extremes, and don't choose any one extreme. Remain available to both the polarities—that is the art, the secret of balancing. Yes, sometimes be utterly happy, and sometimes be utterly sad—both have their own beauties.

The mind is a chooser; that's why the problem arises. Remain choiceless. Whatever happens, and wherever you are—right or left, in the middle or not in the middle—enjoy the moment in its totality. While happy, dance, sing, play music—be happy! And when sadness comes—which is bound to come, which has to come, which is inevitable, you cannot avoid it . . . If you try to avoid it you will have to destroy the very possibility of happiness. The day cannot exist without the night, and the summer cannot exist without the winter. Life cannot be without death. Let this polarity sink deep in your being—there is no way to avoid it. The only way is to become more and more dead; only a dead person can exist in a static middle. The alive person will be constantly moving—from anger to compassion, from compassion to anger—and accepting both, not identified with either but remaining aloof and yet involved, distant yet committed. The alive person enjoys and yet remains like a lotus flower—in the water, yet the water cannot touch it.

Your very effort to be in the middle, and to be in the middle forever and always, is creating unnecessary anxiety for you. In fact, a desire to be in the middle forever is another extreme—the worst kind of extreme, because it is the impossible kind. It cannot be fulfilled. Just think of an old-fashioned clock: If you hold the pendulum exactly in the middle, the clock will stop. The clock works only because the pendulum goes on moving from the left to the right, from the right to the left. Yes, each time it passes through the middle, and there is a moment of that middle-ness, but only a moment.

And it is beautiful! When you pass from happiness to sadness, from sadness to happiness, there is a moment of utter silence, exactly in the middle—enjoy that too.

Life has to be lived in all its dimensions, only then is life rich. The leftist is poor, the rightist is poor, and the middlist is dead! When you are alive you are neither rightist nor leftist nor middlist—you are a constant movement, a flow.

Why do we want to be in the middle in the first place? We are afraid of the dark side of life; we don't want to be sad, we don't want to be in a state of agony. But that is possible only if you are also ready to drop the possibility of being in ecstasy. There are a few who have chosen it—that is the way of the monk. For centuries that has been the way of the monk, ready to sacrifice all possibilities of ecstasy just to avoid agony. He is ready to destroy all the roses just to avoid the thorns. But then his life is just flat . . . a long, long boredom, stale, stagnant. He does not really live. He is afraid to live.

Life contains both; it brings great pain, and it also brings great pleasure. Pain and pleasure are two sides of the same coin. If you exclude one, you have to exclude the other, too. This has been one of the most fundamental misunderstandings down the ages, that you can get rid of pain and save pleasure, that you can avoid hell and have heaven, that you can avoid the negative and can have only the positive. This is a great fallacy. It is not possible in the very nature of things. The positive and negative are together, inevitably together, indivisibly together. They are two aspects of the same energy. We have to accept both.

Include all, be all. When you are on the left, don't miss anything—enjoy it! Being on the left has its own beauty, a beauty you will not find when you are on the right. It will be a different scene. And, yes, to be in the middle has a silence, a peace, and you will not find it on any extreme. So enjoy all of it. Go on enriching your life.

Can't you see any beauty in sadness? Meditate over it. Next time, when you are sad don't fight with it. Don't waste time in fighting—accept it, welcome it, let it be a welcome guest. Look deep into it with love, care . . . be a real host! And you will be surprised—you will be surprised beyond your comprehension—sadness has a few beauties that happiness can never have. Sadness has depth, and happiness is shallow. Sadness has tears, and tears go deeper than any laughter can ever go. Sadness has a silence of its own, a melody, which happiness can never have. Happiness will have its own song but more noisy, not so silent.

I am not saying to choose sadness. I am just saying, enjoy it too. When you are happy, enjoy happiness. Swim on the surface, and sometimes dive deep into the river. It is the same river! On the surface is the play of ripples and waves, and the sun rays and the wind—it has its own beauty. Diving deep into the water has its own quality, its own adventure, its own dangers.

And don't become attached to anything. There are people who have become attached to sadness, too—psychologists know about them, they are called masochists. They go on creating situations in which they can remain miserable forever. Misery is the only thing they enjoy, they are afraid of happiness. In misery they are at home. Many masochists become religious, because religion provides a great protection for the masochist's mind. Religion gives a beautiful rationalization for being a masochist.

Just being a masochist without being religious, you will feel condemned and you will feel ill, ill at ease, and you will know that you are abnormal. You will feel guilty about what you are doing to your life, and you will try to hide it. But if a masochist becomes religious he can exhibit his masochism with great pride, because now it is no longer masochism—it is asceticism, it is austerity. It is "self-discipline," not torture. Only the labels have been changed—now nobody can call the person abnormal, he is a saint! Nobody can call him pathological; he is pious, holy. Masochists have always moved toward religion, it has a great attraction for them. In fact, so many masochists down the ages have moved toward religion—and it was natural, that movement—that ultimately religion grew to be dominated by masochists. That's why so much of religion insists on being life-negative, life-destructive. It is not for life, it is not for love, it is not for joy—it goes on insisting that life is misery. By saying that life is misery, it rationalizes its own clinging to misery.

I have heard a beautiful story—I don't know how far it is correct, I cannot vouch for it.

In paradise one afternoon, in its most famous café, Lao Tzu, Confucius, and Buddha are sitting and chatting. The waiter comes with a tray that holds three glasses of the juice called "Life," and offers them. Buddha immediately closes his eyes and refuses; he says, "Life is misery."

Confucius closes his eyes halfway—he is a middlist, he used to preach the golden mean—and asks the waiter to give him the glass. He would like to have a sip—but just a sip, because without tasting how can one say whether life is misery or not? Confucius had a scientific mind; he was not much of a mystic, he had a very pragmatic, earthbound mind. He was the first behaviorist the world has known, very logical. And it seems perfectly right—he says, "First I will have a sip, and then I will say what I think." He takes a sip and he says, "Buddha is right—life is misery."

Lao Tzu takes all the three glasses and he says, "Unless one drinks totally, how can one say anything?" He drinks all the three glasses and starts dancing!

Buddha and Confucius ask him, "Are you not going to say anything?" And Lao Tzu says, "This is what I am saying—my dance and my song are speaking for me." Unless you taste totally, you cannot say. And when you taste totally, you still cannot say because what you know is such that no words are adequate.

Buddha is on one extreme, Confucius is in the middle. Lao Tzu has drunk all the three glasses—the one that was brought for Buddha, the one that was brought for Confucius, and the one that was brought for him. He has drunk them all; he has lived life in its three-dimensionality.

My own approach is that of Lao Tzu. Live life in all possible ways; don't choose one thing against the other, and don't try to be in the middle. Don't try to balance yourself—balance is not something that can be cultivated. Balance is something that comes out of experiencing all the dimensions of life. Balance is something that *happens;* it is not something that can be brought about through your efforts. If you bring it through your efforts it will be false, forced. And you will remain tense, you will not be relaxed, because how can a person who is trying to remain balanced in the middle be relaxed? You will always be afraid that if you relax you may start moving to the left or to the right. You are bound to remain uptight, and to be uptight is to miss the whole opportunity, the whole gift of life.

Don't be uptight. Don't live life according to principles. Live life in its totality, drink life in its totality! Yes, sometimes it tastes bitter—so what? That taste of bitterness will make you capable of tasting its sweetness. You will be able to appreciate the sweetness only if you have tasted its bitterness. One who knows not how to cry will not know how to laugh, either. One who cannot enjoy a deep laughter, a belly laugh, that person's tears will be crocodile tears. They cannot be true, they cannot be authentic.

I don't teach the middle way, I teach the total way. Then a balance comes of its own accord, and then that balance has tremendous beauty and grace. You have not forced it, it has simply come. By moving gracefully to the left, to the right, in the middle, slowly a balance comes to you because you remain so unidentified. When sadness comes, you know it will pass, and when happiness comes you know that will pass, too. Nothing remains; everything passes by. The only thing that always abides is your witnessing. That witnessing brings balance. That witnessing *is* balance.

Body and Soul: A brief history of religion

Religion has passed through many phases. The first phase of religion was magical, and it has not died yet. Many aboriginal tribes around the world are still living in this first phase of religion, which is based on magic rituals of sacrifice to the gods. It is a kind of bribery so that the gods will help you, protect you. Whatever you think is valuable—in food, clothes, ornaments, whatever—you give to the gods. Of course it is not that any god receives it; the priest receives it—he is the mediator, he profits by it. And the strangest thing is that for at least ten thousand years this magical, ritualistic religion has kept man's mind captured.

There are so many failures—99 percent of the efforts are failures. For example, the rains are not coming at the right time; then the magical religion will have a ritual sacrifice and will believe that the gods will be happy now and the rains will come. Once in a while the rains do come—but they come also to those people who are not praising the gods and doing the ritual. They come even to the enemies of the people who have prayed.

Those rains have nothing to do with the rituals, but the rain becomes a proof that the ritual has succeeded. Ninety-nine times out of a hundred the ritual fails; it is bound to fail because it has nothing to do with the weather. There is no scientific cause-and-effect relationship between the ritual—your fire ceremony, your mantras—and the clouds and the rain.

The priest is certainly more cunning than the people he is exploiting. He knows perfectly well what is really happening. Priests have never believed in God, remember, they cannot, but they *pretend* to believe more than anybody else. They have to, that is their profession. The stronger their faith, the more crowds they can attract, so they pretend. But I have never come across any priest who believes that there is a God. How can he believe? Every day he sees that it is only rarely, by coincidence, that sometimes a ritual or a prayer succeeds; mostly it fails. But he has explanations for the poor people: "Your ritual was not done correctly. While doing it you were not full of pure thoughts."

Now, who is full of pure thoughts? And what is a pure thought? For example, in a Jain ritual, people have to be fasting. But while they are doing the ritual, they are thinking of food—that is an impure thought. Now, a hungry person thinking of food . . . I don't see how it is impure, it is exactly the right thought. In fact, the person is doing wrong at that moment in trying to go on with the ritual; he should run to a restaurant!

But the priest has a very simple explanation for why your ritual failed. God never fails, he always is ready to protect you—he is the provider, the creator, the maintainer; he will never let you down. But *you* fail *him*. While you are saying the prayer or doing the ritual, you are full of impure thoughts. And people know the priest is right—they *were* thinking of food, or a beautiful woman passed by and the idea arose that she was beautiful, and the desire arose to have her. They pushed away the thoughts, but it was too late; it had already happened. Everybody knows their thoughts are impure.

Now, I don't see anything impure about it. If a beautiful woman passes by a mirror, it will also reflect the beautiful woman—is the mirror "impure"? Your mind is a mirror, it simply reflects. And your mind is conscious of everything that is happening around you. It comments, it is continuously making a commentary. If you watch, you will be surprised—you cannot find a better commentator. The mind says the woman is beautiful—and if you feel a desire for beauty, I don't see anything wrong in it. If you feel a desire for ugliness, *then* something is wrong; then you are sick. Beauty has to be appreciated. When you see a beautiful painting, you would like to possess it. When you see anything beautiful, just by the side of it the idea comes as a shadow, "If this beautiful thing could be mine . . ." Now, these are all natural thoughts. But the priest will say, "The rains have not come because of your impure thoughts"—and you are absolutely defenseless. You know it, you are ashamed of yourself. God is always right.

But when the rains do come, then, too, these thoughts were passing through your head; you were exactly the same person. If you were hungry, you were thinking of food; if you were thirsty, you were thinking of water. These ideas were also coming to you when the rains came, but then nobody bothers about the bad thoughts. The priest starts praising you, your great austerity, your deep prayer: "God has heard you." And your ego feels so satisfied that you don't say, "But what about the impure thoughts?" Who wants to mention impure thoughts when you have succeeded and God has heard you?

Most of the time nobody hears, the sky remains empty and no answer comes. But the magical religion goes on and on.

Magical religion is the most primitive religion, but fragments of it remain in the second phase; there is not a very clear-cut demarcation. The second phase is the pseudo-religion: Hinduism, Christianity, Mohammedanism, Judaism, Jainism, Buddhism, Sikhism—and there are more than three hundred "isms" in all. These are pseudo-religions. They have come a little farther than magical religion.

Magical religion is simply ritualistic. It is an effort to persuade God to help you. The enemy is going to invade the country, the rain is not coming, or too much rain has come and the rivers are flooded and your crops are being destroyed—whenever you encounter these difficulties, you ask the help of God. But the magical religion is not a discipline for you. Hence magical religions are not repressive. They are not concerned yet with your transformation, with changing you.

The pseudo-religions shift the attention from God to you. God remains in the picture, but he fades far away. For the magical-religious person God is very close by; he can talk to him, he can persuade him. Pseudo-religions still carry the idea of God, but now God is far away—far, far away. Now the only way to reach him is not through rituals but through a significant change in your lifestyle. The pseudo-religions start molding and changing you.

The magical religions leave people as they are—so the people who believe in magical religions are more natural, less phony, but more primitive, unsophisticated, uncultured. The people who belong to pseudo-religions are more sophisticated, more cultured, more educated. Religion to them is not just ritual, it is their whole life's philosophy.

The use of repression comes here, at this second phase of religion. Why have all the religions used repression as a basic strategy, for what? The phenomenon of repression is tremendously significant to understand, because all the religions differ from each other in every other way, are against all other religions in every other aspect. No two religions agree on anything except repression. So repression seems to be the greatest tool in their hands. What are they doing with it?

Repression is the mechanism for enslaving you, for putting humanity into psychological and spiritual slavery. Long before Sigmund Freud discovered the phenomenon of repression, religions had already used it for five thousand years, and successfully. The methodology is simple—the methodology is to turn you against yourself. But it does miracles. Once you are turned against yourself, many things are bound to happen. First, you will be weakened. You will never be the same strong person you were before. Before, you were one; now you are not only two but many. Before, you were a single, whole entity; now you are a crowd. Your father's voice is speaking in you from one fragment, your mother's voice is speaking from another fragment, and within you they are still fighting with each other—although they may be no longer in the world. All your teachers have their compartments in you, and all the priests you came across, all the monks, all the do-gooders, moralists—they all have made places in you, strongholds of their own. Whomever you have been impressed with has become a fragment in you. Now you are many people—dead, alive, fictitious, from books you have read, from holy books, which are just religious fiction, like science fiction. If you look inside yourself, you will find yourself lost in such a big crowd. You cannot recognize who you are in the midst of this whole crowd, which face is your original face. They all pretend to be you, they all have faces like you. They speak your language and they are all quarrelsome with each other. You have become a battlefield.

The strength of the single individual is lost. Your house is divided against itself and you cannot do anything with wholeness. Some parts within you will be against it, some parts will be for it, and some parts will be absolutely indifferent. If you do something, the parts that were against it will go on telling you that you have done wrong; they will make you feel guilty. The parts that remain indifferent will pretend to be holy, telling you that you are just third rate to listen to these people who don't understand. So whether you do something or you don't do something, in either case you are condemned.

You are always in a dilemma. Wherever you move you will be defeated, and major portions of your being will be against you. You will be always doing things with minority support. That certainly means the majority is going to want to take revenge—and it will take revenge. It will tell you, "If you had not done *this* you could have done *that*. If you had not chosen this, you could have chosen that. But you were a fool, you wouldn't listen. Now suffer, now repent."

But the problem is that you cannot do anything with such wholeness that there is nobody later on to condemn you, to tell you that you are stupid, unintelligent.

So the first thing is that the pseudo-religions have destroyed the integrity, the wholeness, the strength of the human being. That is necessary if you want to enslave people—strong people cannot be enslaved. And this is a very subtle slavery, psychological and spiritual. You don't need handcuffs and chains and prison cells, no—the pseudo-religions have made much more sophisticated arrangements. And they start working from the moment you are born; they don't miss a single moment.

The religions have condemned sex, condemned your love for food—condemned everything that you can enjoy—music, art, singing, dancing. If you look around the world and collect all the condemnations from all the religions, you will see: Together, they have condemned the whole of man. They have not left a single inch uncondemned.

Yes, each religion has done only its own bit—because if you condemn the whole of a person completely, he may simply freak out. You have to maintain some sense of proportion so that he becomes condemned and feels guilty, and then wants to be freed from guilt and is ready to take your help. You should not condemn him so much that he simply escapes from you or jumps into the ocean and finishes himself. That will not be good business.

It is just like the slaves in the old days. They were given food—not enough that they could become too strong and revolt, and not so little that they would die; otherwise you would make a loss. You give them a certain percentage so they are just hanging in the middle between life and death, and they can go on living and working for you. Only that much food is given, not more than that; otherwise there will be energy left after work, and that energy could become a revolution. They might start joining together because they can see what is being done to them.

The same has been done by the religions. Every religion has taken a different segment of man and condemned it, and through it made him feel guilty.

Once guilt is created in you, you are in the clutches of the priest. You cannot escape now because he is the only one who can clean all the shameful parts of you, who can make you capable of standing before God without being ashamed. He creates the fiction of God. He creates the fiction of guilt. He creates the fiction that one day you will have to stand before God, so you have to be clean and be pure, and be in such a state that you can stand before him without any fear and without any shame.

The whole thing is fictitious. But this has to be remembered: it is true about the pseudo-religions. And whenever I say "all religions," I mean pseudo-religions; the plural is indicative of the pseudo.

When religion becomes scientific, it is not going to be plural: then it will be simply religion, and its function will be just the opposite of the pseudo-religions. Its function will be to make you free from God, to make you free from heaven and hell, to make you free from the concept of original sin, to make you free from the very idea that you and nature are separate—to make you free from any kind of repression.

With all this freedom you will be able to learn the expression of your natural being, whatever it is. There is no need to feel ashamed. The universe wants you to be this way, that's why you are this way. The universe needs you this way, otherwise it would have created somebody else, not you. So not being yourself is the only irreligious thing according to me.

Be yourself with no conditions, no strings attached—just be yourself and you are religious, because you are healthy, you are whole. You don't need the priest, you don't need the psychoanalyst, you don't need anybody's help because you are not sick, you are not crippled, paralyzed. All that crippledness and paralysis has gone with the finding of freedom.

Religion can be condensed in a single phrase: total freedom to be oneself.

Express yourself in as many ways as possible without fear. There is nothing to fear, there is nobody who is going to punish you or reward you. If you express your being in its truest form, in its natural flow, you will be rewarded immediately—not tomorrow but today, here and now.

You are punished only when you go against your nature. But that punishment is a help, it is simply an indication that you have moved away from nature, that you have gone a little astray, off the road—come back. Punishment is not a revenge, no. Punishment is only an effort to wake you up: "What are you doing?" Something is wrong, something is going against yourself. That's why there is pain, there is anxiety, there is anguish.

And when you are natural, expressing yourself just like the trees and the birds—who are more fortunate, because no bird has tried to be a priest and no tree has yet got the idea of being a psychoanalyst—just like the trees, and the birds, and the clouds, you will feel at home in existence.

And to be at home is all that religion is about.

Among what you call the pseudo-religions, do you see any significant difference between those that have arisen in the Western context and those that have arisen in the East?

In the past two thousand years Christianity has done more harm to humanity than any other religion. Mohammedanism has tried to compete with it but has not been successful. It came very close, but Christianity still remains on the top. It has slaughtered people, burned people alive. In the name of God, truth, religion, it has been killing and slaughtering people—for their own sake, for their own good.

And when the murderer is murdering you for your own good, then he has no feeling of guilt at all. On the contrary, he feels he has done a good job. He has done some service to humanity, to God, to all the great values of love, truth, freedom. He feels excited. He feels that he is now a better human being. When crimes are being used for people to feel like better human beings, that is the worst that can happen to anybody. Now he will be doing evil, thinking it is good. He will be destroying good, thinking it is good.

This is the worst kind of indoctrination that Christianity has put into people's minds. The idea of the crusade, of a religious war, is a great contribution of Christianity. Mohammedanism learned it from Christianity; they cannot claim to be the originators of the idea. They call it jihad, holy war, but they came five hundred years later than Jesus. Christianity had already created in people's minds the idea that a war too can be religious.

Now, war as such is irreligious.

There cannot be anything like a crusade, a holy war.

If you call war holy, then what is left to be called unholy?

This is a strategy to destroy people's thinking. The moment they think of crusade, they don't think there is anything wrong: they are fighting for God against the devil. And there is no God and no devil—you are simply fighting and killing people. And what business is it of yours anyway? If God cannot destroy the devil, do you think you can? If God is impotent and cannot destroy the devil, then can the pope do it? Can these Christians do it? Can Jesus do it? And for eternity God has lived with the devil.

Even now the forces of evil are far more powerful than the forces of good, for the simple reason that the forces of good are also in the hands of the forces of evil.

Calling war religious, holy, is the cause of war—because the First World War happened in the Christian context, the Second World War happened in the Christian context, and the Third World War is going to happen in the Christian context.

There are other religions also, but why did these two great wars happen in the Christian context? Christianity cannot save itself from taking the responsibility. Once you create the idea that war can be holy, then you cannot monopolize the idea.

Adolf Hitler was saying to his people, "This war is holy"; it was a crusade. He was simply using Christianity's contribution. He was a Christian, and he believed himself to be the reincarnation of the prophet Elijah. He thought himself equal to Jesus Christ, perhaps better, because what Jesus could not do, he was trying to do. All that Jesus succeeded in doing was getting crucified. Adolf Hitler was almost successful. If he had succeeded—which was 99 percent possible, just by one percent he missed—then the whole world would have been purified of all that is Jewish, of all that is non-Christian. What would have remained?

And do you know?—Adolf Hitler was blessed by the German

archbishop, who told him, "You are going to win because Christ is with you and God is with you." And the same fools were blessing Winston Churchill, saying, "God is with you and Christ is with you—you are sure to win." The same fools, even bigger ones, were in the Vatican, because the Vatican is just part of Rome, and Mussolini was being blessed by the pope—a representative, an infallible representative, of Jesus Christ.

One can think the German archbishop is not infallible, the archbishop of England is not infallible—we can forgive them, fallible people—what about the pope, who for centuries has been claimed by the Christians to be infallible? Now, this infallible pope blesses Mussolini for victory because "he is fighting for Jesus Christ and God"—and Mussolini and Adolf Hitler are one party. Together they are trying to win the whole world.

Perhaps the pope was hoping that if Mussolini wins then Christianity will have a chance to become the universal religion. They have been trying for two thousand years to make Christianity the universal religion, to destroy all other religions.

In Jainism there is no question of holy war. Every war is unholy. You may be fighting in the name of religion, but fighting itself is irreligious. Buddhism has no idea of any holy war; hence, Jainism and Buddhism have never contributed to creating any war—and their history is very long. Jainism has been in existence for at least 10,000 years and has not created a single war, holy or unholy. Buddhism is also older than Christianity, 500 years older, and has as big a membership as Christianity—except for India, the whole of Asia is Buddhist—but they have not started a single war.

Christianity deserves all the credit for making war, the most ugly thing in human life, holy. And then behind the name of a crusade you can do everything: rape women, burn people alive, kill innocent children, old people—anything. This is a blanket term, a cover: it is a holy war, a crusade. But all these other things actually happen behind it. All the atomic weapons, nuclear weapons, have been produced in the Christian context.

It is not that the rest of the world lacks intelligence. If China can produce Confucius, Lao Tzu, Chuang Tzu, Mencius, Lieh Tzu, there is no reason why it could not produce an Albert Einstein, a Lord Rutherford. Instead, China was the first in creating the printing press, and it has been in existence for three thousand years.

In India, if they can produce a man like Patanjali, who single-handedly has produced the whole system of yoga; if they could produce Gautam the Buddha, Mahavira the Jain—great philosophers, mystics. Three thousand years ago in India, Sushrut, a great physician and surgeon, existed. In his books he describes some of the most intricate surgery possible today—even brain surgery, and with all the instruments. If these countries could produce those types of people, what was missing? Why were they not trying to produce atom bombs? India produced mathematics, without which no science is possible. Seven thousand years ago they created the basis of mathematics, but they never used their mathematical understanding for destructive purposes. They used it for creative purposes because no religion there was giving them the incentive to war. All their religions were saying war is ugly—about that there was no dispute—and those countries were not going to support any program, any project, any research that was going to lead them into war.

I am saying this to make it clear that it is Christianity that is responsible for giving science the incentive to war. If Christianity had created an atmosphere of nonviolence and had not called war holy, then we would have avoided these two world wars; and without those two, certainly the third could not happen. Those two are absolutely necessary steps for the third; they have led you already towards the third. You are geared for it, and there is no possibility to come back, to turn back.

Not only has science been corrupted by Christianity, Christianity itself has given birth to strange ideologies, either directly or as a reaction. In both ways it is responsible. Poverty has existed in the world for thousands of years, but communism is a Christian contribution. And don't be misguided by the fact that Karl Marx was a Jew, because Jesus was also a Jew. If a Jew can create Christianity. . . . The context of Karl Marx is Christian, it is not Jewish. The idea was given by Jesus Christ. The moment he said, "Blessed are the poor, for they shall inherit the kingdom of God," he sowed the seed of communism.

Nobody has said it so straight, because to say it so straight you need a crazy man like me—who can call a spade not only a spade but a fucking spade! What is there in just calling a spade a spade?

Once Jesus created the idea that "Blessed are the poor for they shall inherit the kingdom of God," it was child's play to change it to the more practical and pragmatic communism. What Marx says in essence is "Blessed are the poor for theirs is the earth." He is simply changing some spiritual jargon into practical politics.

"Kingdom of God"—who knows whether it exists or not? But why waste this opportunity when you can have the kingdom of earth? The whole of communism is based on that single statement of Jesus. It is just a little turn, throwing away the esoteric nonsense and bringing practical politics into it. Yes, blessed are the poor because theirs is the whole kingdom of this earth—that's what Karl Marx is saying.

Strange that nowhere else—in the context of Buddhism, Hinduism, Jainism, Sikhism, Taoism, or Confucianism—does communism appear; it appears only in the context of Christianity. It is not just accidental, because you can see fascism also appears in the context of Christianity. Socialism, Fabian socialism, Nazism—all are Christian children, kids of Jesus Christ. Either directly influenced by him . . . because he is the man who says, "In my kingdom of God a camel can pass through the eye of a needle but a rich man cannot enter through the gates."

What do you think about this man? Is he not a communist? If he is not a communist, then who is? Even Karl Marx, Engels, Lenin, Stalin, or Mao Tse-tung have not made that strong a statement: A rich man cannot enter into the kingdom of God. And you see the comparison he makes? It is possible for a camel—this is impossible—to pass through the eye of a needle. He says even that is possible, but the entrance of a rich man into the kingdom of God is impossible. If it is impossible there, why leave them here?—make it impossible here too. That's what Marx did.

In fact, what theoretically Jesus provided, Marx gave a practical turn. But the original theoretician was Jesus. Karl Marx may not have even recognized it, but in no other context is communism possible. In no other context is Adolf Hitler possible. In India if you want to declare yourself a man of God, you cannot be an Adolf Hitler. You cannot even participate in politics, you cannot even be a voter. You cannot destroy millions of Jews, or millions of people belonging to other religions, and still claim that you are a reincarnation of an ancient prophet Elijah.

In India there have been thousands of people declaring that they are incarnations, that they are prophets, tirthankaras, but they have to prove it by their lives, too. Maybe they are phony, most of them are—but even then, nobody can be an Adolf Hitler and still say that he is a prophet, that he is a religious man.

Once the president of the American Nazi party wrote a letter to me saying, "We have been hearing you speak against Adolf Hitler—that hurts our religious feelings." I am rarely amazed, but I was amazed: their religious feelings! "Because to us Adolf Hitler is the prophet Elijah, and we hope that you will not speak against him in the future."

You cannot think of this happening in India or China or Japan—impossible. But in a Christian context it is possible: not only possible, it happened! And if Hitler had won the war, he would have been proclaimed as having overcome the evil in the world and converted the whole of humanity into Christianity. And he would have done it; he had the power.

I am not paying special attention to Christianity, but it deserves it. It has done so much harm, so much nuisance. It is impossible to believe that people still go on keeping it alive. The churches should be demolished, the Vatican should be completely removed. There is no need of these people. Whatever they have done they have done wrong. Other religions have also done wrong, but proportionately they are nothing compared to Christianity.

It has been exploiting the poverty of people to convert them to Christianity. Yes, Buddhism has converted people, but not because people were hungry and you provided them food, and because you provided them food they started feeling obliged to you. If you provide them clothes, if you provide them other facilities—education for their children, hospitals for their sick people—naturally they feel obliged. And then you start asking them, "What has Hinduism done for you? What has Buddhism done for you?"

Naturally, Buddhism, Hinduism, and Jainism have never opened a hospital, a school; they have never done any such service. This is the only argument. And those people are so obliged that they feel certainly no other religion has been of any help to them, and they become Christians. This is not an honest way, this is bribing people. This is not conversion, this is buying people because they are poor. You are taking advantage of their poverty.

Buddhism has converted millions of people, but that was through Buddhism's intelligence. The conversion happened at the top, through kings, emperors, masters, great writers, poets, and painters. Seeing that the intelligent people had become Buddhist, then others followed. Jains have converted emperors. Their first effort was to change the cream, the highest stratum, because that makes it simple: Then the common people naturally understand that if their topmost intelligentsia are becoming Jains, that meant their old religion had not been able to argue for its doctrines, its standpoint. Something better had arrived—something more sophisticated, something more logical and rational.

But everywhere around the world, Christians have approached the lowest stratum. And the poor have been there always; but to exploit their poverty to increase the population of your religion is sheer politics—ugly, mean. Politics is a game of numbers. How many Christians you have in the world—that is your power. The more Christians there are, the more power is in the hands of Christian priesthood. Nobody is interested in saving anybody, but just in increasing the population. What Christianity has been doing is continually issuing orders from the Vatican against birth control, saying it is sin to use birth control methods; it is sin to believe in abortion or to propagate abortion, or to make it legal.

Do you think they are interested in the unborn children? They are not interested, they have nothing to do with those unborn children. They pursue their interest knowing perfectly well that if abortion is not practiced, if birth control methods are not practiced, then this whole humanity is going to commit a global suicide. And it is not so far away that you cannot see the situation. Within just a few decades the world population might be such that it will be impossible to survive. Either you will have to go into a third world war . . . which will be a safer method to solve the problem; people will die more quickly, more easily, more comfortably with nuclear weapons than with hunger. Hunger can keep you alive for ninety days, and those ninety days will be really a torture. I know about hunger in India. Mothers have sold their children just for one rupee. Mothers have eaten their own children. You cannot conceive where hunger can lead you.

But the Vatican keeps coming out with the same message to humanity—"Abortion is sin. Birth control is sin." Now, nowhere in the Bible is abortion sin. Nowhere in the Bible is birth control a sin, because no birth control was needed. Out of ten children, nine were going to die. That was the proportion, and it was the same proportion in India just thirty or forty years ago: Out of ten children, only one would survive. Then the population was not so great, not so heavy on the resources of the earth. Now, even in India, out of ten children, only one dies. So medical science goes on helping people to survive, and Christianity goes on opening hospitals and distributing medicines, and Mother Teresa is there to praise you and the pope is going to bless you if you don't practice birth control. There are all kinds of associations working in underdeveloped countries to distribute Bibles and to distribute these stupid ideas that birth control is a sin. The whole interest is in bringing many more children into the world, many more orphans into the world. Make it so overcrowded, so poor, that Christianity can become the universal religion. That has been their ambition for two thousand years. It has to be exposed. This ambition is inhuman; and if I have been criticizing Christianity it is not without reason.

Rich Man, Poor Man: A look at the roots of poverty and greed

Just by saying, "Blessed are the poor because theirs is the kingdom of God," you don't change poverty. Otherwise in two thousand years Christianity would have made poverty disappear. Poverty goes on growing, the blessed people go on growing. In fact, there will be so many blessed people that in the kingdom of God, shared by all these blessed people, they will again be poor. Each of them is not going to get much of a share in it. And all these shareholders in the kingdom of God will make God poor, too. It will be a company of impoverished shareholders.

Two thousand years of teaching . . . has it changed the nature of poverty? No. It has done only one thing—it has killed the revolutionary spirit in the poor. Poverty goes on growing in leaps and bounds.

A lawyer made his way to the edge of the excavation where a gang was working, and called the name of Timothy O'Toole.

"Who is wanting me?" inquired a heavy voice.

"Mr. O'Toole," the lawyer asked, "did you come from Castlebar, County Mayo?"

"I did that."

"And your mother was named Bridget and your father Michael?"

"They was."

"It is my duty then," said the lawyer, "to inform you, Mr. O'Toole, that your Aunt Mary has died in Iowa, leaving you an estate of $150,000."

There was a short silence below and then a lively commotion.

"Are you coming, Mr. O'Toole?" the lawyer called down.

"In one minute," was bellowed in answer. "I just have to give a good licking to the foreman before I go." It required just six months of extremely riotous living for O'Toole to expend all of the $150,000. His chief endeavor was to satisfy a huge inherited thirst. Then he went back to his job. There, presently, the lawyer sought him out again.

> *"It is your Uncle Patrick this time, Mr. O'Toole," the lawyer explained. "He has died in Texas and left you $80,000."*
>
> *O'Toole leaned heavily on his pick and shook his head in great weariness.*
>
> *"I don't think I can take it," he declared. "I am not as strong as I once was, and I misdoubt me that I could go through all that money and live."*

That's what has happened in the West. People in the West have succeeded in attaining all the affluence that the whole of humanity has been longing for down the ages. The West has succeeded materially in becoming rich, and now it is weary, tired. The journey has taken all its soul. Outwardly all is available, but the contact with the inner is lost. Now everything that any person needs is there, but the human being is no more. Possessions are there, but the master has disappeared. A great imbalance has happened. Richness is there, but the people are not feeling rich at all; they are feeling, on the contrary, very impoverished, very poor.

Think of this paradox: when you are outwardly rich, only then do you become aware of your inner poverty, in contrast. When you are outwardly poor, you never become aware of your inner poverty because there is no contrast. You write with white chalk on blackboards, not on white boards. Why? Because only on a blackboard will it show. The contrast is needed.

When you are outwardly rich, then suddenly a great awareness happens that "Inwardly I am poor, a beggar." And now a hopelessness also comes as a shadow: "All is attained that we had thought we wanted—all imagination and fantasies fulfilled—and nothing has happened out of it, no contentment, no bliss." People are bewildered, and out of this bewilderment a great desire arises: How can we have contact with ourselves again?

Meditation is nothing but getting your roots again into your inner world, into your interiority. Hence, people in the West are becoming interested in meditation, and in the Eastern traditions of meditation.

The East was also interested in meditation when the East was rich; this has to be understood. That's why I am not against richness, and I don't think poverty has any spirituality in it. I am utterly against poverty because whenever a country becomes poor it loses contact with all meditation, all spiritual efforts. Whenever a country becomes poor outwardly, it becomes unaware of the inner poverty.

That's why among poor people in India you can see a kind of contentment that is not found in the West. It is not real contentment; it is just unawareness of the inner poverty. I have been watching thousands of poor people in the East—they are not truly contented, but one thing is certainly true: They are not aware of their discontent because to be aware of the discontent, outer richness is needed.

Without outer richness nobody becomes aware of the inner discontent. And there are enough proofs for it. All the mystics, the avatars of the Hindus, were kings or sons of kings. All the Jain masters were from royal families; and so was Buddha. All the three great traditions of India give ample proof. Why did Buddha become discontented, why did he start a search for meditation? Because he was rich. He lived in affluence; he lived in all the abundance that was possible, with all the comforts, all the material gadgets. Suddenly he became aware—he was just twenty-nine years old when he became aware that there was a dark hole inside. When the light is outside, it shows your inner darkness. Just a little dirt on a white shirt and it shows. That's what happened. He escaped from the palace. The same happened to Mahavira; he also escaped from a palace. This was not happening to beggars. There were beggars also in Buddha's time, but they didn't renounce anything in search of truth. They had nothing to renounce; they were contented. Buddha became discontented.

When India was rich, many more people were interested in meditation; in fact, everybody was interested in meditation. Then the country became poor, so poor that there was no contrast between the inner and the outer. The inner was poor and the outer was poor. The inner and the outer were in perfect harmony—both were poor.

But people have become accustomed to thinking that poverty has something spiritual in it. I am not in favor of any kind of poverty. Poverty is not spirituality, it forces the disappearance of spirituality.

I would like the whole world to become as affluent as possible. The more people are affluent, the more they will become spiritual. They will have to; they will not be able to avoid it. Only then does real contentment arise. When outer richness meets inner richness, a new kind of harmony happens—then there is real contentment. When outer poverty meets inner poverty, there is false contentment. Harmony is possible in these two ways. When the outer and inner are in harmony, one feels contented. Poor people in India look contented because there is poverty on both sides of the fence. There is perfect harmony, the outer and inner are in tune—but this is an ugly contentment, it is really a lack of life, lack of vitality.

The affluent West is bound to become interested in meditation, there is no way to avoid it. That's why Christianity is losing its hold on the Western mind, because Christianity has not developed the science of meditation in any way. It has remained a very mediocre religion; so has Judaism. The West has been poor in the past; that is the reason these religions remained mediocre. Up till recently most of the West has lived in poverty. When the East was rich, the West was poor. Judaism, Christianity, and Mohammedanism, all the three non-Indian religions, were born in poverty.

They could not develop meditation techniques, because there was no need. And for the most part, they have remained the religions of the poor.

Now the West has become rich and there is a disparity. Their religions were born in poverty, so they have nothing to offer the rich. For the rich person, educated, these religions look childish, they don't satisfy—they can't. The Eastern religions were born in richness—that's why the Western mind is becoming more interested in Eastern religions. Yes, the religion of Buddha is having a great impact; Zen is spreading like wildfire. Why? It was born out of richness. There is a great similarity between the psychology of the affluent contemporary humanity and the psychology of Buddhism. The West is in the same state as Buddha was when he became interested in meditation. His was a rich man's search. And so is the case with Hinduism, so is the case with Jainism. These three great Indian religions were born out of affluence; hence the West now is bound to be attracted to these Eastern religions.

And in the meantime, India lost contact with its own religions. It could not afford to understand Buddha—it had become a poor country. Poor Indians are being converted to Christianity. Rich Americans are being converted to Buddhism, Hinduism, Vedanta—and the untouchables, the poor, the poorest of the poor in India, are becoming Christians. Do you see the point? Those religions have a certain appeal for the poor. These people have been living almost in a state of unconsciousness—too hungry to meditate, their only interest is in bread, shelter, clothing. So when the Christian missionary comes and opens a hospital or opens a school, the Indians are very much impressed—this is "spirituality." When I talk about meditation they are not interested—not only not interested, they are against it: "What kind of spirituality is this? What are you doing to help the poor?" And I understand—they need bread, they need shelter, they need clothes.

But it is because of their mind that they are suffering. On the one hand they need bread, shelter, clothes, better houses, better roads; and on the other hand they go on worshiping poverty as something "spiritual." They are in a double bind. The East cannot yet meditate. First it needs scientific technology to make it a little physically better. Just as the West needs religious technology, the East needs scientific technology.

I am all for one world, where the West can fulfill the needs of the East and the East can fulfill the needs of the West. The East and West have lived apart too long; there is no need anymore. We have come to a critical moment where this whole earth can become one—should become one—because it can survive only if it becomes one.

The days of the nations are over, the days of divisions are over, the days of the politicians are over. We are moving into a tremendously new world, a new phase of humanity, and the phase is that there can be only one world now, only one single humanity. Then there will be a tremendous release of creative energies.

The East has treasures in the spiritual technologies, and the West has treasures in the scientific technologies. If they can meet, this very world can become a paradise. Now there is no need to ask for another world in paradise; we are capable of creating paradise here on this earth, for the first time. And if we don't create it, then except for us, nobody else is responsible.

I am for one world, one humanity, and ultimately one science which will take care of both—a meeting of religion and science—one science, which will take care of the inner and the outer, both.

?

Isn't the human tendency to accumulate and hoard things a hindrance to the meeting of East and West that you envision? Is a system like communism perhaps useful in distributing wealth more evenly around the world?

The poor and the rich depend on each other; the rich cannot exist without the poor. It would be a simple humanitarian gesture—we have enough technology now—to produce so much wealth that there is no need for anybody to be poor and starving. But what we go on doing is just the opposite.

Thirty million people in America, the richest country of the world, are undernourished. And you will be surprised: thirty million people in America are overnourished. They are dieting and trying hard somehow to lose weight. America has some of the fattest people in the whole world. It is simple arithmetic: these thirty million fat people are eating the food of the thirty million who are undernourished!

We can produce enough, more than needed, so that any necessity to hoard disappears. You don't hoard air. Of course, on the moon you will; you will have a container hanging on your shoulder with oxygen, because there is no oxygen on the moon. In a desert you will hoard water. People in the desert will fight for a small oasis, even kill each other for water. Outside the desert you don't fight for water; there is enough available.

I have a different view of society than both communism and capitalism. Society needs a supercapitalistic system, and it will become communistic automatically. There will be no need for any revolution. What is needed is evolution, not revolution. Revolution never betters things. It is evolution, growth, which betters things.

If many people are poor and a few people are rich, that simply means there is not enough wealth. All effort should be made to create more wealth—and it can be created; there is no reason why not. And when wealth is there and it is more than needed, then who bothers to hoard it?

A few things will disappear of their own accord which you have not been able to dispel from the society. The poor will disappear, the thief will disappear. The policeman perhaps may not be needed, the judges can be put to better use. Thousands of lawyers are just wasting their time and people's money; they are not needed.

We don't see things; we simply remove the symptoms and they come back again. We have to look at the very causes. In America there is so much crime—why? There must be temptations for crime. Those temptations can be dropped very easily.

Just look at my wristwatch. Are you tempted or not? You will be tempted because you don't know that it is made just of stones, not diamonds. It has no value. When stones can do the work of diamonds, then only fools will be after diamonds. Can you see any difference? In diamonds, the watch would cost a quarter-million dollars—the same watch exactly. My friends have made it just using stones. It functions as accurately as any watch—just one second's difference in one year—because now to create such accuracy is a very simple phenomenon. Whether you purchase a million-dollar watch or just a ten-dollar watch, they both use the same kind of battery. The electronic battery has changed the whole idea of watches.

But if stones—real, authentic stones—can do the work of diamonds, then why unnecessarily create temptations? Create more watches and jewelry with beautiful stones, and the temptation for diamonds will disappear. The prices of the diamonds will come down. In fact, diamonds are themselves just stones. We create temptations for crime, and then the criminal is punished, not the person who has created the temptation. Both should be punished!

But only symptoms are being addressed, not causes. And the causes will create other symptoms. This is so unscientific! Instead of creating more wealth, every nation is creating more weapons—missiles, rockets, nuclear weapons—and piling them up. For what? Do you want to commit a global suicide? Then why such waste of money and time? If humanity has decided to commit suicide, simpler methods are available.

Seventy-five percent of our energy around the earth is being poured into war efforts. Are we servants of death and destruction? This 75 percent of energy could be poured into life, into the service of life—and there will be laughter, and there will be greater health, and there will be more wealth, more food. There will be no poverty.

There is no need for poverty to exist at all.

? **You've criticized the religions, but don't they play a significant part in helping to deal with poverty? So many religious organizations exist in an unselfish effort to serve the poor.**

All the religions in the world teach service to others, unselfishness. But to me, selfishness is a natural phenomenon. Unselfishness is imposed; selfishness is part of your nature. Unless you come to a point where your "self" dissolves into the universal, you cannot be truly unselfish. You can pretend, but you will be only a hypocrite, and I don't want people to be hypocrites. So it is a little complicated, but it can be understood.

First, selfishness is part of your nature. You have to accept it. And if it is part of your nature it must be serving something essential, otherwise it would not have been there at all. It is because of selfishness that you have survived, that you have taken care of yourself; otherwise humanity would have disappeared long ago.

Just think of a child who is unselfish, born unselfish. He will not be able to survive, he will die—because even to breathe is selfish, to eat is selfish when there are millions of people who are hungry. You are eating? When there are millions of people who are unhealthy, sick, dying, you are healthy? If a child is born without selfishness as an intrinsic part of his nature, he is not going to survive. If a snake comes close to you, what is the need to avoid the snake? Let him bite. It is your selfishness that is trying to protect you; otherwise, you are just in the way of the snake. If a lion jumps upon you and kills you, be killed! That is unselfishness. The lion is hungry, you are providing food—who are you to interfere? You should not protect yourself, you should not fight. You should simply offer yourself on a plate to the lion—that will be unselfishness. All these religions have been teaching things that are unnatural. This is one aspect.

I teach nature. I teach you to be natural, absolutely natural, unashamedly natural. Yes, I teach selfishness. Nobody has said it before me; they had not the guts to say it. And they were all selfish; this is the amazing part of the whole story. Why is a Jain monk torturing himself? There is a motivation. He wants to attain the ultimate liberation and all its pleasures. He is not sacrificing anything, he is simply bargaining. He is a businessman. His scriptures say, "You will get back a thousandfold." And this life is really very small—seventy, eighty years is not much. If you sacrifice seventy years of pleasures for an eternity of pleasures, it is a good bargain! I don't think it is unselfish.

And why have these religions been teaching you to serve humanity? What is the motive, what is the goal? What are you going to gain out of it? You may never have asked the question. It is not service. . . .

I have loved a very ancient Chinese story:

A man falls into a well. It was at a big gathering, a big festival time, and there was so much noise, and people were enjoying, dancing, singing, and all kinds of things were going on, so nobody heard him fall. And at that time in China the wells were not protected by a wall surrounding them. They were without any protection, just open. You could step into a well in the darkness without being aware that it was there.

The man starts shouting, "Save me!"

A Buddhist monk passes by. Of course a Buddhist monk is not interested in the festival, or is not supposed to be interested—I don't know what he was doing there. Even to be there means some unconscious urge to see what is going on, how people are enjoying: "All these people will go to hell, and I am the only one here who is going to heaven."

He passes by the well, and he hears this man. He looks down. The man says, "It's good that you have heard me. Everybody is so busy and there is so much noise, I was afraid I was going to die."

The Buddhist monk says, "You are still going to die, because this is happening because of some past life's evil act. Now you are getting the punishment, so accept it and be finished! It is good; in the next life you will start out clean and there will be no need to fall again into a well."

The man said, "I don't want any wisdom and any philosophy at this moment . . ." But the monk had moved on.

Next an old Taoist man comes by. He is thirsty and looks into the well. The man is still crying for help. The Taoist says, "This is not manly. One should accept everything as it comes—that's what the great Lao Tzu has said. So accept it! Enjoy! You are crying like a woman. Be a man!"

The man said, "I am ready to be called a woman, but first please save me! I am not manly, and you can say anything you want to say to me afterwards—first pull me out."

But the Taoist said, "We never interfere in anybody's business. We believe in the individual and his freedom. It is your freedom to fall in the well, it is your freedom to die in the well. All I can do is just make a suggestion: You can die crying, weeping—that is foolish—or you can die like a wise man. Accept it, enjoy it, sing a song, and go. Anyway, everybody is going to die, so what is the point of saving you? I am going to die, *everybody* is going to die—perhaps tomorrow, perhaps the day after tomorrow—so what is the point of bothering to save you?" And he moves on.

A Confucian comes, and the man sees some hope because Confucians are more worldly, more earthbound. He says, "It is my good fortune that you have come, a Confucian scholar. I know you, I have heard your name. Now do something for me, because Confucius says, 'Help others.'"

Seeing the response of the Buddhist and the Taoist, the man thought, "It is better to talk philosophy if these people are going to be convinced to save me." He said, "Confucius says, 'Help others.'"

The Confucian monk said, "You are right. And I will help. I will go from one city to another, and I will protest and force the government to create a protective wall around every well in the country. Don't be afraid."

The man said, "But by the time those protective walls are made and your revolution succeeds, I will be gone."

The Confucian said, "You don't matter, I don't matter, individuals don't matter—society matters. You have raised a very significant question by falling in the well. Now we are going to fight for it. You just be calm and quiet. We will see that every well has a protective wall around it so nobody falls into it. But just by saving you, what is saved? The whole country has millions of wells, and millions of people can fall into them. So don't be so concerned about yourself, rise above this selfish attitude. I am going to serve humanity. You have already done a great service by falling into the well. I am going to serve by forcing the government to make protective walls." And the Confucian walks on.

But the Confucian has raised a significant point: "You are being selfish. You just want to be saved and waste my time, which I can use for the whole of humanity."

Do you know if anything like "humanity" exists anywhere, if anything like a "society" exists anywhere? These are just words. Only individuals exist.

The fourth man is a Christian missionary, who is carrying a bag with him. He immediately opens the bag, takes out a rope, throws the rope down; before the man even says anything, he throws the rope into the well. The man is surprised. He says, "Your religion seems to be the truest religion."

The missionary says, "Of course. We are prepared for every emergency. Knowing that people can fall into wells, I am carrying this rope to save them—because only by saving them can I save myself. But I am concerned—I have heard what the Confucian was saying—you shouldn't make protective walls around the wells; otherwise how will we serve humanity? How will we pull out people who fall in? They have to fall first, only then can we pull them out. We exist to serve, but the opportunity must be there. Without the opportunity, how can we serve?"

All these religions talking about "service" are certainly interested that humanity remains poor, that people remain in need of service, that there are orphans, widows, old people nobody takes care of, beggars. These people are needed, absolutely needed. Otherwise, what will happen to these great servants of the people? What will happen to all these religions and their teachings, and how will people earn the right to enter into the kingdom of God? These poor and suffering people have to be used as a ladder. Do you call it unselfishness? Is this missionary unselfish? He is saving this man, not for this man's sake; he is saving this man for his own sake. Deep down it is still selfishness, but now it is covered with beautiful words: unselfishness, service.

But why is there any need for service? Why should there be any need? Can't we destroy these opportunities for service? We can, but the religions will be very angry. Their whole ground will be lost if there is nobody poor, nobody hungry, nobody suffering, nobody sick. This is their whole business,

Science can make it possible. It is absolutely in our hands today. It would have happened long ago if these religions had not tried to stop every person who was going to contribute to knowledge that might destroy all the opportunities for service. But these religions have been against all scientific progress—they need these problems to remain. Their need is utterly selfish, it is motivated. There is a goal to be achieved.

Service is a dirty, four-letter word. Never use it. Yes, you can share, but never humiliate people by "serving" them. It is a form of humiliation. When you serve somebody and you feel great, you have reduced the other to a worm, subhuman. You are so superior that you have sacrificed your own interests and you are "serving the poor"—you are simply humiliating them.

If you have something, something that gives you joy, peace, ecstasy, share it. And remember that when you share there is no motive. I am not saying that by sharing it you will reach heaven, I am not giving you any goal. I am saying that just by sharing you will be tremendously fulfilled. In the very sharing is the fulfillment, there is no goal beyond it. It is not end-oriented, it is an end unto itself. You will feel obliged to the person who was ready to share with you. You will not feel that the person is obliged to you—you have not "served."

Only people who believe in sharing instead of service can destroy all the ugly opportunities for service that surround the whole earth. All the religions have been exploiting those opportunities, but they give good names to what they do—they have become very proficient, in thousands of years, in giving good names to ugly things. And when you start giving a beautiful name to an ugly thing, there is a possibility that you yourself may forget that it was just a cover. Inside, the reality is just the same.

All these problems can be solved. There is no need for public servants, missionaries, and their kind. We need more intelligence brought to each problem and how to dissolve it. So I teach selfishness. I want you to be, first, your own flowering. Yes, it will appear as selfishness; I have no objection to that appearance; it is okay with me. But is the rose selfish when it blossoms? Is the lotus selfish when it blossoms? Is the sun selfish when it shines? Why should you be worried about selfishness?

You are born—birth is only an opportunity, just a beginning, not the end. You have to flower. Don't waste it in any kind of stupid service. Your first and foremost responsibility is to blossom, to become fully conscious, aware, alert; and in that consciousness you will be able to see what you can share, how you can solve problems.

Ninety-nine percent of the world's problems can be solved. Perhaps one percent of problems may not be solved. Then you can share with those people whatever you can share—but first you have to have something to share.

? I am beginning to see how big a part greed plays in my life, and the misery it brings with it. Could you please shed more light on what this thing called greed is, where it comes from, and perhaps offer some tools to help me?

Just to understand the nature of greed is enough. You need not do anything else to get rid of it; the very understanding will clarify the whole mess.

You are full if you are in tune with the universe; if you are not in tune with the universe, then you are empty, utterly empty. And out of that emptiness comes greed—greed is to fill it, with money, houses, furniture, with friends, lovers, with anything, because one cannot live as emptiness. It is horrifying, it is a ghost life. If you are empty and there is nothing inside you, it is impossible to live.

To have the feeling that you have much inside you, there are only two ways. You can get in tune with the universe—then you are filled with the whole, with all the flowers and with all the stars. They are within you just as they are without you. That is real fulfillment. But if you don't do that—and millions of people are not doing that—then the easiest way is to fill it with junk.

I used to stay with a man. He was a rich man, and he had a beautiful house, and somehow he became interested in my ideas. He listened to a few of my lectures and he invited me to stay with him, saying, "Why live far away, out of the city? I have a beautiful house in the city and it is so big; you can have half. I will not charge you any rent, I simply want your presence in my house."

I was living outside the city in the mountains, but it was difficult to commute from there to the university, and from his house the university was very close. He had a beautiful garden and the house was in the best neighborhood of the city, so I accepted his invitation. But when I went into the house I could not believe it; he had so much junk collected that there was no place to live. The house was big, but his collection was even bigger—and a collection that was absolutely stupid! Anything he could find in the market he would purchase. I asked him, "What are you going to do with all these things?"

He said, "One never knows, someday one may need it."

"But," I said, "where is one supposed to live in this house?" So much furniture of all different periods . . . When the Europeans left India they had to sell all their things. This man could never have enough; he managed to purchase anything, things he didn't need. A car was in the garage which just sat there because it was old, broken down. I asked him, "Why don't you throw it away? At least to clean up the place . . ."

He said, "It looks good in the garage." All the tires were flat, it was of no use. Whenever it had to be moved from here to there, you had to push it. It was just sitting there rotting. He said, "I got it at a very reasonable price. It belonged to an old woman who used to be a nurse here and now has gone back to England."

I said, "If you were interested in purchasing a car, then at least you should have purchased a car that runs!"

He said, "I am not interested in driving a car, my bicycle is perfectly good." His bicycle was also a marvel. You could know that he was coming from a mile away, because the bicycle made so much noise. It had no mud guards, no chain cover; it must have been the oldest bicycle ever made. It had no horn. He said, "There is no need for a horn. It makes so much noise that at least for a half mile ahead people are already getting out of the way. And it is good, because it cannot be stolen because nobody else can ride it. It has been stolen twice, and the thief was caught immediately—because it makes so much noise, and everybody knows it is my bicycle. I can leave it anywhere. I go to see a movie and I don't put it in a bicycle stand, because then you have to pay money. I can put it anywhere, and it is always there when I come back. Everybody knows that it is too much trouble, so it is better not to bother with it." He said, "It is a rare specimen."

He had all kinds of things in his house . . . broken radios, because he could get them cheap. He was a Jain and he had a broken statue of Jesus on the cross. I asked him, "What have you purchased it for?"

He said, "The woman gave it to me free when I purchased the car—she offered it to me as a present. I don't believe in Jesus Christ or anything, but I could not refuse a piece of art."

I said to him, "If I'm going to stay in this house, my part has to be empty." And he was very happy to take everything. Already the house was so full you couldn't walk, but he took everything to his side. He had so many pieces of furniture that he had piled up on top of the sofa, it could not be used. I asked, "Why?"

He said, "You don't understand—I got all these things for such a good price! And someday I may get married and have children and they may need all these things. Don't be worried, everything will be of some use sometime."

Even on the road, if he found anything lying there that had been thrown out by somebody, he would pick it up. One day he was walking with me from the garden to the house and he found a bicycle handle, and he picked it up. I asked him, "What will you do with a bicycle handle?"

He said, "I will show you." I went with him, and in his bathroom he had almost a complete bicycle—just a few things were missing. He said, "All these pieces I have picked up from the road, and I go on joining them and putting them together. Now only a few things are missing. There is no chain, no seat, but I will get them. Somebody will throw them away someday. I have a long life ahead of me, and what is the harm? It looks perfectly good in the bathroom."

Greed simply means you are feeling a deep emptiness and you want to fill it with anything possible—it doesn't matter what it is. Once you understand it, then there is no need to do anything about greed. You have to do something about coming into communion with the whole, so the inner emptiness disappears. With it, all greed disappears.

That does not mean that you start living naked; it simply means you do not live just to collect things. Whenever you need something you can have it. But there are mad people all over the world, and they are collecting things. Somebody is collecting money, although he never uses it. It is strange—a thing has to be used; if it is not used then there is no need for it. But this situation can take any direction: People are eating; they are not feeling hungry and still they go on swallowing. They know it is going to create suffering, they will be sick, they will get fat, but they cannot prevent themselves. This eating is also a filling-up process. So there can be many ways to try and fill the emptiness, although it is never full—it remains empty, and you remain miserable because it is never enough. More is needed, and the "more" and the demand for more is unending.

I don't see greed as a desire—it is some existential sickness. You are not in tune with the whole. And only a tuning with the whole can make you healthy; that tuning with the whole can make you holy. It is interesting that the word *health* and the word *holy* both come from the same root as "wholeness." When you are feeling one with wholeness, all greed disappears. Otherwise, what have the religions been doing? They have misunderstood greed as a desire, so they try to repress it: "Don't be greedy." Then one moves to the other extreme, to renounce. One collects—the greedy person—and the one who wants to get rid of greed starts renouncing. There too, there is no end.

The Jain master, Mahavira, could never recognize Gautam Buddha as enlightened for the simple reason that he still carried three sets of clothes—just three sets of clothes, which are absolutely necessary. One you are using, one has to be washed, and one for emergency reasons; someday the clothes may not come back from being washed or they are not dry, or it has rained the whole day. So three seems to be the minimum—just one emergency and the third will be needed. Mahavira is absolutely against greed, and he has taken it to an extreme—he lives naked. Buddha carries a begging bowl. Mahavira cannot accept it because even a begging bowl is a possession, and an enlightened man, according to Mahavira, should not possess anything. A begging bowl . . . it is made of coconut. You cut the coconut across the middle, take all of the fruit out, and then you have two bowls from the shells. It is the cheapest possible thing, because otherwise the shells are thrown away; you cannot eat them. To have a begging bowl like this and to call it being "possessive" is not right.

But when you see greed as a desire and you become stubborn in going against it, then everything is a possession. Mahavira lived naked, and instead of a begging bowl he used to make a bowl of his two hands. Now, it was a difficult thing: his two hands are full of the food, and he has to eat just like the animals because he cannot use his hands—he has to use his mouth directly to take the food from the bowl of his hands.

Everybody in the world eats sitting down, but Mahavira's idea is that when you eat sitting, you eat more. So he was teaching his monks that they should eat food standing—standing, with the food in their hands. And whatever can fit in your two hands at one time is one meal. You have to eat it standing, and everything has to be taken together, sweet, salty, and they all get mixed. That was Mahavira's idea of making it tasteless, because to enjoy taste is to enjoy the body, is to enjoy the material world.

To me, greed is not a desire at all. So you need not do anything about greed. You have to understand the emptiness that you are trying to fill and ask the question, "Why am I empty? The whole existence is so full, why am I empty? Perhaps I have lost track—I am no longer moving in the same direction, I am no longer existential. That is the cause of my emptiness."

So be existential.

Let go, and move closer to existence in silence and peace, in meditation. And one day you will see you are so full—overfull, overflowing—of joy, of blissfulness, of benediction. You have so much of it that you can give it to the whole world and yet it will not be exhausted. That day, for the first time, you will not feel any greed—for money, for food, for things, for anything. You will live, not with a constant greed that cannot be fulfilled, a wound that cannot be healed. You will live naturally, and whatever is needed you will find it.

BELIEF VS. EXPERIENCE

Understanding the Difference Between Knowledge and Knowing

The true religion can only be one, just like science. You don't have a Mohammedan physics, a Hindu physics, a Christian physics; that would be nonsense. But that's what the religions have done—they have made the whole earth a madhouse.

If science is one, then why should the science of the inner not be one, too? Science explores the objective world and religion explores the subjective world. Their work is the same, just their direction and dimensions are different. In a more enlightened age there will be no such thing as religion, there will be only two sciences: objective science and subjective science. Objective science deals with things, subjective science deals with being.

I am against the religions but not against religiousness. But that religiousness is still in its birth pangs. All the old religions will do everything in their power to kill it, to destroy it—because the birth of a science of consciousness will be the death of all these so-called religions that have been exploiting humanity for thousands of years. What will happen to their churches, synagogues, temples? What will happen to their priesthood, their popes, their imams, their shankaracharyas, their rabbis? It is a big business, and these people are not going to easily allow the true religion to be born.

But the time has come in human history when the grip of the old religions is loosening. More and more people are only formally paying respect to Christianity, Judaism, Hinduism, Mohammedanism, but basically anybody who has any intelligence is no longer interested in all that rubbish. They may go to the synagogue and to the church and to the mosque for other reasons, but those reasons are not religious; those reasons are social. It pays to be seen in the synagogue; it is respectable, and there is no harm. It is just like joining the Rotary Club or the Lions Club. These religions are old clubs that have a religious jargon around them, but look a little deeper and you will find they are all hocus-pocus with no substance inside.

I am for religion, but that religion will not be a repetition of any religion that you are acquainted with. That religion will be a rebellion against all those old religions. It will not carry their work further; it will stop their work completely and start a new work—the real transformation of human beings.

The most fundamental error of all the religions is that none of them was courageous enough to accept that there are things we don't know. They all pretended to know everything, pretended they were omniscient. Why did this happen? Because if you admit that you are ignorant about something, then doubt arises in the minds of your followers. If you are ignorant about one thing, who knows? You may be ignorant about other things also. What is the guarantee? To make it foolproof, they have all pretended that they are omniscient.

The most beautiful thing about science is that it does not pretend to be omniscient. Science accepts its human limits. It knows how much it knows, and it knows that there is much more to know. And the greatest scientists know of something even deeper. They know the boundaries of the known; the knowable they will know sooner or later, they are on the way. But the greatest scientists, people like Albert Einstein, will be aware of the third category, the unknowable—which will never be known; nothing can be done about it, because the ultimate mystery cannot be reduced to knowledge.

We are part of existence—how can we know its ultimate mystery? We have come very late; there was nobody present in the beginning as an eyewitness. And there is no way for us to separate ourselves completely from existence and become just observers. We live, we breathe, we exist with existence; we cannot separate ourselves from it. The moment we are separate, we are dead. And without being separate, as just a watcher with no involvement, with no attachment, you cannot know the ultimate mystery; it is impossible. There will remain something always unknowable. Yes, it can be felt, but it cannot be known. Perhaps it can be experienced in different ways, but it is not like knowledge.

You fall in love—can you say you know love? It seems to be a totally different phenomenon. You feel it. If you try to know it, perhaps it will evaporate in your hands. You cannot reduce it to knowledge. You cannot make it an object of knowledge because it is not a mind phenomenon. It is something to do with your heart. Yes, your heartbeats know it, but that is a totally different kind of knowing; the intellect is incapable of understanding those heartbeats.

But there is something more than the heart in you—your

being, your life source. Just as you know through the mind, which is the most superficial part of your individuality, you know something through your heart that is deeper than the mind. The mind cannot go into it, it is too deep for the mind to comprehend. But behind the heart, still deeper, is your being, your very life source. That life source also has a way of knowing.

When mind knows, we call it knowledge.

When heart knows, we call it love.

And when being knows, we call it meditation.

But all three speak different languages, which are not translatable into each other. And the deeper you go the more difficult it becomes to translate, because at the very center of your being there is nothing but silence. Now, how to translate silence into sound? The moment you translate silence into sound you have destroyed it. Even music cannot translate it. Perhaps music comes closest, but still it is sound.

Poetry does not come quite as close as music because words, howsoever beautiful, are still words. They don't have life in them, they are dead. How can you translate life into something dead? Yes, perhaps between the words you may have a glimpse here and there—but it is *between* the words, between the lines, not *in* the words, not in the lines.

This is the most fundamental error of all religions: They have deceived humanity by blatantly posing as if they know all.

But every day they have been exposed and their lack of knowledge has been exposed; hence, they have been fighting against any progress of knowledge. If Galileo finds that the earth moves around the sun, the pope is angry. The pope is infallible—he is only a representative of Jesus, but he is infallible. What to say about Jesus, he is the only begotten son of God, and what to say about God? But in the Bible—which is a book descended from heaven, written by God—the sun goes around the earth. Now Galileo creates a problem. If Galileo is right, then God is wrong.

God's only begotten son is wrong. And the only begotten son's representatives for these two thousand years, all the infallible popes, are wrong. Just a single man, Galileo, destroys the whole pretension, he exposes the whole hypocrisy. His mouth has to be shut. He was old, dying, on his deathbed, but he was forced, almost dragged to the court of the pope to apologize. The pope demanded: "You change it in your book, because the holy book cannot be wrong. You are a mere human being; you can be wrong, but Jesus Christ cannot be wrong, God himself cannot be wrong, hundreds of infallible popes cannot be wrong. . . . You are standing against God, his son, and his representatives. You simply change it!"

Galileo must have been a man with an immense sense of humor—which I count to be one of the great qualities of a religious man. Only idiots are serious; they are bound to be serious. To be able to laugh you need a little intelligence.

Galileo must have been intelligent. He was one of the greatest scientists of the world, but he must be counted as one of the most religious persons also. He said, "Of course God cannot be wrong, Jesus cannot be wrong, all the infallible popes cannot be wrong, but poor Galileo can always be wrong. There is no problem about it—I will change it in my book. But one thing you should remember: The earth will still go around the sun. About that I cannot do anything; it does not follow my orders. As far as my book is concerned I will change it, but in a footnote I will have to write this: 'The earth does not follow my orders, it still goes around the sun.'"

All the religions of the world are bound to pretend that whatever there is, they know it. And they know it exactly as it is; it cannot be otherwise.

Jains say their prophet, their messiah, is omniscient. He knows everything, past, present and future, so whatever he says is the absolute truth. Buddha has joked about Mahavira, the Jain messiah. They were contemporaries twenty-five centuries ago.

Mahavira was getting old, but Buddha was young and was still capable of joking and laughing. He was still young and alive; he was not yet established. Once you become an established religion, then you have your vested interests. Buddhism was just starting with Buddha. He could afford to joke and laugh, so he jokes against Mahavira and his omnipotence, omniscience, and omnipresence. He says, "I have seen Mahavira standing before a house begging"—because Mahavira lived naked and used to beg for his food. Buddha says, "I have seen him standing before a house that was empty. There was nobody in the house and yet this man, Jains say, knows not only the present, but the past and the future."

Buddha says, "I saw Mahavira walking just ahead of me, and he stepped on a dog's tail. It was early morning and it was not yet light. Only when the dog jumped, barking, did Mahavira come to know that he had stepped on his tail. This man is omniscient, and he does not know that a dog is sleeping right in his way, and he is going to step on his tail?"

But the same happened with Buddha when he became established. Three hundred years after his death, when his sayings and statements were collected and published for the first time, the disciples made it absolutely clear that "everything written here is absolutely true, and it is going to remain true forever."

The basic mistake that all the religions have committed is that they have not been courageous enough to accept that there are limits to their knowing. They have not been able to say on any point, "We don't know." They have been so arrogant that they go on saying they know, and they go on creating new fictions of knowledge.

That's where the true religion will be different, fundamentally different.

Yes, once in a while there have been single individuals who had the quality of true religion; for example, Bodhidharma. One of the most lovable human beings, he went to China fourteen hundred years ago. He remained for nine years in China, and a following gathered around him. But he was not a man belonging to the stupidity of the so-called religions. Formally he was a Buddhist monk, and China was already converted to Buddhism. Thousands of Buddhist monks had already reached China before Bodhidharma, and when they heard Bodhidharma was coming they rejoiced, because he was almost equal to Buddha. His name had reached them long before he came. Even the king of China, the great Emperor Wu, went to receive Bodhidharma on the boundary of China and India.

Wu was the person who had been responsible for converting the whole of China into Buddhism, from Confucius to Gautam Buddha. He had put all his forces and all his treasures in the hands of Buddhist monks, and he was a great emperor. When he met Bodhidharma he said, "I have been waiting to see you. I am old, and I am fortunate that you have come; all these years we have been waiting. I want to ask a few questions."

The first question he asked was: "I have devoted all my treasures, my armies, my bureaucracy—everything I have—to convert this vast land to Buddhism, and I have made thousands of temples for Buddha." He had made one temple in which there were ten thousand statues of Buddha; a whole mountain was carved out to create this temple. He asked, "What will be my benefit in the other world?"

That's what the monks had been telling him: "You have done so much to serve Gautam Buddha that perhaps when you reach the other world, he himself will be standing there to welcome you. You have earned so much virtue that an eternity of pleasures is yours."

Bodhidharma said, "All that you have done is absolutely meaningless. You have not even started on the journey, you have not taken even the first step. You will fall into the seventh hell—take my word for it."

Emperor Wu could not believe it: "I have done so much, and you say I will fall into the seventh hell?!"

Bodhidharma laughed and he said, "Whatsoever you have done is out of greed, and anything done out of greed cannot make you religious. You have renounced so many riches, but you have not renounced them unconditionally. You are bargaining; it is a business transaction. You are making a purchase in the other world. You are putting your bank balance from this world into the other world, transferring it. You are cunning, because this world is momentary—tomorrow you may die—and these monks have been telling you the other world is eternal. So what are you really doing? Giving up momentary treasures to gain eternal treasures—it's really a good deal! Whom are you trying to deceive?"

When Bodhidharma spoke to Wu in this way, in front of all the monks and the generals and the lesser kings who had come with Wu and his whole court, Wu was angry. Nobody had spoken in this way to him before. He said to Bodhidharma, "Is this the way for a religious person to talk?"

Bodhidharma said, "Yes, this is the only way a religious person can talk; all other ways are the ways of people who want to cheat you. These monks here have been cheating you; they have been making promises to you. You don't know anything about what happens after death, nor do they, but they have been pretending that they do."

Wu asked, "Who are you to speak with such authority?"

And do you know what Bodhidharma said? He said, "I don't know. That is one point that I don't know. I have been into myself, I have gone to the very center of my being and come out as ignorant as before. I do not know." Now, this I call courage.

No religion has been courageous enough to say, "We know this much, but there is much we don't know; perhaps in the future we may know it. And beyond that, there is a space which is going to remain unknowable forever."

If these religions had been that humble, the world would have been totally different. Humanity would not have been in such a mess; there would not have been so much anguish. All around the world everybody is full of anguish. What to say about hell—we are already living in hell here. What more suffering can there be in hell? And the people responsible for it are your so-called religious people. They still go on pretending, playing the same game. After three hundred years of science continually demolishing their territory, continually destroying their so-called knowledge, bringing forth new facts, new realities, still the pope is infallible, still the Hindu shankaracharya is infallible.

A true religion will have the humbleness to admit that only a few things are known, much more is unknown, and something will always remain unknowable. That "something" is the target of the whole spiritual search. You cannot make it an object of knowledge, but you can experience it, you can drink of it, you can have the taste of it—it is existential.

The scientist remains separate from the object he is studying. He is always separate from the object; hence knowledge is possible, because the knower is different from the known. But the religious person is moving into his subjectivity, where the knower and the known are one. When the knower and the known are one, there is no possibility of knowledge. Yes, you can dance it, but you cannot say it. It may be in the way you walk; it may be in your eyes, the way you see; it may be in your touch, the way you touch—but it cannot be put into words. Words are absolutely impotent as far as religion is concerned. And all these so-called religions are full of words. I call it all crap! This is their fundamental mistake.

That brings me to the second point, that all these religions have been against doubt. They have been really *afraid* of doubt. Only an impotent intellect can be afraid of doubt; otherwise doubt is a challenge, an opportunity to inquire.

They have all killed doubt and they have all forced on everybody's mind the idea that if you doubt you will fall into hell and you will suffer for eternity: "Never doubt." Belief is the thing, faith, total faith—not even partial faith will do, but total faith. What are you asking from human beings? something absolutely inhuman. An intelligent human being—how can he believe totally? And even if he tries to believe totally, it means doubt is there; otherwise against what is he fighting? Against what doubt is he trying to believe totally?

There is doubt, and doubt is not destroyed by believing. Doubt is destroyed by experiencing.

They say, believe. I say, explore. They say, don't doubt; I say, doubt to the very end, till you arrive and know and feel and experience. Then there is no need to repress doubt; it evaporates by itself. Then there is no need for you to believe. You don't believe in the sun, you don't believe in the moon—why do you believe in God? You don't need to believe in ordinary facts because they are there. A rose flower is there in the morning; in the evening it is gone. You *know* it, there is no question of doubt. This "belief" in a rose flower is a simple belief, not against doubt. Just so that you don't get confused between a simple belief and a complicated belief, I have a different word for it: it is trust. You trust a rose flower. It blooms, it releases its fragrance, and it is gone. By the evening you will not find it; its petals have fallen and the wind has taken them away. And you know again there will be roses, again there will be fragrance. You need not believe; you simply know from experience, because yesterday also there were roses and they disappeared. Today again they appeared—and tomorrow nature is going to follow its course.

Why believe in God? Neither yesterday did you have any experience of God, nor today . . . and what certainty is there about tomorrow? From where can you get certainty for tomorrow?—

because yesterday was empty, today is empty, and tomorrow is only an empty hope, hoping against hope. But that's what all these religions have been teaching—destroy your doubt, and believe.

The moment you destroy doubt, you have destroyed something of immense value, because it is doubt that is going to help you to inquire and find. In destroying doubt you have cut the very root of inquiry; now there will be no inquiry. That's why there is rarely, once in a while, a person in the world who has the feel of the eternal, who has breathed the eternal, has found the pulse of the eternal—it is very rare. And who is responsible? All your rabbis and popes and shankaracharyas and imams—they are responsible because they have cut the very root of inquiry.

In Japan they grow a strange tree. There are, in existence, three-hundred- or four-hundred-year-old trees, five inches tall. Four hundred years old! If you look at the tree, it is so ancient but such a pygmy of a tree, just five inches tall. They think it is an art. What they have done is to go on cutting the roots. The earthen pot that holds the tree has no bottom, so once in a while they take up the pot and cut the roots. When you cut the roots, the tree cannot grow up. It grows old, but it never grows up. It becomes older and older, but you have destroyed it. It may have become a big tree, because mostly those trees are bo trees.

Japan is a Buddhist country, and Gautam Buddha became enlightened under a bo tree. The bo tree is called a bo tree in English too, because under it Gautam Siddartha became a Buddha, attained *bodhi*, enlightenment. The full name is the bodhi tree, but in ordinary use it is called a bo tree. So most of those trees in Japan are bo trees. Now, no Buddha can sit under these tiny bo trees. You have stopped who knows how many Buddhas from becoming Buddhas by cutting these trees!

But what these people in Japan are doing shows something significant: it is what religions have done with man. They have been cutting your roots so you don't grow up—you only grow old. And the first root they cut is doubt; then your inquiry stops.

The second root they cut turns you against your own nature, condemns your nature. Obviously when your nature is condemned, how can you help your nature to flow, grow, and take its own course like a river? No, they don't allow you to be like a river, moving zigzag. All the religions have turned you into railway trains, running on rails, running from one station to another—and mostly just shunting, not going anywhere but still on rails. Those rails they call discipline, control, self-control.

Religions have done so much harm that it is almost incalculable—their pot of sins is full, overflowing. It just needs to be thrown into the Pacific, five miles deep, so deep that nobody can find it again and start again the same idiotic process. The small number of people in the world who are intelligent should get rid of all that their religions have done to them without their knowing. They should become completely clean of Jewishness, of Hinduism, of Christianity, of Jainism, of Buddhism. They should be completely clean—just to be human is enough.

Accept yourself. Respect yourself. Allow your nature to take its own course. Don't force, don't repress. Doubt—because doubt is not a sin, it is the sign of your intelligence. Doubt and go on inquiring until you find.

One thing I can say: whosoever inquires, finds. It is absolutely certain; it has never been otherwise. Nobody has come empty-handed from an authentic inquiry.

The greatest harm that the so-called religions have done to humanity is to prevent humanity from finding the true religion. They all pretended to be the true religion. All the religions of the world have conditioned the human mind from the very childhood to believe that theirs is the true religion—the religion in which you are born. A Hindu believes his religion is the only true religion in the world, all other religions are false. The same is the case with the Jew, with the Christian, with the Buddhist, with the Mohammedan. They are in agreement on one point, and that is that there is no need to find the true religion; the true religion is already available to you—you are born in it.

I call this their greatest harm because when you are without authentic religiousness you can only vegetate, not really live. You remain a superficial being; you cannot attain any profundity, authenticity. You know nothing about your own depths. You know about yourself through others, what they say. Just the way you know your face through the mirror, you are acquainted with yourself through other people's opinions; you don't know yourself directly. And the opinions that you depend on are of those people who are in a similar position; they don't know themselves.

These religions have created a society of blind people, and they go on telling you that you don't need eyes. Jesus had eyes; what is the need for Christians to have eyes? All you have to do is to believe in Jesus; he will lead the way to paradise, you have simply to follow. You are not allowed to think, because thinking may take you astray. Thinking is bound to take you on different paths than they want you to take, because thinking means sharpening your doubt, your intellect. And that is very dangerous for the so-called religions. The so-called religions want you dull, dead, somehow dragging; they want you without intelligence. But they are clever in finding good names; they call it "faith." It is nothing but the suicide of your intelligence.

A true religion will not require faith from you; a true religion will require *experience*. It will not ask you to drop your doubt, it will help you to sharpen your doubt so that you can inquire to the very end. The true religion will help you to find your truth.

And remember, my truth can never be your truth because there is no way of transferring truth from one person to another.

Mohammed's truth is Mohammed's truth; it cannot be yours just by your becoming a Mohammedan. To you it will remain only a belief. And who knows whether Mohammed knows or not? Who knows, Jesus may be simply a fanatic, neurotic. That's what many psychiatrists and psychologists and psychoanalysts agree upon, that Jesus is a mental case. To declare oneself to be the only begotten son of God, to declare, "I am the messiah who has come to redeem the whole world from suffering and sin"—do you think it is normal?

Even if a Gautam Buddha knows the truth, there is no way for you to know whether he knows it or not. Yes, you can recognize somebody who knows the truth if you also know it; then you will have the capacity to smell it. Otherwise you are simply believing in public opinion: you are believing in mass psychology, which is the lowest.

Truth comes to the highest intelligence. But if from the very beginning you are taught to believe, then you are crippled, you are destroyed. If from the very beginning you are conditioned to have faith, you have lost your soul. Then you will vegetate, you will not live. And that's what millions of people around the world are doing: vegetating.

What life can you have? You don't even know yourself. You don't know from where you are coming, to where you are going, what the purpose of all this is. Who has prevented you from knowing? Not the devil but the popes, the priests, the rabbis, the shankaracharyas—these are the real devils.

As far as I can see, all these synagogues, temples, mosques, churches, are all dedicated to the devil, not to God, because what they have done is not divine. It is sheer murder, the slaughter of the whole human mind.

No religion has been courageous enough to say, "There are things about which you can ask a question, but don't expect the answer. Life is a mystery." We can manage to live better, we can manage to live longer, we can manage to live more comfortably—but we cannot know what life is. That question will remain a question until the very end.

My whole effort here is to help you again to become ignorant.

The religions have been making you knowledgeable, and that is the harm they have done. They hand over to you so easily and so simply the whole Christian catechism which you can learn by rote within an hour and can repeat like a parrot. But you will not come to know the truth, the real, the one that surrounds you within and without. That catechism is not going to give it to you.

But to drop knowledge is one of the greatest problems, because knowledge gives so much nourishment to the ego. The ego wants all knowledge within its power. And when I say you have to drop knowledgeability and become again a child, I mean you have to start from that point where the rabbi or the priest distracted you. You have to come back to that point again.

You have to be again innocent, ignorant, not knowing anything, so that the questions can start arising again. Again the inquiry becomes alive, and with the inquiry becoming alive you cannot vegetate. Then life becomes an exploration, an adventure.

Learned and Natural: Reclaiming the Self You Were Born With

In the past, all over the world, people were pagans—simple nature-worshipers. There was no concept of sin, there was no question of guilt. Life was accepted as it is. There was no evaluation, no interpretation—reason had not interfered yet.

The moment reason starts interfering, condemnation comes in. The moment reason enters, division starts and man becomes split. Then you start condemning something in your being—one part becomes higher, another part becomes lower, and you lose balance. But this had to happen; reason had to come in, this is part of growth. As it happens to every child, it had to happen to the whole of humanity too.

When the child is born, he is a pagan. Each child is a born pagan, he is happy the way he is. He has no idea what is right and what is wrong; he has no ideals. He has no criteria, he has no judgment. Hungry, he asks for food. Sleepy, he falls asleep. That's what Zen masters say is the utmost in religiousness—when hungry eat, when feeling sleepy go to sleep. Let life flow; don't interfere.

Each child is born as a pagan, but sooner or later he will lose that simplicity. That is part of life; it has to happen. It is part of our growth, maturity, destiny. The child has to lose it and find it again. When the child loses it he becomes ordinary, worldly. When he regains it he becomes religious.

The innocence of childhood is cheap; it is a gift from existence. We have not earned it and we will have to lose it. Only by losing it will we become aware of what we have lost. Then we will start searching for it. And only when we search for it and earn it, achieve it, become it—then we will know the tremendous preciousness of it.

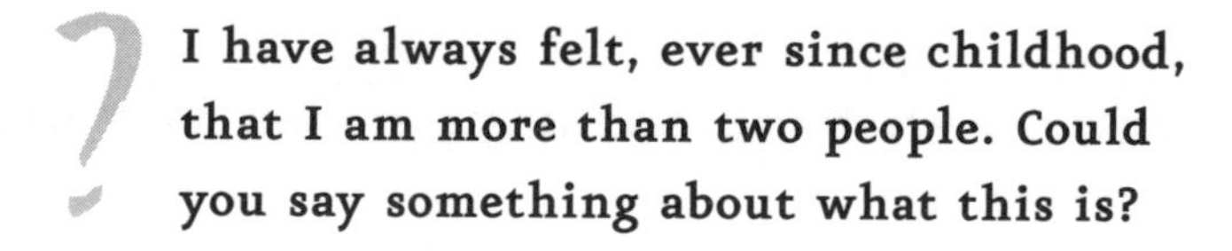

I have always felt, ever since childhood, that I am more than two people. Could you say something about what this is?

Everybody is born as one single individual, but by the time he is mature enough to participate in life he has become a crowd. It is not anything special that you are feeling; it is the case with almost everybody. The only difference is that you are becoming aware of it, which is good. People are not aware of it.

If you just sit silently and listen to your mind, you will find so many voices. You will be surprised, you can recognize those voices very well. Some voice is from your grandfather, some voice is from your grandmother, some voice is from your father, another voice is from your mother. Some voice is from the priest, another from the teacher, from the neighbors, from your friends, from your enemies. All these voices are jumbled up in a crowd within you, and if you want to find your own voice, it is almost impossible; the crowd is too thick.

In fact, you have forgotten your own voice long ago. You were never given freedom enough to voice your opinions. You were always taught obedience. You were taught to say yes to everything that your elders were saying to you. You were taught that you have to follow whatever your teachers or your priests are doing. Nobody ever told you to search for your own voice, "Have you got any voice of your own or not?" So your voice has remained very subdued and other voices are very loud, commanding, because they were orders and you followed them—in spite of yourself. You had no intention to follow, you could see "This is not right." But one has to be obedient to be respected, to be acceptable, to be loved.

Naturally only one voice is missing in you, only one person is missing in you, and that is you. Otherwise there is a whole crowd, and that crowd is constantly driving you mad, because one voice says, "Do this," another voice says, "Never do that! Don't listen to that voice!" and you are torn apart.

This whole crowd has to be withdrawn. This whole crowd has to be told, "Now please leave me alone!" The people who have gone to the mountains or to the secluded forests were really not going away from the society; they were trying to find a place where they could disperse their crowd inside.

Those people who have made a place within you are obviously reluctant to leave. But if you want to become an individual in your own right, if you want to get rid of this continuous conflict and mess within you, then you have to say good-bye to them—even when they belong to your respected father, your mother, your grandfather. It does not matter to whom they belong. One thing is certain: they are not your voices. They are the voices of people who have lived in their time, and they had no idea what the future was going to be. They have loaded their children with their own experience; their experience is not going to match with the unknown future. They think they are helping their children to be knowledgeable, to be wise, so their life can be easier and more comfortable, but they are doing just the wrong thing. With all the good intentions in the world, they are destroying the child's spontaneity, his own consciousness, his own ability to stand on his feet and respond to a new future, which their old ancestors had no idea of.

The child is going to face new storms, is going to face new situations, and he or she needs a totally new consciousness to respond. Only then is the response going to be fruitful; only then can one have a victorious life, a life that is not just a long, long drawn-out despair but a dance from moment to moment, which goes on becoming deeper and deeper to the last breath. Then the person enters into death dancing, and joyously.

It is good that you are becoming aware that it seems you are more than one person. Everybody is! And by becoming aware, it is possible to get rid of this crowd.

Be silent, and find your own self. Unless you find your own self, it is difficult to disperse the crowd because all those different people in the crowd are pretending "I am your self," and you have no way to agree or disagree. So don't create any fight with the crowd. Let them fight amongst themselves—they are quite efficient in fighting amongst themselves! You, meanwhile, try to find yourself. And once you know who you are, you can just tell them to get out of the house—it is actually that simple! But first you have to find yourself. Once you are there, once the master is there, the owner of the house is there and all these people, who have been pretending to be masters themselves, start dispersing. Once you are yourself, unburdened of the past—discontinuous with the past, original, strong as a lion, and innocent as a child—you can reach the stars, or even beyond the stars; your future is golden.

Up to now people have always talked about the golden past. Now we have to learn the language of the golden future. There is no need for you to change the whole world; just change yourself and you have started changing the whole world, because you are part of the world. If even a single human being changes, that change will radiate to thousands and thousands of others. You will become a trigger point for a revolution that can give birth to a new kind of humanity.

? You have said knowledge is not any use in the process of coming to know ourselves. So please explain what is included in the development of being.

Being never develops. Being simply is. There is no evolution, there is no time involved in it. It is eternity, it is not "becoming." Spiritually, you never develop; you cannot. As far as the ultimate goal is concerned, you are already there. You have never been anywhere else.

Then what is development? Development is only a kind of awakening to the truth that you are. The truth does not grow; only recognition grows, remembrance grows.

That's why I don't talk about the "development of being." I talk about all the hindrances that are preventing your recognition. And knowledge is the greatest hindrance; hence I have talked about it extensively. It is the barrier.

If you think you already know, you will never know. If you think you already know, what is the point of searching? You can go on sleeping and dreaming. The moment you recognize that you don't know, that recognition of ignorance goes like an arrow into the heart, it pierces you like a spear. In that very piercing, one becomes aware—in that very shock.

Knowledge is a kind of shock absorber. It does not allow you to be shaken and shocked. It goes on protecting you, it is an armor around you. I speak against knowledge so that you can drop the armor, so that life can shock you into awareness.

Life is there, ready to shock you every moment. Your being is there inside you, ready to be awakened any moment. But between these two there is knowledge. And the more of it there is, the more your self-awakening will be delayed.

Become unknowledgeable.

And never think of spirituality as a process of growth. It is not a growth. You are already gods, buddhas from the very beginning. It is not that you have to become buddhas—the treasure is there, only you don't know where you have put it. You have forgotten the key, or you have forgotten how to use the key. You are so drunk with knowledge that you have become oblivious of all that you are. Knowledge is alcoholic; it makes people drunk. Then their perception is blurred, then their remembrance is at the minimum. Then they start seeing things that are not, and they stop seeing things that are.

That's why I have not talked about how to evolve your being. Being is already as it should be, it is perfect. Nothing needs to be added to it, nothing *can* be added to it. It's a creation of existence. It comes out of perfection, hence it is perfect. Just withdraw all the hindrances that you have created.

And our whole society goes on working, endeavoring to create hindrances. A child is born and immediately we start creating hindrances in him. We create comparison in him: "Somebody is more beautiful than you, and somebody else is healthier than you, and somebody else's child—look, look at their grades, at their intelligence, and what are you doing?" We start creating comparison. Comparison brings with it the idea of inferiority and superiority—and both are illnesses, hindrances. Now the child will never think just about himself; he will always think in comparison to somebody else. The poison of comparison has entered. Now the person is going to remain miserable; now the bliss of being will become more and more impossible.

Everyone is born unique. No comparison is possible. You are you, and I am I. A Buddha is a Buddha, and a Christ is a Christ, and no comparison is possible. If you compare, you create superiority, inferiority—the ways of the ego. And then, of course, a great desire arises to compete, a great desire arises to defeat others. You remain in fear of whether you are going to make it or not, because it is a violent struggle and everybody is trying to do the same, to become the first. Millions of people are trying to become the first. Great violence, aggression, hatred, enmity arise. Life becomes a hell. If you are defeated, you are miserable . . . and there are many more chances of being defeated than of winning. And even if you succeed you are not happy because the moment you succeed you become afraid: Now somebody else might take it from you. Competitors are all around, violently coming after you.

Before you succeeded you were afraid about whether you were going to make it or not; now you have succeeded, you have the money and the power, and you are afraid somebody is going to take it away from you. Before you were trembling and now you are trembling. Those who are failures are miserable, and those who succeed are miserable.

In this world, it is very difficult to find a happy person, because nobody is fulfilling the conditions for being happy. The first condition is that one has to drop all comparison. Drop all these stupid ideas of being superior and inferior. You are neither superior nor inferior. You are simply yourself! There exists no one like you, no one with whom you can be compared. Then, suddenly, you are at home.

But we start poisoning the children's minds with knowledge. We start teaching them things they don't know and haven't experienced. We teach them about God—we are teaching them a lie. This God is not going to be a true God—they don't *know*; we are forcing them to believe, and this belief will become their knowledge. Belief cannot become real knowing; it will be only a pretension. Their whole life they will think they know, and they will never know. The foundation has been laid in untruth.

We teach children, "You have an immortal soul." What nonsense you are teaching to them! And I am not saying there is no immortal soul, I am not saying there is no such thing as godliness, mind you. I am saying these things should not be taught as beliefs. They are existential experiences. The child has to be helped to explore into his inner world.

Rather than helping children in exploration we hand them ready-made knowledge. That ready-made knowledge becomes the greatest problem. How to drop it?

That's why I have spoken on the stupidity of knowledge—because it is ignorance masquerading as knowledge. The moment you drop it you will be again a child—fresh, alive, vibrant, curious; your eyes will be full of wonder and your heart will start throbbing again with the mystery of life. Then the exploration begins, and with that, the awareness. More and more you become aware of this inner consciousness that you have been carrying all along, but it has become too stuffed with knowledge, so whenever you go in you never find consciousness; you always find some content floating in consciousness.

Knowledge is like clouds in the sky. Right now, there are so many clouds in the sky. If you look at the sky you will not find the sky at all, only clouds and clouds. That is the state of a knowledgeable person's mind: thoughts, scriptures, great theories, dogmas, doctrines—they all float like clouds, and you cannot see the pure sky.

Let these clouds disappear. And they are there because you are clinging to them. They are there because you go on holding on to them. Loosen your grip, let them go. Then there is a pristine clarity of the sky, the absolute infinity of the sky. That is freedom. That is consciousness. That is true knowing.

A great Western philosopher, David Hume, has written, hearing again and again from the great mystics, "Know thyself!" he says, "I also tried one day to know myself. I closed my eyes and went in. I found a few desires, a few thoughts, memories, dreams, imaginations and things like that. But I could not find anybody else there. I could not find myself."

This is the true depiction of almost everybody's mind, except a few buddhas. If you go in, what will you find? Contents, clouds moving around.

Even such an intelligent person as David Hume could not see the point: Who is it that is looking at the contents? Who is this awareness that finds a few memories, desires floating around? Of course, this witness cannot be a desire, this witness cannot be an imagination. This witness cannot be any thought. All is passing in front of this witness . . . and Hume was looking for the witness! Now, you cannot look for the witness as an object. The only way to know the witness is to drop all content and become utterly empty. When there is nothing to see, your capacity to see turns upon itself.

That's what Jesus calls conversion. When there is nothing there to see, one starts seeing oneself. When there is nothing to hinder, the consciousness is pure, and in that purity it becomes self-conscious.

And when I use the term "self-conscious" I don't mean your "self-consciousness." Your self-consciousness is not the consciousness of your self, it is just ego-consciousness. You don't know who you are; how can you be self-conscious? Your self-consciousness is a disease. You become self-conscious only when you are facing other people. If you are to deliver a speech you become self-conscious, and because of that self-consciousness you become disturbed, almost paralyzed. Or if you are playing a part in a drama, you become self-conscious. Your self-consciousness is nothing but the desire of the ego to perform a thing so perfectly that everybody appreciates it.

When I say "self-consciousness," I mean when all has disappeared and there is no other content left—when the mirror reflects itself. It is like a small candle burning in a room. It reflects off the walls, it reflects off the furniture, it reflects off the painting on the wall, it reflects off the ceiling. For a moment imagine that the walls have disappeared, the painting is no more, the roof has disappeared—all has disappeared, only the small candle is burning. Now what will reflect its light? It will only reflect itself; it will only be self-luminous.

This is the state of being.

Drop knowledge. Drop comparison. Drop false identities. This whole process is negative! Drop this, drop that, and go on dropping. Go on dropping till nothing is left to drop—and then it is there, your pure consciousness is there.

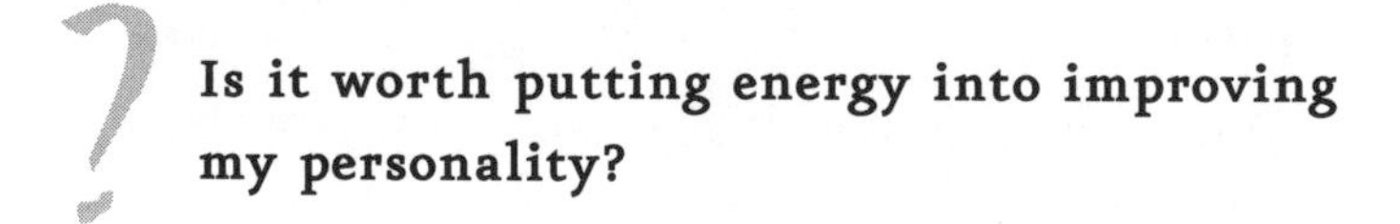

Is it worth putting energy into improving my personality?

The personality has to be dropped so that your individuality can be discovered. What we call the personality is not you; it is a mask people have put over you. It is not your authentic reality, it is not your original face. You are asking me, "Is it really worth putting any energy into improving my personality?" Put your energy into destroying your personality! Put your energy into discovering your individuality, and make the distinction very clear: individuality is that which you have brought from your very birth. Individuality is your essential being, and personality is what the society has made of you, what they wanted to make of you.

No society up to now has been able to give freedom to their children to be themselves. It seems risky. They may prove rebellious. They may not follow the religion of their forefathers; they may not think the great politicians are really great; they may not trust in your moral values. They will find their own morality, and they will find their own lifestyle. They will not be replicas, they will not repeat the past; they will be beings of the future.

This has created fear that they may go astray. Before they go astray, every society tries to give them a certain direction how to live, a certain ideology of what is good and what is evil, a certain religion, a certain holy scripture. These are ways to create the personality, and the personality functions like an imprisonment.

But millions of people in the world know only their personality; they don't know that there is anything more. They have completely forgotten themselves, and they have forgotten even the way to reach themselves. They have all become actors, hypocrites. They are doing things they never wanted to do, and they are not doing things they are hankering to do. Their life is so split that they can never be at peace. Their nature will assert itself again and again, will not leave them at peace. And their so-called personality will go on repressing it, forcing it deeper into the unconscious. This conflict divides you and your energy—and a house divided cannot stand long. This is the whole misery of human beings—why there is not much dance, much song, much joyfulness.

People are so engaged in warfare with themselves. They don't have energy, and they don't have time to do anything else except fight with themselves. Their sensuality they have to fight, their sexuality they have to fight against, their individuality they have to fight against, their originality they have to fight against. And they have to fight *for* something that they don't want to be, which is not part of their nature, which is not their destiny. So they can pretend to be false for a time—but again and again the real asserts.

Their whole life goes on, up and down, and they cannot figure out who they really are: the repressor or the repressed? the oppressor or the oppressed? And whatever they do, they cannot destroy their nature. They can certainly poison it; they can certainly destroy its joy, they can destroy its dance, they can destroy its love. They can make their life a mess, but they cannot destroy their nature completely. And they cannot throw away their personality because their personality carries their forefathers, their parents, their teachers, their priests, their whole past. It is their heritage; they cling to it.

My whole teaching is, don't cling to personality. It is not yours, and it is never going to be yours. Allow your nature full freedom. And respect yourself, be proud of being yourself, whatever you are. Have some dignity! Don't be destroyed by the dead.

People who have been dead for thousands of years are sitting on your head. They are your personality—and you want to improve on them? So call in a few more of the dead! Dig up more graves, bring out more skeletons, surround yourself with all kinds of ghosts. You will be respected by the society. You will be honored, rewarded; you will have prestige, you will be thought to be a saint. But surrounded by the dead, you will not be able to laugh—it will be so out of place—you will not be able to dance, you will not be able to sing, you will not be able to love.

Personality is a dead thing. Drop it! In a single blow, not in fragments, not slowly, today a little bit and then tomorrow a little bit, because life is short and tomorrow is not certain. The false is false. Discard it totally!

Every real human being has to be a rebel . . . and rebel against whom? Against his own personality.

The Japanese-American was a longtime customer at a Greek restaurant, because he had discovered that they made especially tasty fried rice. Each evening he would come in the restaurant, and he would order "flied lice." This always caused the Greek restaurant owner to roll on the floor with laughter. Sometimes he would have two or three friends stand nearby just to hear the Japanese customer order his "flied lice."

Eventually the customer's pride was so hurt that he took a special diction lesson just to be able to say "fried rice" correctly. The next time he went to the restaurant he said very plainly, "Fried rice, please."

Unable to believe his ears, the Greek restaurant owner said, "Sir, would you repeat that?"

The Japanese-American replied, "You heard what I said, you Gleek plick!"

How long can you go on pretending? The reality is going to come up some day or other, and it is better that it comes sooner. There is no need to improve your diction—just drop that whole personality thing. Just be yourself. However raw and however wild it appears to be in the beginning, soon it starts having its own grace, its own beauty.

And the personality . . . you can go on polishing it, but it is just polishing a dead thing, which is going to destroy not only your time, your energy, your life, but also the people around you. We are all affecting each other. When everybody is doing something, you also start doing it. Life is very contagious, and everybody is improving his personality—that's why the idea has arisen in your mind.

But there is no need to do that. You are not part of a herd, not part of a mob. Be respectful of yourself, and be respectful of others. Be proud of your freedom. When you are proud of your freedom you want everybody else to be free, because your freedom has given you so much love and so much grace. You would like everybody else in the world to be free, loving, and graceful.

This is possible only if you are original—not something put together, not something false, but something that grows within you, which has roots in your being, which brings flowers in its time. And to have one's own flowers is the only destiny, is the only significant way of life.

But the personality has no roots; it is plastic, it is phony. Dropping it is not difficult; it needs just a little courage. And my feeling of thousands of people is that everybody has that much courage, just people are not using it. Once you start using your courage, sources within you that are dormant become active, and you become capable of having even more courage, more rebelliousness. You become a revolution in yourself.

When you are a revolution unto yourself it is a joy to see, because you have fulfilled your destiny. You have transcended the ordinary mob, the sleeping crowd.

? **What does it mean when you say, "Just be yourself"? How can I be myself when I don't know who I am? I know many of my preferences, likings, dislikings, and tendencies, which seem to be the outcome of a programmed biocomputer called the mind. Does just being oneself mean that one totally lives out the whole content of the mind as watchfully as possible?**

Yes, it exactly means that—to live as an awareness. An awareness of all the programs the mind has been conditioned for, awareness of all the impulses, desires, memories, imaginations . . . all that the mind can do. One has to be not part of it, but separate—*seeing* it but not *being* it—watching it.

And one of the most essential things to remember is that you cannot watch your watchfulness. If you watch your watchfulness, then the *watcher* is you, not the watched. So you cannot go beyond watchfulness. The point that you cannot transcend is your being; the point that you cannot go beyond is you. You can watch very easily any thought, any emotion, any sentiment. Just one thing you cannot watch, and that is your watchfulness. If you manage to watch it, that means you have shifted: the first watchfulness has become just a thought; now you are the second watcher. You can go on shifting back, but you cannot get out of watchfulness because it is *you*; you cannot be otherwise.

So when I say, "Just be yourself," I am saying to you, "Just be unprogrammed, unconditioned awareness." That's how you have come into the world, and that's how the enlightened person leaves the world. He lives in the world but remains totally separate.

One of the great mystics, Kabir, has a beautiful poem about it. All his poems are just perfect; nothing can be better. One of his poems says, "I will give back the soul that was given to me at the time of my birth as pure, as clean, as it was given to me. I will give it back that way when I die." He is talking about awareness, saying that it has remained unpolluted. The whole world was there to pollute it, but he has remained watchful.

All you need is just to be watchful, and nothing will affect you. This unaffectedness will keep your purity, and this purity has certainly the freshness of life, the joy of existence—all the treasures you have been endowed with.

But you become attached to the small things surrounding you and forget the one that you are. It is the greatest discovery in life and the most ecstatic pilgrimage to truth. And you need not be an ascetic, you need not be antilife; you need not renounce the world and go to the mountains. You can be where you are, you can continue to do what you are doing. Just a new thing has to be evolved: Whatever you do, you do with awareness, even the smallest act of the body or the mind—and with each act of awareness you will become aware of the beauty and the treasure and the glory and the eternity of your being.

Outer and Inner: In search of where the twain shall meet

There have been many civilizations before ours that have reached high peaks but destroyed themselves because they grew in a deep imbalance. They developed great technologies, but they forgot that even the greatest technological progress is not going to make people more blissful, more peaceful, more loving, more compassionate.

Our consciousness has not grown at the same pace as our scientific progress, and that has been the cause of many civilizations destroying themselves. We have created monsters as far as machines are concerned, and at the same time we have remained retarded, unconscious, almost asleep. And it is very dangerous to give so much power to unconscious people.

That's what is happening now. Politicians are of the lowest kind as far as consciousness is concerned. They are clever, they are cunning. They are mean, too, and they make every effort for a single goal, which is to be more powerful. Their only desire is for more power—not for more peace, not for more being, not for more truth, not for more love.

What do you need more power for?—to dominate others, to destroy others. All the power accumulates in the hands of unconscious people. So on the one hand, politicians in all the civilizations that have developed and died—it would be better to say committed suicide—had all the power in their hands. On the other hand, the genius of human intelligence was searching for more and more technology, scientific improvements, and all they discovered finally had to go into the hands of the politicians.

The destruction of our earth will not come from some other planet—we are preparing our own graves. We may be aware, we may not be aware, but we are all gravediggers and we are digging our own graves. Right now there are only a few nations in possession of nuclear weapons. Soon many more nations will also be nuclear powers. It is going to be beyond control, with so many nations having so much destructiveness that a single nation could destroy the whole earth. A single crazy person, a single politician, just to show his power, can destroy the whole of civilization and you will have to begin from ABC. And the destruction is not only of humanity. With humanity will die all the companions of humanity—the animals, the trees, the birds, the flowers. Everything could disappear, everything that is alive.

The reason is an imbalance in our evolution. We go on developing scientific technology without bothering at all that our consciousness should also evolve in the same proportion. In fact, our consciousness should be a little ahead of our technological progress.

If our consciousness were in the state of enlightenment . . . In the hands of a Gautam Buddha nuclear power would no longer be dangerous. In the hands of a Gautam Buddha nuclear power would be turned towards some creative force—because force is always neutral; either you can destroy with it or you can find ways to create something. But right now our powers are great and our humanity is very small. It is as if we have put bombs in the hands of children to play with.

Human beings have gone through this struggle since the very beginning. It is the imbalance between the inner and the outer.

The outer is easier, and the outer is objective. For example, one man, Thomas Alva Edison, discovers electricity and the whole of humanity uses it; there is no need for everyone to discover it again and again. Inner growth is a totally different phenomenon. A Gautam Buddha may become enlightened, but that does not mean that everybody else becomes enlightened. Each individual has to find the truth by himself or herself. So whatever happens on the outside goes on accumulating, piling up; all the scientific progress goes on piling up because each scientist is standing on the shoulders of other scientists. But the evolution of consciousness does not follow the same law. Each individual has to discover it by himself; he cannot stand on the shoulders of somebody else.

Anything objective can be shared, can be taught in the schools, colleges, universities. But the same is not true about subjectivity. I may know everything about the inner world; still I cannot hand that over to you. It is one of the fundamental laws of existence that the inner truth has to be discovered by each individual through his or her own efforts. It cannot be purchased in the marketplace, nor can it be stolen. Nobody can give it to you as a gift. It is not a commodity, it is not material; it is an immaterial experience.

One can give evidence for this immaterial experience by one's individuality, by one's presence, compassion, love, silence. But these are only indications that something has happened inside a person. That person can encourage you, can tell you that you are not going inside in vain: "You will find treasures, as I have found." Each master is nothing but an argument, evidence, an eyewitness. But the experience remains individual.

Science becomes social, technology becomes social; the subjective realm remains individual. That is the basic problem, how to create a balance.

In one of the most beautiful forests in Germany, the famous Black Forest, trees were simply dying for no visible reason. The government of Germany tried to hide the facts, but you cannot cover things up forever. The forest was dying, and the reason was not "natural causes." The reason was the production of certain gases by the factories and those gases mixing with the atmosphere, so that when it rains the water becomes acidic. When it falls on a tree, that tree starts to die, it is poisoned. By now perhaps half the Black Forest is completely dead.

There is a layer of ozone around the earth, which is protective; it protects life on the earth. All of the sun's rays are not good for life, and the ozone layer reflects a few of those rays. They are death rays; if they enter the atmosphere they begin to destroy life. Only those rays are allowed through by the ozone which are not against life but which are life-enhancing. But stupidly we have made holes in this layer. One way is by sending rockets to the moon—which is a simple exercise in stupidity. When the rockets go outside the atmosphere, they create holes in the ozone layer, and when they came back they again create holes. Now those death rays from the sun are entering the atmosphere.

When this civilization is destroyed, people may think it was a natural calamity. It is not, we have created it. Because of the accumulation of carbon dioxide and other gases, the temperature of the earth's atmosphere has begun to rise, and that is creating new problems. The ice at both the poles, south and north, is melting because the temperature is going so high. Anybody researching the phenomenon hundreds of years later on might think it was a natural calamity. It is not. It is our own stupidity.

We can learn much, seeing what is happening, and then we can think introspectively about other civilizations that have disappeared, either through war or through calamities that were apparently natural. But they weren't necessarily natural. Those civilizations might have done something stupid that caused the calamities. There have been highly developed civilizations living on this earth, but they all got into the same mess we are entering.

They all got into the same darkness we are entering. Their consciousness was not lost—they had no consciousness. They had just the same superficial consciousness as we have.

What are you doing to prevent the calamity that is coming closer every day? The death of this earth is not far away—at the most a few decades, and that is an optimistic estimate; for the pessimists it might happen as early as tomorrow. But even if we give a hundred years to you, what are you going to do to help human consciousness rise in such a way that we can prevent the global suicide that is going to happen? It is coming from many directions. Nuclear weapons are one direction that is completely ready. Any moment and there could be a push-button war. It will not be a question of sending armies and airplanes to respond. If the oceans are filled with all the ice that the Himalayas hold, and that of the South and North Poles, and the Alps and other mountains, we will be drowned.

The only possible way to avoid it is to create more meditativeness in the world. But it is such an insane world that sometimes it seems almost unbelievable.

If, in the coming years, we can go through a revolution, attain a new consciousness, perhaps the consequences of what has been happening up to now can be avoided. We should make every effort to avoid it. It is a particularly dark period, and it will become darker and darker unless everybody becomes a light unto himself or herself and radiates light. Unless everyone starts sharing their light and their fire with those who are thirsty and hungry for it, the dawn is not going to come automatically. We have to be fully alert to make every possible effort in helping consciousness evolve.

It is a great struggle against darkness, but also a great opportunity and challenge and excitement. You do not have to become serious about it. You have to do it lovingly, dancingly, with all your songs and with all your joy, because only in that way is it possible to bring the dawn and dispel the darkness.

There is a cosmic law that says, "Only out of the mud the lotus can grow." The politicians, and the priests of all the religions, the governments and the bureaucracies—all are creating enough mud. Now we have to grow lotuses. You have not to be drowned in their mud; you have to sow seeds for lotuses.

The lotus seed is a miracle: it transforms the mud into the most beautiful flower. In the East the lotus has been almost worshiped for two reasons. One, that it arises out of the mud. The English word *human* simply means mud. The Arabic word *admi* simply means mud, because God made human beings out of mud. But there is a possibility of growing a lotus flower. It is a big flower, and it opens its petals only when the sun rises and the birds start singing and the whole sky becomes colorful. As the darkness comes and the sun sets, it again closes its petals. It is a lover of light.

Secondly, its petals and even its leaves are so velvety that in the night, dewdrops gather on the petals, on the leaves. In the early morning sun, those dewdrops shine almost like pearls—far more beautiful, creating rainbows around themselves. But the most beautiful thing is that although they are resting on the petals and on the leaves, the dewdrops don't touch the leaf. Just a small breeze comes and they slip back into the water, leaving no trace.

The lotus flower has been symbolic in the East, because the East says you should live in the world but remain untouched by it. You should remain in the world, but the world should not remain in you. You should pass through the world without carrying any impression, any impact, any scratch. If by the time of death you can say that your consciousness is as pure, as innocent, as you brought it at birth, you have lived a religious life, a spiritual life.

Hence, the lotus flower has become a symbol of a spiritual style of living. It grows from the mud and yet remains untouched. It is a symbol of transformation. Mud is transformed into the most beautiful and the most fragrant flower the planet knows. Gautam Buddha was so in love with the lotus that he talked about "the lotus paradise."

With our deep meditation and gratitude for existence, it is possible that this earth can remain growing with more consciousness, with more flowers; it can become a lotus paradise.

But a tremendous struggle for a great revolution in human consciousness is needed, and everybody is called to that revolution. Contribute all that you can. Your whole life has to be given to the revolution. You will not have another chance, another challenge for your own growth and for the growth of this whole beautiful planet.

This is the only planet in the whole of existence that is alive; its death would be a great tragedy. But it can be avoided.

? **The scientific vision of objective reality and the subjective experience of existence seem to be two completely separate and unbridgeable dimensions. Is this because of the nature of things, or is it only an illusion of our mind?**

The scientific approach to existence and the religious approach have been in the past separate and unbridgeable. The reason was the insistence of old religions on superstitions, belief systems, denial of inquiry, and doubt. In fact, there is nothing unbridgeable between science and religion, and there is no separation either. But religion insisted on belief—science cannot accept that.

Belief is covering up your ignorance. It never reveals to you the truth; it only gives you certain dogmas, creeds, and you can create an illusion of knowledge through them. But that knowledge is nothing but a delusion. Anything based on belief is bogus. Because religions insisted continuously on belief and the basic method of science is doubt, the separation happened and it became unbridgeable. It will remain unbridgeable if religion does not rise to face the challenge of doubt.

In my vision, there is only science, with two dimensions. One dimension approaches the outside reality, the other dimension approaches the interior reality. One is objective, the other is subjective. Their methods are not different, their conclusions are not different. And both start from doubt.

Doubt has been condemned so much that you have forgotten the beauty of it, you have forgotten the richness of it.

The child is born not with any belief but is born with a very curious, doubting, skeptical consciousness. Doubt is natural, belief is unnatural. Belief is imposed by the parents, society, the educational systems, religions. All these people are in the service of ignorance, and they have served ignorance for thousands of years. They have kept humanity in darkness, and there was a reason for it: If humanity is in darkness, knows nothing of reality, then it can be exploited easily, enslaved easily, deceived easily, kept poor, dependent. All these things were involved.

The old religions were not concerned with truth. They talked about it, but their concern was how to keep people away from truth. Up to now they have succeeded, but now those religions are all on their deathbed. And the sooner they die the better.

Why do you need a belief in the first place? You don't believe in a rose. Nobody asks you, "Do you believe in the rose?" You will simply laugh, you will say, "The question of belief does not arise; I know the rose." Knowing needs no belief.

But the blind believe in light; they have to, they have no eyes. And belief keeps a religious person blind. If he were not given belief, if he were told that he is blind and his eyes had to be cured, then perhaps he would be able to see. The moment you see the light, the question of belief does not arise: you know it. Any belief just indicates your ignorance, your blindness—but it gives you a false sense that you know.

If you inquire, meditate, go deeper into yourself, you will find a tremendous reality, but you will not find God. You will find consciousness in its ultimate flowering, eternal, but you will not find an old man with a long beard—and the beard must be by this time really long, miles long; for centuries he has been sitting there! You will not find God. All religions are frightened of inquiry—that's why the separation from science happened. And all the religions have been against science, because sooner or later science is going to prove—it has proved already—that its method of doubt brings you closer to reality. It opens secrets of life; it makes you really intelligent, alert, knowing what the truth is.

But science up to now has remained concerned only with the objective world that surrounds you. I condemn the religions because they have kept humanity in darkness, and I condemn the scientists because they are doing such a stupid thing—they are aware of everything, inquiring into everything in the world except themselves. The scientist in his lab is the only person who is left out of inquiry. Everything else he inquires about—and inquires deeply, without any prejudice. But he forgets who the inquirer is.

Is there any inquiry possible without an inquirer? Is there any possibility of observing objective reality without an observer? And that's what science has been doing for three hundred years. The religions are criminal, but science has also to take the burden of that crime—not that big, because science is only three hundred years old. But science cannot say anything about the subjective world, for or against, because it has not inquired.

Religions have to disappear completely—they are a kind of

cancer on the human soul—and science has to extend its inquiry, to make it complete. It is only half. You are just looking at the object and forgetting the person looking at it. Science has to grow a new dimension that goes inwards. Doubt will be the method for both, so there is no question of bridging. Doubt is the center. From that center you can move into objective reality—that's what science has been doing up to now. You can move from the same doubt into your interiority, which science has not done up to now. And because science has not done it, the subjective world is left in the hands of religions.

Religions pretend to inquire into the subjective world, the world of consciousness; but it is a pretension because it starts with belief. Once you believe in a thing your inquiry is finished. You have already destroyed the question, you have killed the quest.

From belief you cannot move into investigation. Every inquiry, either objective or subjective, needs an open mind—and doubt gives you that tremendous quality of an open mind. And remember, because there is a possibility to be confused—doubt does not mean *disbelief*, because disbelief is again belief standing on its head. Karl Marx and his followers, the communists, say there is no God. This is their belief. Neither Karl Marx nor Lenin nor any other communist ever bothered to inquire whether God really does not exist. They have accepted it in the same way as Christians and Hindus and Mohammedans and Jews have accepted that there is a God. I don't make any distinction between the atheist and the theist; they are traveling in the same boat.

I don't make any distinction between a Christian, a Hindu, and a communist. On the surface there seems to be a great distinction. The communist does not believe in God; religions believe in God. That is very superficial; if you look just a little bit deeper, scratch just a little bit, you will be surprised: disbelief is as ignorant as belief. Both have accepted something on faith, without any inquiry. Hence I say communism is an atheist religion. Mohammedans have their Mecca, Jews have their Jerusalem, communists have their Kremlin. And it is very amusing to see a picture of the Kremlin—it looks like a church! Perhaps it was a church before the revolution. It was not made by the communists, certainly. It may have been the biggest church in Russia. They captured it and they made it their central office. But the architecture shows simply that it is a church.

Not only the architecture of the Kremlin but the minds of people who dominated people from the Kremlin are exactly the same as the popes, as ayatollahs, as the shankaracharyas—no difference! On the fundamentals they would agree. Communists believe in *Das Kapital*, and Christians believe in the Bible, but where is the difference? Those books are different, but the person who believes, the mind that believes, is the same.

Because science has denied—strangely—the very existence of the scientist, it goes on playing games with rats, experimenting. They go on working with rats, monkeys, with everything else in the world. The scientific inquiry has reached into molecules, atoms, electrons. But in all this search, the scientist has forgotten one thing: that he exists too. Without the scientist, the lab is meaningless. Who is experimenting? Certainly there is a consciousness, a certain awareness, a certain entity with the capacity to observe. This is such a simple fact; but for three hundred years science has not been able to accept this simple fact. I find them guilty because, if they had accepted this fact and made it also a subject of scientific inquiry, the religions would have died long ago. If religions are still in existence, science has to accept some of the responsibility.

The very word *science* explains my approach. *Science* means knowing. Any knowledge, any knowing, needs three things: an object to know, a subject to know it, and between the subject and the object, knowing arises.

If human beings were not on the earth, trees will be here, rose bushes will be here, but they will not know they are rose bushes and trees. The clouds will come, but nobody will know this is the rainy season. The sun will rise, but there will be no sunrise because there will be nobody to describe it. A knower is the most valuable phenomenon in existence, and, because science has denied the knower, religions have had absolute freedom to go on insisting on all their old beliefs.

My work is to help all the religions die peacefully. The area they have been occupying should be occupied by science. We can keep two names, science for objective reality and religion for subjective reality, but really there is no need for two names. It is better to have one name, science, with two dimensions—one moving outward, one moving inward.

The scientific method starts with doubt. It goes on doubting till it comes to a point where doubt is impossible. When it faces reality, doubt falls.

Religions have been repressing doubt. I have not come across a single religious leader who does not have, deep down in himself, a doubt that is still alive. All his beliefs may have repressed it, but they cannot destroy it. You can look into your own mind. You believe in God, but don't you have a doubt about it? In fact, if you don't have a doubt, why should you believe? You don't have the disease, then why are you carrying the whole load of medicines? The belief proves the existence of doubt; and the belief remains only on the surface; it pushes, forces the doubt deeper into your unconscious. But it cannot destroy doubt.

Belief has no power, it is impotent. Doubt is immense energy. Belief is already something dead, a corpse. You can carry the corpse as long as you want, but remember, the corpse is an unnecessary burden on you. Soon you will start stinking just like the corpse, and finally the corpse is going to make you also a corpse. It is not good to keep company with the dead. It is dangerous. Belief has to disappear from all the languages. Doubt should be enthroned and belief should be dethroned.

Doubt immediately bridges the objective and the subjective. They are two poles of the same reality, and doubt is the bridge.

Why do I praise doubt so much?—because it leads you into inquiry, it raises questions, it takes you into new adventures. It never allows you to remain ignorant. It goes on and on moving till you have found the light.

People have asked me again and again, "Do you believe in this? Do you believe in that?" And I have been telling them that this is a nonsense question. Either I know something or I don't know. Belief has no place in my being, anywhere. If I don't know, then I will try to know—that's what doubt is, that's what inquiry is. And if I know, then there is no need to believe; I know it on my own authority. Why should I believe in Jesus Christ or Gautam Buddha? There is no need.

Science should open the doors of devices that religions have been keeping closed. There is a vast universe outside you—it is infinite. You can go on and on exploring it, there is no end. But there is a bigger universe within you, and so close—just within you! And you can go on exploring that, too. You will come to know who you are, but that is not the end; the experience goes on deepening infinitely.

A person can be both scientific and religious, and that will be the total human being. I have defined the new humanity in many ways, from different angles. Let this also be included in the definition of the new humanity: we will be complete, entire, acquainted with the outside world and acquainted with the inside world. And the moment you know both, you know they are not two; it is the same energy extending into two polarities. One becomes the object, the other becomes the subject. I would like to call it the science of the inner. And whatever is known as science today, I will call the science of the outer. But the inner and the outer are two sides of the same coin. The outer cannot exist without the inner, the inner cannot exist without the outer. So there is no separation and there is no question of bridging.

The question of bridging science and religion arises because we tend to think of a science that is half, and of bogus religions that depend on belief and not on inquiry.

You have to be inquirers. And it should be your only responsibility to know yourself. You have been taught so many responsibilities, but not this one. You have been told to be responsible to your parents, to your wife, to your husband, to your children, to the nation, to the church, to humanity, to God. The list is almost endless. But the most fundamental responsibility is not in that list.

I would like to burn that whole list! You are not responsible to any nation, to any church, to any God. You are responsible only for one thing, and that is self-knowledge. And the miracle is, if you can fulfill this responsibility, you will be able to fulfill many other responsibilities without any effort. The moment you come to your own being, a revolution happens in your vision. Your whole outlook about life goes through a radical change. You start feeling new responsibilities—not as something to be done, not as duty to be fulfilled, but as a joy to do.

You will never do anything out of a sense of duty, out of feeling a responsibility, because it is expected of you. You will do everything out of your happiness, out of your own sense of love and compassion. It is not a question of duty, it is a question of sharing. You have so much love and so much bliss, you would like to share it.

So I teach only one responsibility, and that is towards yourself. Everything else will follow of its own accord without any effort on your part. And when things happen effortlessly, they have a tremendous beauty to them.

Science has to accept that it has been neglecting the most important part of existence: human consciousness. And once science starts moving into man's interiority, religions will start disappearing of their own accord. They will become meaningless. When knowing is available, who is going to believe? When experience is available, who is going to read about it in a Bible, in a Koran? When you have food available to eat, I don't think you will choose a cookbook and read it. That you can do later on, or perhaps you may not need to do it.

You have within you the secret key, and now it is science's responsibility to help you to find the key. My vision of religiousness is scientific. That's why I don't offer any belief system. I offer methods, just as science has methods. They explore objects by their methods; we explore our consciousness with our methods.

Our methods are called meditations. They are absolutely scientific. No prayer is scientific, because first you have to believe in a God and only then can you pray, because a prayer has to be addressed.

Meditation is not to be addressed to anybody; it is just a method of digging within yourself. And you are there! There is no need to believe that you exist. In fact, even if you want to, you cannot deny yourself. The very denial will prove your existence. This is the only thing that is undeniable. Everything else can be denied. Perhaps it is a mirage in the desert, perhaps it is a dream, perhaps you are hallucinating, perhaps you are hypnotized and you are seeing things that are not there. Everything in the world can be denied, except you. You are the most fundamental reality—undeniable, indubitable.

And finding it is a scientific experience.

In the coming world, the new humanity, we will not have to bother about how to bridge religion and science, how to bring them closer, how to stop them fighting and destroying each other—there is no need. We can create a science with the same methodology as all other sciences are created. We can establish meditation as a scientific method, which is not difficult, everybody can do it.

It does not need a big lab, you are the lab! And nothing else is needed, no tubes and burners and chemicals—nothing else is needed.

Everything that you need to know yourself is provided from your very birth. Just a little 180-degree turn.

If the truth of our own being is already inside us, why are there so few people who have found it? And how can we recognize the difference between that truth and all the other clutter we see when we go inside to look?

Our ignorance is the only reason. Not that we don't have it—it has been always there—but we have forgotten it. We have become oblivious to it, our eyes have become clouded. The vision has lost the crystal clarity that is needed to rediscover it.

Have you watched? Sometimes you are trying to remember somebody's name. You know it, and still it is not coming. You feel very much at a loss. You say it is just on the tip of your tongue. You say, "I *know* it." But if somebody insists—"If you know it, then why don't you tell it?"—you say, "It is not coming."

Have you watched it? You know the name, you know that you know it, but there is a gap. But that gap is not empty, that gap is not passive. That gap is very active, intensely active. That gap is searching, that gap itself is in search for the forgotten name.

And another thing you will notice if you watch: Somebody suggests some name, and you say, "No, it is not that." This is beautiful! You don't know what is true, but you know what is false. You say, "That is not it." Somebody suggests some other name. You say, "No, I know what it is, and that is not it." The gap is not just a dead gap; it is dynamic. It knows what is false, it knows what is not true, but it has forgotten the truth.

So if somebody is teaching you a false god, you will immediately understand. There is no problem about it. If somebody is giving you a false thing, you will immediately understand it. You don't know what is true, you don't know what truth is, but you can immediately sense what is untrue because the truth is hidden within you. You may have forgotten it, but you have not forgotten it is there.

That's why, whenever you hear truth, suddenly something in you immediately perceives it. It is not a question of time. Others who cannot perceive it will think you have been hypnotized. They think one has to argue, reason, think about it, brood, and then believe. But whenever you hear truth, the very quality of it is such that immediately it fills your gap because your own truth has been called forth.

Whenever you hear a truth, it is not coming from the outside. The outside is just an opportunity for the inside to open. Immediately you know that this is true. Not that you can argue about it, not that you can prove it, not that you are convinced by it, no. You are transformed by it, not convinced. It is a conversion, not a conviction.

Clever and Wise: Untangling the Knots of the Mind

Mind cannot be still. It needs continuous thinking, worrying. The mind functions like a bicycle; if you go on pedaling it, it continues. The moment you stop the pedaling, you are going to fall down. Mind is a two-wheeled vehicle just like a bicycle, and your thinking is a constant pedaling.

Even sometimes if you are a little bit silent you immediately start worrying, "Why am I silent?" Anything will do to create worrying, thinking, because the mind can exist only in one way—in running. Running after something, or running from something, but always running. In the running is the mind. The moment you stop, the mind disappears.

Right now you are identified with the mind. You think you are it. From there comes the fear. If you are identified with the mind, naturally if the mind stops you are finished, you are no more. And you don't know anything beyond the mind.

The reality is you are not the mind. You are something beyond the mind. Hence it is absolutely necessary that the mind stop, so that for the first time you can know that you are not the mind . . . because you are still there. The mind is gone; you are still there—and with greater joy, greater glory, greater light, greater consciousness and greater being. The mind was pretending . . . and you had fallen into the trap.

What you have to understand is the process of identification—how one can get identified with something that one is not.

An ancient parable in the East is that a lioness was jumping from one hillock to another and just in the middle she gave birth to a kid. The kid fell down into the road where a big crowd of sheep was passing. Naturally he mixed with the sheep, lived with the sheep, behaved like a sheep. He had no idea, not even in his dreams, that he was a lion. How could he have? All around him were sheep and only sheep. He had never roared like a lion; a sheep does not roar. He had never been alone like a lion; a sheep is never alone. She is always in the crowd—the crowd is cozy, secure, safe. If you see sheep walking, they walk so close together that they are almost stumbling on each other. They are so afraid to be alone.

But the lion started growing up. It was a strange phenomenon. He was identified mentally with being a sheep, but biology does not go according to your identification; nature is not going to follow your mind. He became a beautiful young lion, but because things happened so slowly, the sheep became accustomed to him, just as he became accustomed to the sheep.

The sheep thought he was a little crazy, naturally. He was not behaving just right—a little cuckoo—and he went on growing. It was not supposed to be so. Pretending to be a lion! But they knew he was not a lion; they had seen him from his very birth. They had brought him up, they had given their milk to him. He was a non-vegetarian by nature—no lion is vegetarian, but this lion was, because sheep are vegetarian. He used to eat grass with great joy. They accepted these small differences, that he was a little big and looked like a lion. A very wise sheep had said, "It is just a freak of nature. Once in a while it happens."

And the lion himself also accepted that it was true. His color was different, his body was different—he must be a freak, abnormal. But the idea that he was a lion was impossible! All those sheep surrounded him, and sheep psychoanalysts gave him explanations: "You are just a freak of nature. Don't be worried. We are here to take care of you."

But one day an old lion passed by and saw this young lion standing far above the crowd of sheep. He could not believe his eyes! He had never seen such a thing nor had he ever heard that in the history of the whole past a lion had been in the middle of a crowd of sheep but no sheep was afraid. And this lion was walking exactly like the sheep, grazing on grass!

The old lion could not believe his eyes. He forgot he was going to catch a sheep for his breakfast. He completely forgot breakfast. It was something so strange that he determined to catch hold of the young lion and find out what was happening. But he was old, and the young lion was young—he ran away. Although he believed that he was a sheep, when there was danger this much of the identification was forgotten. He ran like a lion, and the old lion had great difficulty in catching him.

Finally the old lion got hold of him. He was crying and weeping and saying, "Just forgive me, I am a poor sheep. Please let me go."

The old lion said, "You idiot! You simply stop this nonsense and come with me to the pond." Just nearby there was a pond. He took the young lion there. The young lion was not going willingly, he went reluctantly, but what can you do against a lion if you are only a sheep? He may kill you if you don't follow him, so he went. The pond was silent, with no ripples, almost like a mirror.

The old lion said to the young, "Just look. Look at my face and look at your face. Look at my body and look at your body in the water."

In a second there came a great roar! All the hills echoed it. The sheep disappeared; he was a totally different being—he recognized himself. The identification with sheep was not a reality, it was just a mental concept. Now he had seen the reality. The old lion said, "Now I don't have to say anything more. You have understood."

The young lion could feel a strange energy he had never felt before—as if it had been dormant. He could feel a tremendous power, and he had always been a weak, humble sheep. All that humbleness, all that weakness, simply evaporated.

This is an ancient parable about the master and the disciple. The function of the master is only to bring the disciple to see who he is, and that what he goes on believing about himself is not true.

Your mind is not created by nature. Always try to keep the distinction: your brain is created by nature. Your brain is the mechanism that belongs to the body, but your mind is created by the society in which you live—by the religion, by the church, by the ideology that your parents followed, by the educational system that you were taught in, by all kinds of things.

That's why there is a Christian mind and a Hindu mind, a Mohammedan mind and a communist mind. Brains are natural, but minds are a created phenomenon. It depends on which flock of sheep you belong to. Was the flock of sheep Hindu? Then naturally you will behave like a Hindu.

Meditation is the only method that can make you aware that you are not the mind; and that gives you a tremendous mastery. Then you can choose what is right with your mind and what is not right with your mind, because you are distant, an observer, a watcher. Then you are not so attached to the mind . . . and that is your fear. You have completely forgotten yourself; you have become the mind. The identification is complete.

When I say, "Be silent, be still. Be alert and watchful of your thought processes," you can freak out, you can become afraid; it looks like death. In a way you are right, but it is not your death, it is the death of your conditionings. Combined, they are called your mind.

Once you are capable of seeing the distinction clearly—that you are separate from the mind and the mind is separate from the brain—it immediately happens, simultaneously: As you withdraw from the mind you suddenly see that the mind is in the middle; on either side there is the brain and there is your consciousness.

The brain is simply a mechanism. Whatever you want to do with it, you can do. The mind is the problem because others have created it for you. It is not you, it is not even your own; it is all borrowed.

The priests, the politicians—the people who are in power, the people who have vested interests—don't want you to know that you are above the mind, beyond the mind. Their whole effort has been to keep you identified with the mind because the mind is managed by them, not by you. You are being deceived in such a subtle way. The managers of your mind are outside you.

When the consciousness becomes identified with the mind, then the brain is helpless. The brain is simply mechanical. Whatever the mind wants, the brain does. But if you are separate from it, then the mind loses its power; otherwise it is sovereign.

It seems scary to think about the mind losing its power. How can a person function without the mind?

An enlightened person can use the mind more efficiently than the greatest intellectual can, for the simple reason that he is outside the mind and has an overall view. Perhaps the parts of the brain that are not functioning in normal human beings start functioning when your consciousness goes beyond your normal reason, as you transcend the confinements of your rationality. The other parts function only with your transcendence.

This is the experience of all those who have become enlightened. And when I say this, I say it on my own authority. I would not believe it if Buddha had said it. Perhaps he was lying, perhaps he was misguided; perhaps he was not lying, but what he said was not right. Perhaps there was no intention to lie but he could be confused; he could have made a mistake.

But I know it from my own experience, because it is such a tremendous change that you cannot miss it. It is almost as if half of your body was paralyzed; then one day suddenly you feel you are no longer paralyzed. Both sides of your brain are fully functioning. Can you miss it? If a person who has been paralyzed suddenly finds he is not paralyzed, can he miss it? There is no possibility of missing it.

I know perfectly well the difference in the moment before enlightenment happened to me, and the moment after. With absolute certainty, I knew that something within my mind—which I was not even aware existed—had stirred and had started functioning. Since then there has been no problem for me. Since then

I have existed without a problem, without a worry, without any tension.

All these qualities come from the other parts of the mind that are not functioning. And when the whole mind functions and you are outside of it, you are the master. The mind is the best servant you can find, and the worst master you can find. But ordinarily the mind is the master—and that too, only about half of it. The master—and half paralyzed! When you become the master, the mind is the servant and it is fully healthy, fully recovered.

The enlightened man is "out of his mind" but has full control of the mind. Just his awareness is enough. If you observe anything minutely, you will have a little experience of the enlightened person . . . not the full experience but a little taste, just a tongue-tip taste. If you observe your anger minutely, the anger disappears. You are feeling a sexual urge: watch it closely, and soon it disappears.

If just by your watching, things evaporate, what to say about the person who is always above the mind, simply aware of the whole mind? Then all those ugly things that you would like to drop simply evaporate. And remember, they all have energy. Anger is energy—when anger evaporates, the energy that is left behind turns into compassion. It is the same energy. Through observation the anger has left—that was the mode, the form surrounding the energy—but the energy remains. Now, the energy of anger, without anger, is compassion. When sex disappears, the tremendous energy of love is left behind. And each ugly thing in your mind, disappearing, leaves a great treasure behind.

The enlightened person has no need to drop anything and has no need to practice anything. All that is wrong drops of its own accord because it cannot stand up to awareness. And all that is good evolves of its own accord because awareness is nourishment for it.

The enlightened person has gone above the mechanical mind

into a nonmechanical consciousness. You can destroy the brain, then the mind will be finished, but you cannot destroy consciousness because it is not dependent on the brain or the brain system. You can destroy the body, you can destroy the brain, but if you have been able to free your consciousness from both, you know you are intact, untouched. Not even a dent has been made in you.

There is an intrinsic law: thoughts don't have their own life. They are parasites; they live on your identifying with them. When you say, "I am angry," you are pouring life energy into anger, because you are getting identified with anger. But when you say, "I am watching anger flashing on the screen of the mind within me," you are not anymore giving any life, any energy to anger. You will be able to see that because you are not identified, the anger is absolutely impotent. It has no impact on you, it does not change you, does not affect you. It is absolutely hollow and dead. It will pass on by and leave the sky clean and the screen of the mind empty.

Slowly, slowly you start getting out of your thoughts. That's the whole process of witnessing and watching. In other words—George Gurdjieff used to call it nonidentification—you are no longer identifying with your thoughts. You are simply standing aloof and away—indifferent, as if they might be anybody's thoughts. You have broken your connections with them. Only then can you watch them.

Watching needs a certain distance. If you are identified, there is no distance, they are too close. It is as if you are putting the mirror too close to your eyes: you cannot see your face. A certain distance is needed; only then can you see your face in the mirror.

If thoughts are too close to you, you cannot watch. You become impressed and colored by your thoughts: anger makes you angry, greed makes you greedy, lust makes you lustful because there is no distance at all. They are so close that you are bound to think that you and your thoughts are one.

Watching destroys this oneness and creates a separation. The more you watch, the bigger is the distance. The bigger the distance, the less energy your thoughts are getting from you. And they don't have any other source of energy. Soon they start dying, disappearing. In these disappearing moments you will have the first glimpses of no-mind.

In the West, psychoanalysis has grown through Freud, Adler, Jung, and Wilhelm Reich, to solve problems arising from the mind such as frustrations, conflicts, schizophrenia, and madness. In comparison to your meditation techniques, please explain the contributions, limitations, and incompleteness of the system of psychoanalysis in solving the human problems rooted in the mind.

The first thing to be understood is that any problem rooted in the mind cannot be solved without transcending the mind. You can postpone the problem, you can bring in a little normality, you can dilute the problem, but you cannot solve it. You can make a person function more efficiently in the society through psychoanalysis, but psychoanalysis never solves a problem. And whenever a problem is postponed, shifted, it creates another problem. It simply changes its place, but it remains. A new eruption will come sooner or later, and each time the new eruption of the old problem happens it will become more difficult to postpone and shift it.

Psychoanalysis is a temporary relief, because it cannot conceive of anything that transcends mind. A problem can be solved only when you can go beyond it. If you cannot go beyond it, then *you* are the problem. Then who is going to solve it? Then how is one going to solve it? Then you are the problem; the problem is not something separate from you.

Yoga, Tantra, and all meditation techniques are based upon a different premise. They say that the problems are there, the problems are around you, but you are never the problem. You can transcend them; you can look at them like an observer looks down from the hill into the valley. This witnessing self can solve the problem. Really, just by witnessing a problem it is half solved already, because when you can witness a problem—when you can observe it impartially, when you are not involved in it—you can stand by the side and look at it. The very clarity that comes out of this witnessing gives you the clue, gives you the secret key. And almost all problems exist because there is no clarity through which to understand them. You do not need solutions, you need clarity.

A problem rightly understood is solved, because a problem arises through a nonunderstanding mind. You create the problem because you don't understand. So the basic thing is not to solve the problem; the basic thing is to create more understanding. And if there is more understanding, more clarity, and the problem can be encountered impartially—observed as if it doesn't belong to you, as if it belongs to someone else—if you can create a distance between the problem and you, only then can it be solved.

Meditation creates a distance, it gives you a perspective. You go beyond the problem. The level of consciousness changes. Through psychoanalysis you remain on the same level. The level never changes; you are adjusted back to the same level again. Your awareness, your consciousness, your witnessing capacity doesn't change. As you move in meditation, you go higher and higher. You can begin to look down at your problems. They are now in the valley, and you have come to a hill. From this perspective, this height, all problems look different. And the greater the distance grows, the more you become capable of observing them as if they do not belong to you.

Remember one thing: if a problem doesn't belong to you, you can always give good advice on how to solve it. If it belongs to someone else, if someone else is in difficulty, you are always wise. You can give good advice, but if the problem belongs to you, you simply don't know what to do. What has happened? The problem is the same, but now you are involved in it. When it was someone else's problem, you had a distance from which to look at it impartially. Everyone is a good advisor for others, but when it happens to oneself then all your wisdom is lost because the distance is lost.

Someone has died and the family is in anguish: you can give good advice. You can say the soul is immortal; you can say nothing dies, that life is eternal. But when someone has died whom you loved, who means something to you, who was near, intimate, now you are crying and weeping. Now you cannot give the same advice to yourself—that life is immortal and no one ever dies. Now it looks absurd.

So remember, while advising others you may look foolish. When you say to someone whose beloved has died that life is immortal, he will think you stupid. You are talking nonsense to him. He knows what it feels like to lose a beloved. No philosophy can give consolation. And he knows why you are saying this thing—it is because the problem is not yours. You can afford to be wise; he cannot afford it.

Through meditation you transcend your ordinary being. A new point arises in you from where you can look at things in a new way. The distance is created. Problems are there, but they are now very far away, as if happening to someone else. Now you can give good advice to yourself, but there is no need to give it. The very distance will make you wise.

So the whole technique of meditation consists of creating a distance between the problems and you. Right now, as you are, you are so entangled with your problems that you cannot think, you cannot contemplate, you cannot see through them, you cannot witness them.

Psychoanalysis only helps readjustment. It is not a transformation; that is one thing. And another thing: in psychoanalysis you become dependent. You need an expert and the expert will do everything. It will take three years, four years, or even five years if the problem is very deep, and you will become just a dependent—you are not growing. Rather, on the contrary, you are becoming more and more dependent. You will need this psychoanalyst every day, or twice a week, or thrice a week. Once you miss an appointment you will feel lost. If you stop psychoanalysis you will feel lost. It becomes an intoxicant, it becomes alcoholic. You start being dependent upon someone—someone who is an expert. You can tell that person your problem and they will solve it. They will discuss it and will bring the unconscious roots out of you. But the other person will do it; the solving will be done by someone else.

Remember, a problem solved by someone else is not going to give you more maturity. A problem solved by someone else may give that person some maturity, but it cannot give you maturity. You may become more immature; then whenever there is a problem you will need some expert advice, some professional advice. And I do not think that even psychoanalysts grow mature through your problems because they go for psychoanalysis to other psychoanalysts. They have their own problems. They solve your problems, but they cannot solve their own problems. Again, the question of distance.

Every psychoanalyst goes to someone else with his own problems. It is just like the medical profession. If the doctor himself is ill, he cannot diagnose himself. He is so near that he is afraid, so he will go to someone else. If you are a surgeon, you cannot operate upon your own body—or can you? The distance is not there. It is difficult to operate upon one's own body. But it is also difficult if your wife is really ill and a serious operation has to be done—you cannot operate because your hand will tremble. The intimacy is so great that you will be afraid; you cannot be a good surgeon. You will have to call some other surgeon to operate on your wife.

What is happening? You are a surgeon, you have done many operations. But you cannot do it on your child or your wife because the distance is not great enough—it is as if there is no distance at all, and without distance you cannot be impartial. So a psychoanalyst can help others, but when he is in trouble he will have to take advice, he will have to be psychoanalyzed by someone else.

And it is really strange that even a person like Wilhelm Reich goes mad in the end. We cannot conceive a Gautam Buddha going mad—or can you conceive of it? If a Buddha can go mad, then there is no way out of this misery. It is inconceivable that a Buddha goes mad.

Look at Sigmund Freud's life. He is the father and founder of psychoanalysis; he went on talking about problems very deeply. But as far as he himself was concerned not a single problem was solved. Not a single problem was solved! Fear was as much a problem for him as for anybody else. He was so afraid and nervous. Anger was as much a problem for him as for anybody else. He would get so angry that in anger he would fall unconscious in a fit. This man knew so much about the human mind, but as far as he himself was concerned, that knowledge seems to have been of no use.

Jung would also fall unconscious when in deep anxiety; he would have a fit. What is the problem? Distance is the problem. They had been thinking about problems, but they had not been growing in consciousness. They thought intellectually, keenly, logically, and they concluded something. Sometimes those conclusions may have been right, but that is not the point. They did not grow in consciousness, they did not in any way transcend. And unless you transcend, the problems cannot be solved; they can only be adjusted.

Freud said, in the last days of his life, that man is incurable. At the most we can hope that he can exist as an adjusted being; there is no other hope. This is at the most! Man cannot be happy, Freud says. At the most we can arrange it so that he is not so very unhappy. That's all. What type of solution can come out of such an attitude? And this is after forty years' experience with human beings! He concludes that the human being cannot be helped, that we are by nature miserable and we will remain in misery.

But the approach of meditation says that it is not the human being that is incurable; it is our minimal consciousness that creates the problem. Grow in consciousness, increase in consciousness, and problems decrease. They exist in the same proportion: if there is a minimum of consciousness, there are a maximum of problems; if there is a maximum of consciousness, there are a minimum of problems. With total consciousness, problems simply disappear just like the sun rises in the morning and dewdrops disappear. With total consciousness there are no problems, because with a total consciousness problems cannot arise. At the most psychoanalysis can be a cure, but problems will go on arising; it is not preventive.

Meditation goes to the very depth. It will change you so that problems cannot arise. Psychoanalysis is concerned with problems. Meditation is concerned with you directly, it is not concerned with problems at all. That is why the greatest of Eastern psychologists—Buddha, Mahavira, or Lao Tzu—do not talk about problems. Because of this, Western psychology thinks that psychology is a new phenomenon. It is not!

It was just in the first part of the twentieth century that Freud could prove scientifically that there is such a thing as the unconscious. Buddha talked about it twenty-five centuries ago. But

Buddha has never tackled any problem because, he says, problems are infinite. If you go on tackling every problem, you will never really be able to tackle them. Tackle the person, forget the problems. Tackle the being itself and help the being to grow. As the being grows, as it becomes more conscious, problems go on dropping; you need not be worried about them.

For example, a person is schizophrenic, split, divided. Psychoanalysis will deal with this split—with how to make this split workable, with how to adjust this man so that he can function, so that he can live in the society peacefully. Psychoanalysis will tackle the problem, the schizophrenia. If this man comes to Buddha, Buddha will not talk about the schizophrenic state. He will say, "Meditate so that the inner being becomes one. When the inner being becomes one, the split on the periphery will disappear." The split is there, but it is not the cause, it is just the effect. Somewhere deep in the being there is a duality, and that duality has created this crack on the periphery. You can go on cementing the crack, but the inner split remains. Then the crack will appear somewhere else. Then you cement that crack; then somewhere else the crack will appear. So if you treat one psychological problem, another problem arises immediately; then you treat the other and a third arises. This is good as far as the professionals are concerned because they live off it. But this is not a help. We will have to go beyond psychoanalysis, and unless we come to the methods of growing consciousness, of the inner growth of being, of expansion of consciousness, psychoanalysis cannot be of much help.

Now, this is happening already; psychoanalysis is already out of date. The keen thinkers of the West are now thinking about how to expand consciousness and not about how to solve problems—about how to make people alert and aware. Now it has come; the seeds have sprouted. The emphasis has to be remembered.

I am not concerned with your problems. There are millions, and it is just useless to go on solving them, because you are the creator and you remain untouched. I solve one problem and you will create ten. You cannot be defeated, because the creator remains behind them. And as I go on solving, I am just wasting my energy.

I will push aside your problems; I will simply deal with *you*. The creator must be changed. And once the creator is changed, the problems on the periphery drop. Now no one is cooperating with them, no one is helping to create them, no one is enjoying them. You may feel this word "enjoy" is strange, but remember well that you enjoy your problems; hence you create them. You enjoy them for so many reasons.

The whole of humanity is sick. There are basic reasons, basic causes, which we go on overlooking. Whenever a child is sick he gets attention; whenever he is healthy no one gives him any attention. Whenever a child is sick, the parents love him—or at least they pretend. But whenever he is okay, no one is worried about him. No one thinks to give him a kiss or a good hug. The child learns the trick. And love is a basic need and attention is a basic food. For the child, attention is potentially even more necessary than milk. Without attention something will die within him.

You may have heard about the research in laboratories where they have experimented with plants. Even plants grow faster if you give them attention, just look at them lovingly. Two plants are used for the experiment. One plant is given attention, love—just a smiling, loving approach—the other is not given any attention. Everything else is provided to both—the necessary water, fertilizers, sun; they give everything equally to each, but to one they give attention. To the other they do not give any attention; whenever they pass by they just don't look at it. And they have seen that the one grows faster, brings bigger flowers, and the other plant's growth is delayed, and it brings smaller flowers.

Attention is energy. When someone looks lovingly at you, he is giving you food—a very subtle food. So every child needs attention, and you give attention only when he is ill, when there is some problem. So if the child needs attention he will create problems, he will become a creator of problems.

Love is a basic need. Your body grows with food, your soul grows with love. But you can get love only when you are ill, when you have some problem; otherwise no one is going to give you love. The child learns your ways and then he starts creating problems. Whenever he is ill or has a problem, everyone gives attention.

Have you ever observed? In your house the children are playing silently, peacefully. Then if some guests come they start creating trouble. This is because your attention goes to the guests, and now the children are hankering for attention. They want your attention, your guests' attention, everybody's attention to turn toward them. They will do something, they will create some trouble. This is unconscious, but then it becomes a pattern. And when you are grown up, you still go on doing it.

A psychoanalyst is a professional attention-giver. For one hour he looks at you attentively. Whatever you say, whatever nonsense, he listens as if scriptures are being preached. And he persuades you to talk more, to say anything, relevant or irrelevant, to bring your mind out. Then you feel so good.

Most patients fall in love with their psychoanalysts. And how to protect the client–therapist relationship is a great problem because sooner or later it becomes a lovers' relationship. Why? Why does a woman patient fall in love with a male psychoanalyst? Or the reverse: Why does a male patient fall in love with a woman psychoanalyst? The reason is that for the first time in their lives, so much attention is given. The love need is fulfilled.

Unless your basic being is changed, nothing will come out of solving problems. You have an infinite potential to create new ones. Meditation is an effort to make you independent, first; and second, to change your type and quality of consciousness. With a new quality of consciousness old problems cannot exist, they simply disappear. You were a small child; you had different types of problems. When you became older they simply disappeared. Where have they gone? You never solved them, they simply disappeared. You cannot even remember what the problems were that belonged to your childhood. But you have grown and those problems disappeared.

Then you were a little older, you had a different type of problem; when you become old they will not be there. Not that you will be able to solve them—no one is able to solve problems—one can simply grow out of them. When you are old you will laugh at all those problems you used to have, so urgent, so destructive that you had many times contemplated committing suicide because of them. And now that you have grown old, you simply laugh. Where have those problems gone? Have you solved them? No, you have simply grown. Those problems belonged to a particular state of growth.

Similar is the case as you grow deeper into consciousness. Then, too, problems go on disappearing. A moment comes when you are so aware that problems do not arise. Meditation is not analysis. Meditation is growth. It is not concerned with problems; it is concerned with the being.

LEADER VS. FOLLOWER

Understanding the Responsibility of Being Free

There is a prophetic saying of Nietzsche's: "God is dead and man is free." He had tremendous insight into the matter. Very few people have been able to understand the depth of his statement. It is a milestone in the history of consciousness. If there is a God, man can never be free—that is an impossibility. With God, man will remain a slave and freedom will remain just an empty word. Only without God does freedom start having meaning.

But Friedrich Nietzsche's statement is only half; nobody has tried to make it complete. It looks complete, but Friedrich Nietzsche was not aware that there are religions in the world that have no

God, yet even in those religions man is not free. He was not aware of Buddhism, Jainism, Taoism—the most profound religions of all. For all these three religions there is no God. For the same reason as Nietzsche did, Lao Tzu, Mahavira, and Gautam Buddha denied God—because they could see that with God, man is just a puppet. Then all efforts for enlightenment are meaningless; you are not free, how can you become enlightened? And there is somebody omnipotent, all-powerful—he can take away your enlightenment. He can destroy anything!

But Nietzsche was not aware that there have been religions that are godless. For thousands of years there have been people who have understood that God's existence is the greatest barrier to man's freedom—they removed God. But still man is not free.

What I am trying to help you to understand is that just by making God dead you cannot make man free. You will have to make one more thing dead, and that is religion.

Religion also has to die; it has to follow God. We have to create a religiousness that is godless and religionless, which has nobody above, more powerful than you, and no organized religion to create different kinds of cages—Christian, Mohammedan, Hindu, Buddhist. Beautiful cages . . .

With God and religion both dead, one more thing dies automatically, and that is the priesthood, the leader, the different forms of religious leader. Now he has no function. There is no organized religion in which he can be a pope or a shankaracharya or Ayatollah Khomeini. He has no God whom he can represent; his function is finished.

Buddha, Mahavira, and Lao Tzu dropped God in the same way as Friedrich Nietzsche—not knowing, not aware that if religion remained, then even without God, the priest would manage to keep man in slavery.

To complete the insight of Friedrich Nietzsche, religion has to die. There is no point to an organized religion if there is no God.

For whom does the organized religion exist? The churches, the temples, the mosques, the synagogues have to disappear. And with that the rabbis and the bishops and all kinds of religious leaders become simply jobless, they become futile. But then a tremendous revolution happens: humanity becomes utterly free.

But before you can understand the implications of this freedom, you have to understand the limitations of Friedrich Nietzsche's insight. If his insight is complete, then what kind of freedom will be available? God is dead, man is free . . . free for what? His freedom will be just like any other animal's. It is not right to call it freedom—it is licentiousness. It is not freedom because it does not carry any responsibility, any consciousness. It will not help man to raise himself upwards, to become something higher than he is in his slavery. Unless freedom takes you higher than what you were in your slavery, it is meaningless.

It is possible your freedom may take you lower than your slavery, because the slavery had a certain discipline, it had a certain morality, it had certain principles. It had a certain organized religion to look after you, to keep you afraid of punishment and hell, to keep you greedy for rewards and heaven, and to keep you a little above the wild animal—who has freedom, yes, but that freedom has not made the animal a higher being. It has not given him any quality of consciousness that you can appreciate.

Nietzsche had no idea that just to give freedom is not enough—not only not enough, it is dangerous, it may reduce man to animality. In the name of freedom he may lose his path towards higher states of consciousness.

When God is dead, religion as an organized body is dead—and man is free to be himself. For the first time he is free to explore his innermost being with no hindrances. He is free to dive into the depths of his being, rise to the heights of his consciousness. There is nobody to hinder him, his freedom is total. But this freedom is possible only if we can save something that I call the quality of religiousness, so that a quality of religiousness is alive and is perfectly harmonious with human freedom; it enhances human growth.

By "religiousness" I mean that the human being, as he is, is not enough. We can be more, We can be enormously more. Whatever the human being is, is only a seed. We do not know what potential we are carrying within ourselves.

Religiousness simply means a challenge to grow, a challenge for the seed to come to its ultimate peak of expression, to burst forth in thousands of flowers and release the fragrance that was hidden in it. That fragrance I call religiousness. It has nothing to do with your so-called religions, it has nothing to do with God, it has nothing to do with priesthood: it has something to do with you and your possibilities of growth.

So I use the word "religiousness" just to remind you that God can die, religions can disappear, but religiousness is something interwoven into existence itself. It is the beauty of the sunrise, it is the beauty of a bird on the wing. It is the beauty of an opening lotus. It is all that is truthful, all that is sincere and authentic, all that is loving and compassionate. It includes everything that pulls you upwards, that does not make you stop at where you are but always keeps reminding you that you have yet far to go. Every place that you stop for a rest is only a rest for the night; in the morning we go again on the pilgrimage. It is an eternal pilgrimage, and you are alone—and you are totally free.

So it is a great responsibility—which is not possible for one who believes in God, which is not possible for one who believes in the priest, who believes in the church, because he wants to give his responsibility to other people. The Christian thinks Jesus is the savior, so it is Jesus' responsibility: "He will come and deliver us from our misery, from this hell." Freedom simply makes you absolutely responsible for everything that you are and that you are going to be.

Hence I have kept the word "religiousness." It is beautiful. It is not organization; it is not Hindu, Mohammedan, Christian. It is simply a fragrance just to keep you going.

And there is nowhere to stop. In life there is no full stop, not even a semicolon—just small commas. Just for a while you can rest, but the rest is just to gather energy to go forward, to go upward.

SHEPHERD AND SHEEP: CUTTING YOURSELF LOOSE FROM THE PUPPETEER

The very idea of God gives you a sense of relief—that you are not alone, that somebody is looking after affairs; that this cosmos is not just a chaos, it is *really* a cosmos; that there is a system behind it, there is logic behind it; that it is not an illogical jumble of things, that it is not anarchy. Somebody rules it; the sovereign king is there looking after each small detail—not even a leaf moves without his moving it. Everything is planned. You are part of a great destiny. Maybe the meaning is not known to you, but the meaning is there because God is there. God brings a tremendous relief. One starts feeling that life is not accidental; there is a certain undercurrent of significance, meaning, destiny. God brings a sense of destiny.

There is no God—it simply shows that man knows not why he is here. It simply shows man is helpless. It simply shows that man has no meaning available to him. By creating the idea of God he can believe in meaning, and he can live this futile life with the idea that somebody is looking after it.

Just imagine: you are on an airplane flight and somebody comes and says, "There is no pilot." Suddenly there will be a panic. No pilot?! No pilot simply means you are doomed. Then somebody says, "The pilot must be there—invisible, we may not be able to see the pilot, but he is there; otherwise how is this beautiful mechanism functioning? Just think of it: Everything is going so beautifully—there must be a pilot! Maybe we are not capable of seeing him, maybe we are not yet prayerful enough to see him, maybe our eyes are closed, but the pilot is there. Otherwise, how is it possible? This airplane has taken off, it is flying perfectly well; the engines are humming. Everything is proof that there is a pilot."

If somebody can convince you, you can relax again into your chair. You close your eyes, you start dreaming again—you can fall asleep. The pilot is there, you need not worry.

The pilot exists not, it is a human creation. Man has created God in his own image. It is man's invention. God is not a discovery, it is an invention. And God is not the truth—it is the greatest lie there is.

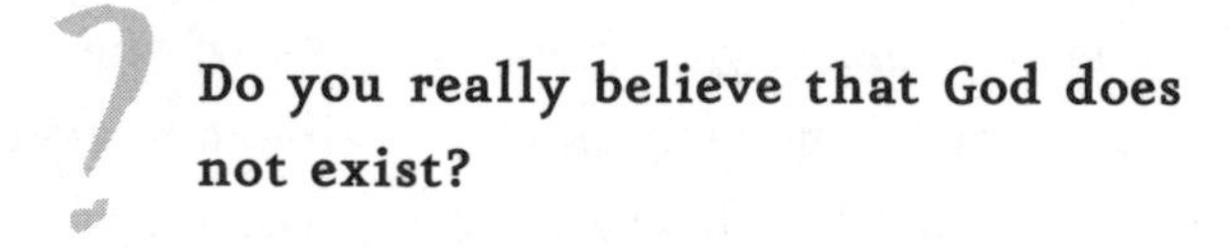

Do you really believe that God does not exist?

I do not believe that God does not exist, I know for sure he does not exist. And thank God that he does not exist, because the existence of God would have created so many problems, difficulties, that life would have been almost impossible. You may not have looked at it from this angle I am going to talk about—perhaps nobody has ever tried to look at it from this angle.

The Christians say God created the world. In fact, the hypothesis of God is needed for the creation. The world is there; somebody must have created it. Whoever created it, that creator is God. But do you see the implication? If the world is created, then there can be no evolution: Evolution means that creation continues.

Think of the Christian story: God created the world in six days, and then on the seventh day he rested; since then he has been resting. The whole creation was completed in six days. Now, from where can evolution possibly appear? Creation means finished! The full stop has arrived. On the sixth day, the full stop, and after that there is no possibility of evolution.

Evolution implies that creation is not complete; hence the possibility of evolving. But God cannot create an incomplete world; that will be going against God's nature. He is perfect, and whatever he does is perfect. Neither he is evolving, nor is the world evolving; everything is at a standstill, dead. This is the reason why the church was against Charles Darwin, because that man was bringing in an idea that was going to kill God sooner or later. Those church leaders were perceptive in a way: they could see the faraway implications of the idea of evolution.

Ordinarily, you would not connect creation and evolution. What connection is there between God and Charles Darwin? There is a connection. Charles Darwin is saying that the creation is an ongoing process, that existence is always imperfect, that it is never going to be perfect; only then can it go on evolving, reaching new peaks, new dimensions, opening new doors, new possibilities.

God finished his work in six days—and not long ago, just 4,004 years before Jesus Christ was born. It must have been the first of January, a Monday, because we manage to fit God into everything that we have created. He has to follow our calendar. If you ask me, I will say it must have been Monday, the first of April, April Fools' Day, because that day seems to be absolutely suitable for creating a complete, ready-made existence.

If evolution becomes impossible, life loses all meaning, life loses all future; then it has only a past.

It is not unnatural that religious people are constantly past-oriented—they have only the past. Everything has been already done; there is nothing to be done in the future, the future is empty, blank, and yet you have to live in that future. Everything that had to happen, happened 4,004 years before Jesus was born. After that there has been no addition, no evolution, no development.

God created the world just as a potter creates a pot, a dead thing out of mud. But you have to remember, the potter can destroy the pot any moment. If you give the power of creation to God, you are simultaneously giving him the power of un-creation too. These are the implications that have not been looked into. God can un-create. April Fools' Day comes every year; any year on the first of April he can un-create. At the very most it may take six days again.

The very idea that you have been created makes you a thing, it takes away your being.

You can be a being only if there is no God. God, and you as a being, cannot coexist. That's why I say I am sure God does not exist, because I see beings everywhere.

The presence of beings is enough proof that God does not exist, cannot exist. Either you can exist or God can exist; you cannot both exist. The person who starts believing in God unknowingly is losing his beinghood; he is becoming a thing. So there are Christian things, Hindu things, Mohammedan things, but not beings. They have dropped their being of their own accord; they have given their being to God. The fiction has become alive, and the alive has become a fiction. I am simply putting things right side up.

When I say God does not exist, I have no grudge against God. I don't care a bit about God, whether he exists or not—it is none of my business. When I say God does not exist, my purpose is to give back your lost beinghood; to show you that you are not a thing created by somebody arbitrarily.

Why did he decide, on a certain day, 4,004 years before Jesus was born, to create the world? What caused the idea of creation? Was there something else that was forcing him to create? Was there some serpent seducing him to create? Why on a certain day, and not before? I want you to see the point. It is arbitrary, whimsical. If the story is true, God is insane. What was he doing for the whole of eternity that the idea of creation came so late to him?

The very idea of creation makes us arbitrary, whimsical, whereas evolution is not arbitrary, whimsical. Evolution is eternal; it has been always going on. There was not a time when existence was not, and there will never be a time when existence will not be: Existence means eternity.

God makes everything silly, small, arbitrary, meaningless, whimsical. Just that old man, and he must have been really old—really, really old—and then this idea of creation came to him and in six days he completed it. That's why the Church was against Charles Darwin: "You are saying that it is not yet completed, it is evolving. You are against the Bible, the holy scriptures. You are against God, against the idea of creation."

Charles Darwin was saying simply, "I am not against any God, I don't know any God." He was a very fearful person, and he was a Christian. He used to pray; in fact he started to pray more after he wrote the theory of evolution. He became very much afraid: who knows, perhaps he was doing something against God. He had believed that God created the world, but the facts of nature were telling a different story—everything is evolving, life never stays the same.

So if anybody believes in God, he cannot believe that you are a being. Only *things* are created; they have a beginning and an end—beings are eternal.

Because of this fact, two religions in India, Jainism and Buddhism, dropped the idea of God because to keep that idea simply meant you were dropping the idea of being, which is far more significant. They would have liked to keep both, but it was logically impossible. Once you accept that you have been created, you accept the other part of it, that the same whimsical man, any day, can uncreate you. So what meaning do you have—just a toy in the hands of some magical old man? So whenever he wants, he plays with the toys, and whenever he wants, he destroys them? It was really a great, courageous step on the part of Mahavira and Buddha to choose being and drop the idea of God—and that too, twenty-five centuries ago. They could simply see that you cannot manage both; they are against each other. But they were not aware of evolution; that was a later development. Now we know that creation goes against the idea of evolution, too.

Creation and evolution are absolutely against each other. Creation means completion; evolution means constant growth. Growth is possible only if things are imperfect, and they remain imperfect. Howsoever they grow, there is always a possibility of growing more.

There are a few other things which have to be considered.

If you are created, you can't have freedom. Have you seen any machine having freedom, any "thing" having freedom? Anything that is created is in the hands of the creator, just like a puppet. He has the strings in his hands; he pulls one string . . . you must have seen a puppet show. The strings are pulled—the man is behind the screen; you don't see him, you simply see the puppets—and the puppets dance and they fight, but it is all false. The puppeteer is the reality.

These puppets cannot have freedom to fight, to love, to get married—all these things happen in a puppet show. To dance or not to dance, or when they don't want to dance, to say, "No! I am not going to dance." The puppet cannot say no. And all the religions have been teaching you not to say no: don't say no to God, to his messiah, to his holy book; never, never think in terms of saying no.

Why? If you cannot say no, what is the meaning of your yes? It is a corollary—yes has meaning only when you are capable of saying no. If you *have* to say yes, then there is no other alternative except yes. I have heard that when Ford first started manufacturing cars, he himself used to go to the showroom and take an interest in the customers, talk to them. He would say to them, "You can choose any color provided it is black"—because at that time only black cars were available. You are free, provided your answer is yes. What kind of freedom is this?

Puppets cannot have freedom. And if God has simply made you, you are a puppet. It is better to revolt against God and be a being than to submit and be a part of a puppet show, because the moment you accept yourself as a puppet, you have committed suicide.

You see puppets the whole world over, with different colors, different names, different rituals. Hindus say that without God's will even a leaf in the tree cannot move—so what about you? Everything happens according to God. In fact, he has determined everything the moment he created; it is predestined. Now, it is so strange that intelligent people also go on believing in such garbage.

Just see the garbage: On one hand God has created you; on the other hand, when you do something wrong you will be punished.

If God has created you, and he has determined your nature and you cannot go against it, you don't have any freedom. There is no possibility, with God, to have freedom; then how can you commit a crime, how can you be a sinner? And how can you be a saint, either? Everything is determined by him. He is responsible; you are not.

But people go on believing in both things together: God creating the world, God creating man, woman, everything—and then throwing all responsibility on you? If there is something wrong in you, God is responsible and should be punished. If you are a murderer, then God has created a murderer; then he should be responsible for the Adolf Hitlers and the Joseph Stalins and the Mao Tse-tungs. He created these people.

But no, the religious mind loses intelligence, becomes rusted, forgets completely that these are incompatible things; God and freedom are incompatible. If you are free, then there is no God.

You may not have thought about it. How you can be free with a creator who is continuously watching you, who is continuously maintaining you and directing you? In the first place he has put everything in you as a fixed program. And you will follow that program; you cannot do otherwise. Just what you feed to the computer—the computer can only answer with that. If you start asking things that you have not fed to the computer before, the computer cannot answer it. The computer is a mechanism: first you have to feed it all the information, then whenever you need, you can ask the computer and the information will be available.

If there is a creator, then you are just a computer. The creator has put certain information in you, he has programmed you, and you are doing things accordingly. If you are a saint, you are not to take the credit for it—it was in the program. If you are a sinner, you need not feel condemned and bad—it was in the program. If there is a God who has created the world, then nobody is responsible except him. And to whom can he be responsible?—there is nobody above him. You are not responsible because he has created you; he is not responsible, because there is nobody else to whom he can be responsible. God means the world loses all responsibility, and responsibility is the very center of your life.

So to accept God is not to be religious, because without responsibility how can you be religious? Without freedom how can you be religious? Without an independent being of your own, how can you be religious? God is the most antireligious idea.

If you look into it from every aspect, then those who believe in God are not religious, cannot be religious. So when I say there is no God, I am trying to save religiousness.

There is no danger from the devil, the real danger comes from God. The devil is only his shadow. If God disappears, the shadow will disappear automatically. The real problem is God.

When I say God is the greatest enemy of religiousness, it is going to shock the so-called religious people, because they think praying to God, worshiping God, surrendering to God is what religion is. They have never thought about responsibility, freedom, growth, consciousness, being; they have never bothered—and yet these are the real religious questions. These people are not aware of what they are losing. They are losing all that is valuable, everything that is beautiful, everything that can become a blessing to them. The so-called religious person starts focusing on a fiction and forgets his own reality, forgets himself and thinks of somebody there, above, in the sky. That person above in the sky is nonexistential, but you can focus on any nonexistential thing and forget yourself in that focusing. And that is where real religion happens—within you.

Hence prayer has nothing to do with religion. What are you doing in prayer? You are creating first an image of your own imagination, surrendering to your own imagination, then talking to that image. You are just performing an insane act. In all the churches, in all the synagogues, in all the temples and in all the mosques of the world, these people are doing something insane; but the whole earth is full of these insane people.

Because they have been doing this for centuries and you have accepted them as religious, it shocks you when I say that they are not religious. They are not even normal—to be religious is far away. They are below normal. They are doing something so stupid that if they go on doing it, whatsoever little intelligence is left in them, by and by will go down the drain. Perhaps it has already gone.

To me, religiousness is a tremendous phenomenon. It is not fictitious. It is entering into the very heart of reality. It is knowing existence from its very center. But you will have to drop your fictions. Those fictions will never allow you to enter into yourself, because those fictions are projected outwards, and you get completely identified with them. You know it. You watch a movie or a television show, and you know perfectly well that many times tears have come to your eyes, although you know that it is only a television screen and there is nobody there. You forget completely that you are only a watcher; you become identified with someone, so much so that if the other person is in great suffering tears will come to your eyes. And this is what your so-called religious people have been doing! They have become involved in imagining gods and goddesses of all kinds and types, and they have completely forgotten themselves. They are worshiping something that is not there, but they have been worshiping so intently that they have created the hallucination of it.

It is possible for a Christian to see Jesus with open eyes; it is possible for a Hindu to see Krishna with open eyes. But the greatest difficulty would be for Jesus to appear to a Hindu. For a Hindu, Jesus never appears—never, even by mistake—and Krishna never appears to a Christian. Once in a while it wouldn't do much harm, but Jesus and Krishna never commit that mistake. The Christian will not allow the mistake to be committed; his hallucination is of Jesus, he cannot hallucinate Krishna. Only what you are projecting appears on the screen.

If you are projecting a film, only that film appears on the screen; if you project another film, then another film appears on the screen. It is not possible to project one film and have a different film start appearing on the screen. That's why it is not possible for Krishna to appear to a Christian, or a Mohammedan, or a Jew. It is not possible for Jesus to appear to anybody else except Christians.

Still we go on and on strengthening, enforcing our imagination and hallucinations. And what have you got out of it? From thousands of years of hallucination, what have you got—this humanity that you see around the world, this mess? This is the result of thousands of years of religious practices, disciplines, ritual, prayer? Millions of churches, synagogues, temples, all around the earth—and this is the result? The human being that you see, the actual people, this humanity has come out of this whole effort?

It was bound to be so, because we have wasted all these years in sheer stupidity, calling it religion. We have wasted so much time in which we could have grown to heights unknown, to depths unfathomable; to the freedom of the spirit, the compassion of the soul, integrity, individuality. If all these thousands of years had not been wasted chasing after a bogus God, just hocus-pocus—of no worth, not a single penny—and you ask me, "Do you really not believe?"

It is not a question of believing or not believing—there is no one to believe in or not to believe in! There is no God.

So please remember: don't start saying that I am an unbeliever. I am neither a believer nor an unbeliever. I am simply saying that the whole thing is a mere projection of the human mind and it is time that we stopped this game against ourselves. It is time that we said good-bye to God forever.

? Where does religious fundamentalism come from? What is the psychology behind it, and how does that psychology change in relation to other forms of religion that seem to be more tolerant and loving?

Religion is a very complex phenomenon, and its complexity has to be understood.

There are seven types of religions in the world. The first type is ignorance-oriented. Because people cannot tolerate their ignorance, they hide it. Because it is difficult to accept that one does not know, it is against the ego, people believe. Their belief systems function to protect their egos. The beliefs seem to be helpful, but in the long range they are very harmful. In the beginning they seem to be protective, but finally they are very destructive. The very orientation lies in ignorance.

A major part of humanity remains in the first type of religion. It is simply to avoid the reality, to avoid the gap that one feels in one's own being, to avoid the black hole of ignorance. The people of the first type are the fanatics. They cannot even tolerate that there can be other sorts of religions in the world. Their religion is *the* religion. Because they are so afraid of their ignorance, if there is some other religion besides theirs, then they might become suspicious, then doubt might arise. Then they will not be so certain. To gain certainty they become stubborn, madly stubborn. They cannot read others' scriptures, they cannot listen to other nuances of truth, they cannot be tolerant to other revelations of God. Their revelation is the only revelation, and their prophet is the only prophet. Everything else is absolutely false. These people talk in terms of absolutes, while a person of understanding is always relative.

These people have done great harm to religion. Because of these people, religion itself looks a little stupid. Remember not to be a victim of this first sort. Almost 90 percent of humanity lives in this first sort of religion, and that is in no way better than being irreligious. Maybe it is worse, because an irreligious person is not a fanatic. An irreligious person is more open, at least ready to listen, ready to talk things out, ready to argue, ready to seek and inquire. But the first type of religious person is not even ready to listen.

When I was a student in the university I used to stay with one of my professors. His mother was a very devout Hindu, completely uneducated but very religious.

One day on a cold winter night, a fire was burning in the room in the fireplace, and I was reading the Rig Veda. She came into the room and she asked, "What are you reading so late in the night?" Just to tease her, I said, "This is the Koran." She jumped on me, took away the Rig Veda, and threw it in the fireplace and said, "Are you a Mohammedan? How do you dare to bring the Koran in my house!"

Next day I told her son, my professor, "Your mother seems to be a Mohammedan"—because this sort of thing has mostly been known to be done by Mohammedans. Mohammedans burned one of the greatest treasures of the ancient world, the library of Alexandria. The fire continued for almost six months; the library was so big that it took six months for it to burn down completely. And the man who burned it was a Mohammedan caliph. His logic was the logic of the first type of religion. He came with a Koran in one hand and with a burning torch in the other, and he asked the librarian, "I have a simple question. In this big library, millions of books are there . . ." Those books contained all that humanity had learned up to that time, and it was really more than we know now. That library contained information about Lemuria, Atlantis, and all the scriptures of Atlantis, the continent that disappeared into the sea. It was the most ancient library, a great preserve. Had it still existed, humanity might have been totally different, because we are still rediscovering many things that had already been discovered.

This caliph said, "If this library contains only that which is contained in the Koran, then it is not needed; it is superfluous. If it contains more than is contained in the Koran, then it is wrong. Then it has to be destroyed immediately." Either way it had to be destroyed. If it contains the same as the Koran, then it is superfluous. Why manage such a big library unnecessarily? The Koran is enough. And if you say that it contains many more things than the Koran, then those things are bound to be wrong, because the Koran is the truth. Holding the Koran in one hand, he started the fire with the other hand—in the name of the Koran. Mohammed must have cried and wept that day in heaven, because in his name, the library was being burned.

This is the first type of religion. Always remain alert, because this stubborn man exists in everybody. It exists in Hindus, it exists in Mohammedans, it exists in Christians, Buddhists, Jains—it exists in everybody. And everybody has to be aware not to get caught. Only then can you rise to higher sorts of religion.

The problem with this first type of religion is that we are almost always brought up in it. We are conditioned in it, so it looks almost normal. A Hindu is brought up with the idea that others are wrong. Even if he is taught to be tolerant, that tolerance is of one who knows towards others who don't know. A Jain is brought up with the belief that only he is right; others are all ignorant, stumbling and groping in darkness. This conditioning can become so deep that you may forget that it is a conditioning and that you have to go above it. One can become used to a certain conditioning, and one can start thinking it is one's nature, or it is the truth. So one has to be very alert and watchful to find this lowest possibility in oneself and not get caught in it.

Sometimes we go on working hard in transforming our lives, yet we go on believing in the first type of religion. The transformation is not possible, because you are trying in a context that is so low that it cannot be really religious. The first type of religion is just religion in name; it should not be called religion.

The characteristic of the first type is imitation. It insists on imitation: imitate Buddha, imitate Christ, imitate Mahavira—but imitate somebody. Don't be yourself, be somebody else. And if you are very stubborn you can force yourself to be somebody else.

You will never be somebody else. Deep down you cannot be. You will remain yourself, but you can force so much that you almost start looking like somebody else.

Each person is born with a unique individuality, and each person has a destiny of his or her own. Imitation is crime, it is criminal. If you try to become a Buddha, you may look like Buddha, you may walk like him, you may talk like him, but you will miss. You will miss all that life was ready to deliver to you. Buddha happens only once. It is not in the nature of things to repeat. Existence is so creative that it never repeats anything. You cannot find another human being in the present, in the past, or in the future who is going to resemble you exactly. It has never happened. The human being is not a mechanism like Ford cars on an assembly line. You are a soul, individual. Imitation is poisonous. Never imitate anybody, otherwise you will be a victim of the first sort of religion, which is not religion at all.

Then there is the second type. The second type is fear-oriented.

Man is afraid, the world is a strange world, and man wants to be secure, safe. In childhood the father protects, the mother protects. But there are many people, millions of them, who never grow beyond their childhoods. They remain stuck somewhere and they still need a father and a mother. Hence God is called the "Father" or the "Mother." They need a divine parent to protect them; they are not mature enough to be on their own. They need some security.

You may have watched small children with their teddy bears, or their toys, their special toy or blanket, anything that has a special personality to the child. The teddy bear you cannot replace. You may say that you can find a better one, but that doesn't matter. There is a love relationship between the child and "his" teddy bear. His teddy bear is unique; you cannot replace it. It becomes dirty, it becomes smelly, rotten, but the child goes on carrying it. You cannot give him a new, a fresh one. Even the parents have to tolerate it. Even they have to respect it because a child feels offended otherwise. If the family is going to travel, they have to tolerate the teddy bear also; they have to treat it almost as a member of the family. They know it is foolish, but for the child it has significance.

What significance does the teddy bear have for the child? It is objective in a way. It is there, outside the child; it is part of reality. Certainly it is not just imagination, it is not just subjective; it is not a dream, it is actually there. But it is not only objective; many of the child's dreams are involved in it. It is an object, but much subjectivity is involved in it. For the child it is almost alive. The child talks to the teddy bear, sometimes he becomes angry and throws it away, then says, "I'm sorry" and takes it back. It has a personality, almost human. Without the teddy bear the child cannot go to sleep. Holding it, hugging it, he goes to sleep; he feels secure. With the teddy bear the world is okay, everything is okay. Without the teddy bear he is suddenly alone.

Many children grow physically, but they never grow spiritually, and they need teddy bears all their lives. Your images of God in the temples and churches are nothing but teddy bears.

So when a Hindu goes into the Hindu temple, he sees something which a Mohammedan cannot see. The Mohammedan can only see a stone statue. The Hindu sees something nobody else can see; it is his teddy bear. It is objectively there, but it is not only objective. Much subjectivity of the worshiper is projected on it; it functions as a screen.

Or you may be a Hindu, and in a Jain temple you will not feel any reverence arising in you. Sometimes you may even feel a little offended, because the statues of Mahavira are nude, naked. You may feel a little offended. But then there comes a Jain with tremendous respect; it is his teddy bear, and he feels protected.

So whenever you are in fear, you start remembering God. Your God is a by-product of your fear. When you are feeling good, unafraid, you don't bother. There is no need.

The second type of religion is fear-oriented. It is ill, it is almost neurotic—because maturity only comes to you when you realize that you are alone, and you have to be alone and face the reality as it is. These transitory teddy bears are just of your imagination; they are not going to help. If something is going to happen, it is going to happen; the teddy bear cannot protect you. If death is going to happen, it is going to happen. You go on calling out to God, but protection cannot come to you. You are calling to nobody, you are simply calling out of fear. Maybe calling out gives you a certain courage.

Maybe prayer gives you a certain courage, but there is no God to respond to it. There is nobody who is going to respond to your prayer, but if you have an idea that somebody is there to respond to your prayer, you may feel a little relieved, relaxed.

The fear-oriented religion is the religion of "Don't"—don't do this, don't do that—because fear is negative. The Ten Commandments are all fear-oriented—don't do this, don't do that—as if religion is nothing but avoiding things. Don't do this, don't do that—closing oneself in safety and security, never taking any risk, never moving on the dangerous path, in fact not allowing yourself to be alive. Just as the first type of religion is fanatic, the second type of religion is negative. It gives a certain stiffness, uptightness. It is a search for security which is nowhere possible, because life exists as insecurity. It exists as insecurity, danger, and risk.

The key word for the fear-oriented religion is "hell" and, of course, repression: "Don't do this." The second type of person is always afraid—and whatever you repress, you are never free of it; in fact, you are more in its power because when you repress a thing it goes deeper into your unconscious. It reaches to your very roots and poisons your whole being.

Remember, repression is not a way towards freedom. Repression is worse than expression, because through expression a person is bound to become free one day or other. But through repression, one always remains obsessed. Only life gives you freedom. A lived life gives you freedom. The unlived parts of life remain very attractive, and the mind goes on roaming around whatever you have repressed.

A real religion gives you fearlessness: let that be the criterion. If religion gives you fear, then it is not really religion.

The third type of religion is based in greed.

It is a "Do" religion. Just as the fear-oriented is a "Don't" religion, the greed-oriented is a "Do" religion: "Do this." And just as the fear-oriented religion has the key word "hell," the religion of greed has the key word "heaven." Everything is to be done in such a way that the world—the other world—is completely secure and your happiness beyond death is guaranteed.

The greed religion is formal, ritualistic, ambitious, desire-oriented. It is full of desires. See the Mohammedan concept of paradise, or the Christian concept, or the Hindu concept. Degrees may be different, but this is the strange thing: everything that these people say one has to deny oneself in this life, they go on providing in heaven in great quantities. You are supposed to be celibate here just to achieve heaven, where beautiful girls, always young, stuck at the age of sixteen, are available. Mohammedans say not to take any alcoholic beverage. But in their heaven they have rivers of wine! This seems to be absurd. If something is wrong, it is wrong. How can it become good and right in heaven? Then Omar Khayyám is right. He says, "If in heaven rivers of wine are available then let us practice here, because if we go unpracticed it will be difficult to live in paradise. Let this life be a little rehearsal, so that we develop the taste and the capacity." Omar Khayyám seems to be more logical. In fact, he is joking about the Mohammedan concept of paradise. He is saying the whole concept is foolish. But people become religious out of greed.

One thing is certain: that whatever you accumulate here will be taken away; death will take it away. So the greedy person wants to accumulate something that cannot be taken by death. But the desire to accumulate remains. Now the person accumulates virtue; virtue is the coin of the other world. Go on accumulating virtue so you can live in the other world forever and forever in lust.

This type of person is basically worldly. His concept of the other world is nothing but a projection of this world. He will "do" because he has desires, and ambition, and a lust for power, but his doing will not be of the heart. It will be a sort of manipulation.

> *Mulla Nasruddin and his young son were driving in the country one winter. It was snowing; their bullock-cart broke down. They finally reached a farmhouse and were welcomed for the night. The house was cold and the attic in which they were invited to spend the night was like an icebox. Stripping to his underwear, the Mulla jumped into a feather bed and pulled the blankets over his head. The young man was slightly embarrassed.*
>
> *"Excuse me, Dad," he said. "Don't you think we ought to say our prayers before going to bed?"*
>
> *The Mulla stuck one eye out from under the covers. "Son," he said, "I keep prayed up ahead for situations just like this one."*

Things are just on the surface. Greed and fear and ignorance are just on the periphery. These are three sorts of religions, and they are all mixed together. You cannot find a person who is absolutely, purely of the first type or the second or the third type. Wherever greed is, there is fear; wherever fear is, there is greed; and wherever greed and fear exist, there is ignorance—because they cannot exist without each other. So I am not talking about pure types. I am classifying simply so that you can understand well. Otherwise they are all mixed.

These three are the lowest types of religion. They should not be called religious.

Then there is the fourth type: the religion of logic, calculation, cleverness. It is "Do" plus "Don't" religion: worldly, materialistic, opportunistic, intellectual, theoretical, scriptural, traditional. This is the religion of the pundit, the learned scholar who tries to prove God through logic, who thinks that the mysteries of life can be understood through the head. This type of religion creates theology. It is not really religion, just a faint carbon copy of it. But all the churches are based on theology. When a Buddha exists in the world, or a Mohammed, or a Krishna, or a Christ, then pundits and scholars and learned people, intellectually clever and cunning people, gather together around them. They start working hard to figure out: "What does Jesus mean?" They start creating a theology, a creed, a dogma, a church. They are very successful people because they are very logical people. They cannot give you any light, they cannot give you truth, but they give you great organizations. They give you the Catholic Church, the Protestant Church. They give you great theologies—just clevernesses, nothing of the real experience; just intellectual, head-oriented. Their whole edifice is built of cards: a small breeze and the house is gone. Their whole edifice, as if one is trying to sail in a boat of paper. It looks like a real boat, the form is of a boat, but it is a paper boat. It is doomed, it is already doomed. Logic is a paper boat. Life cannot be understood through logic. Through logic a philosophy is born, but not real religion.

These four are ordinarily known as religion.

The fifth, sixth, and seventh are the real religions. The fifth is the religion based on intelligence; not on logic, not on intellect, but on intelligence. And there is a lot of difference between intellect and intelligence.

Intellect is logical; intelligence is paradoxical. Intellect is analytical; intelligence is synthetical. Intellect divides, cuts into pieces to understand a thing. Science is based on intellect, dissection, division, analysis. Intelligence joins things together, makes a whole out of parts—because this is one of the greatest understandings: that the part exists through the whole, not vice versa. And the whole is not just the sum of the parts, it is more than the sum.

For example, you can have a rose, and you can go to a scientist, to a logician. You can ask him, "I want to understand this rose flower." What will he do? He will dissect it, he will separate all the elements that go into making it a flower. When you go next, you will find the flower gone. Instead of the flower there will be a few labeled bottles. The elements have been separated, but one thing is certain—there will not be any bottle where the label says "beauty."

Beauty is not material, and beauty does not belong to parts. Once you dissect a flower, once the wholeness of the flower is gone, beauty is also gone. Beauty belongs to the whole, it is the grace that comes to the whole. It is more than the sum of parts. You can dissect a human being; the moment you dissect, life disappears. Then you know only a dead body, a corpse. You can find out how much aluminum is there, and how much iron and how much water; you can find the whole mechanism—the lungs, the kidneys, everything—but one thing is not there and that is life. One thing is not there and that was the most valuable. One thing is not there and that is what we wanted to understand really. Everything else is there.

Where is that fragileness? Where is that aliveness, that throb of life? When it was in the rose flower, it was in a totally different arrangement and life was present. It was full of presence; life was there beating in its heart. All the parts are there, but you cannot say the parts are the same. They cannot be, because the parts exist in the whole.

Intellect dissects, analyzes. It is the instrument of science. Intelligence is the instrument of religion; it joins together. Hence, one of the greatest sciences of spirituality we have called Yoga. Yoga means a methodology to join. Yoga means to put things together. God is the greatest totality, all things together. God is not a person, God is a presence, the presence when the total is functioning in a great harmony—the trees and the birds and the earth and the stars and the moon and the sun and the rivers and the ocean—all together. That togetherness is God. If you dissect it, you will never find God. Dissect a man; you cannot find the presence that was making him alive. Dissect the world; you cannot find the presence that is God.

Intelligence is the method to join things together. An intelligent person is very synthetical. He always looks for a higher whole, because the meaning is always in the higher whole. He always looks for something higher in which the lower is dissolved and functions as a part, functions as a note in the harmony of the whole, gives its own contribution to the orchestra of the whole but is not separate from it. Intelligence moves upwards, intellect moves downwards. Intellect goes to the cause.

Please follow it; the point is delicate.

Intellect goes to the cause; intelligence goes to the goal. Intelligence moves into the future, intellect moves in the past. Intellect reduces everything to the lowest denominator. If you ask what love is, intellect will say it is nothing but sex—the lowest denominator. If you ask what prayer is, the intellect will say it is nothing but repressed sex.

Ask intelligence what sex is, and intelligence will say it is nothing but the seed of prayer. It is the potential love. Intellect reduces to the lowest; it reduces everything to the lowest. Ask intellect what a lotus is, and it will say it is nothing, just an illusion; the reality is the mud—because the lotus comes out of the mud and again falls back into the mud. The mud is the real, the lotus is just an illusion. Mud remains, the lotus comes and goes. Ask intelligence what mud is, and intelligence will say, "It is the potentiality of being a lotus." Then mud disappears and millions of lotuses flower.

Intelligence goes to the higher and the higher, and its whole effort is to reach to the ultimate, to the pinnacle of existence. Because things can be explained only through the higher, not through the lower. You don't explain through the lower, you explain away. And when the lower becomes too important, all beauty is lost, all truth, all good. Everything that has any significance is lost. Then you start crying, "Where is meaning in life?"

In the West, science destroyed every value and reduced everything to matter. Now everybody is worried about what is the meaning of life, because meaning exists in the higher whole. See, you are alone; you feel, "What is the meaning of life?" Then you fall in love with a woman; a certain meaning arises. Now two have become one—a little higher. A single person is a little lower than a couple. A couple is a little higher. Two have joined together. Two opposite forces have mingled, the feminine and the male energies. Now it is more of a circle.

That's why in India we have the concept of *Ardhanarishwar*. Shiva is painted as half woman and half man. The concept of *Ardhanarishwar* says that man is half, and woman is half. When a man and woman meet in deep love, a higher reality arises: certainly greater, more complex, because two energies are meeting. Then a child is born; now there is a family—more meaning. Now the father feels a meaning in his life: the child has to be brought up. He loves the child, he works hard, but work is now no longer work. He is working for his child, for his beloved, for his home. He works, but the hardness of the work has disappeared. He is not dragging himself through it. Tired from the whole day, he comes home dancing. Seeing the smile on his child's face, he is tremendously happy. A family is a higher unit than the couple, and so on and so forth. And God is nothing but the communion of all, the greatest family of all. You become part of a greater unity, bigger than you. Meaning arises immediately whenever you become part of a greater unity.

When a poet writes a poem, meaning arises—because the poet is not alone; he has created something. When a dancer dances, meaning arises. When a mother gives birth to a child, meaning arises. Left alone, cut off from everything else, isolated like an island, you are meaningless. Joined together you are meaningful. The bigger the whole, the bigger is the meaning. At this level of understanding, God is the biggest conceivable whole, and without God you cannot attain the highest meaning. God is not a person; God is not sitting somewhere. Those ideas are just stupid. God is the total presence of existence, the being, the very ground of being. God exists wherever there is union; wherever there is yoga, God comes into existence. You are walking alone; God is fast asleep. Then suddenly you see somebody and you smile; God is awakened, the other has come in. Your smile is not isolated, it is a bridge. You have thrown a bridge towards the other. The other has also smiled, there has been a response. Between you both arises that space called God—a little throb. When you come to the tree and you sit by the side of the tree, completely oblivious to the existence of the tree, God is fast asleep. Then suddenly you look at the tree, and there is an upsurge of feeling for the tree—God has arisen. Wherever there is love, God is; wherever there is response, God is. God is the space; it exists wherever union exists. That's why it is said that love is the purest possibility of God, because it is the subtlest union of energies.

Hence the insistence of some of the mystic traditions that love is God: "Forget God, love will do. But never forget love, because God alone won't do." Intelligence is discrimination, understanding. Truth is the key word, *sat*. One who moves through intelligence moves towards *sat*, truth.

Higher than intelligence is the sixth type of religion. I call it the religion of meditation.

Meditation is awareness, spontaneity. Freedom—it is nontraditional, it is radical, revolutionary, individual. The key word is *chit*, consciousness. Intelligence is still the highest form of intellect, the purest form of intellect. The ladder is the same. Intellect is going downwards on the same ladder, intelligence is going upwards, but the ladder is the same. In meditation the ladder is thrown. Now there is no more movement on the same ladder, neither upwards nor downwards. Now, no more movement but a state of no-movement inside, a drowning into oneself, a sinking in.

Intellect is other-oriented; intelligence is also other-oriented. Intellect cuts the other apart, intelligence joins together with the other, but both are other-oriented. So if you understand rightly, the first four types of religion I don't call religious. They are pseudo-religions. Real religion starts with the fifth type—and the fifth is the lowest, but it is real.

The sixth type of religion is that of meditation, consciousness, *chit*. One simply moves into oneself. All directions are dropped, all dimensions dropped. One simply tries to be oneself, one simply tries just to be. That is where Zen exists, in the sixth type. The very word "Zen" comes from *dhyana*, meditation.

Then comes the highest type, the seventh: the religion of ecstasy, *samadhi*, enlightenment. Just as the fifth type has the key word *sat*, truth, and the sixth type, the religion of meditation, has the key word *chit*, consciousness, the seventh and highest has *anand*, bliss, ecstasy. Together they are the key word *satchitananda*—truth, consciousness, ecstasy.

The seventh type is joy, celebration, song, dance, ecstasy—*anand*. Meditation becomes tremendously joyful—because a person can be meditative and can become sad. A person can be meditative and can become very silent, and may miss bliss. Because meditation can make you silent, absolutely still, but unless dance happens in it, something is missing. Peace is good, peace is very beautiful, but something is lacking in it; bliss is lacking. When peace starts dancing it is bliss. When peace becomes active, overflowing, it is bliss. When bliss is enclosed in a seed it is peace. And when the seed has sprouted, and not only that, but the tree has bloomed and the flowers have come and the seed has become a bloom, then it is enlightenment. That is the highest type of religiousness.

Peace has to dance and silence has to sing. And unless your innermost realization becomes a laughter, something is still lacking. Something still has to be done.

Power and Corruption: The roots of inner and outer politics

One of the fundamentals of fascism is that individuals are not important, it is the group that determines what is real. But then the problem arises: where will you put a stop to it? If the group is real and individuals are not real, or are just parts of the group, then the church is far more real—it is a bigger group; then the nation is far more real because it is an even bigger group; then the whole of humanity is still more real because it is an even bigger group. The individual is completely lost. And whenever there is a conflict between the individual and the group, of course the individual has to sacrifice himself—because he is unreal. He exists only as a part of the group.

This is the way to destroy any possibility of revolution completely, totally. But all societies love fascism. No society wants individuals, because the very existence of the individual is a question mark on many things the society goes on doing.

An individual is bound to be a rebel. An individual is a nonconformist, he cannot conform. He can say yes only to things he feels are worth saying yes to, but it depends on his own feeling, his own intuitive understanding, his own intelligence. He cannot be forced to yield. He can surrender out of love, but he cannot be made to surrender; he would rather die than surrender. He cannot be an obedient slave—not that he does not know how to obey. When he feels for something, when he is committed to something, involved with something, he obeys, he obeys totally, but he is really obeying his own inner light; he is not following any commandments from the outside.

To be an individual is to be nonpolitical. The whole of politics depends on people who are not individuals, who are only phony individuals, who appear to be separate but are not separate—they are dependent on the group, utterly dependent for their safety, security, respectability, power, prestige: for their ego.

The real individual has no ego, hence he need not depend on the society. The society gives you the ego, and if you want to be on an ego trip you have to depend on other people; only they can nourish your ego. The individual knows his real self, hence he needs no ego. To be an individual is to be whole and healthy.

Psychoanalysis has become very important and significant because we have taken away people's individuality. We have given them phony egos which don't satisfy. They are like junk food—colorful, appealing, but not giving any nourishment. And the man who lives with the ego is always missing himself; he is always feeling empty, meaningless. He wants to fill his being with something: he may become obsessed with food just as a way to feel full; he can eat too much, he can become obsessed with food. Or he can become obsessed with money, with gold, with power. These are all ways to somehow feel significant. But nothing succeeds, everything fails. You can hope only while things are far away; when you achieve them, suddenly you see you have been chasing shadows.

You don't feel empty because you don't have much money. You feel empty because you have not yet encountered your real self, you have not come to your authentic individuality. Individuality makes you a light unto yourself.

An individual is a universe in himself. But no society wants individuals, hence for centuries individuality has been destroyed and a plastic thing has replaced it. That plastic thing is called personality.

People are very confused about personality and individuality. They think personality is individuality. It is not—in fact it is the barrier. You will never attain individuality if you are not ready to drop your personality. Individuality is born with you, it is your being. Personality is a social phenomenon, it is given to you. When you are sitting in a cave in the Himalayas you don't have any personality, but you have individuality. Personality can exist only in reference to others. The more people know you, the more personality you have—hence, the desire to have name and fame. The more people respect you, the more you enjoy the personality; it becomes strengthened.

Hence, a great longing for respectability. You can attain it through money, you can attain it by renouncing money. You can attain it by eating too much or you can attain it by eating too little, by fasting. You can attain it by accumulating things or you can attain it by accumulating knowledge. But the whole idea is: you are looking in others' eyes to see how they are feeling about you. You can become very virtuous, very moral, just to attain a personality, but the personality is not going to fulfill you. And down the centuries individuality has been destroyed, and people are carrying personalities.

The people who have lost contact with their beings, the people who are too confined to their personalities and have no idea of any individuality, are ready to become part of a group. They feel very at ease in becoming part of a group, because the moment they become part of a group they have no responsibility. They can relax, they have no anxiety. Now the group takes the responsibility.

That's why people are Hindus and Christians and Mohammedans. Why? Why do people belong to rotten, utterly out-of-date, so-called ideologies? For a single reason: it gives you security, a feeling that you belong, that there are people who are with you—you are not alone. The Christian knows that millions of people are

Christians. The Hindu knows that he is not alone, millions of people are with him—how can he be wrong? How can millions of people be wrong? He must be right! He knows nothing of what is right and what is wrong, but the crowd around him gives him the feeling that he does—a false feeling, obviously.

Truth has nothing to do with the crowd; truth has always been attained by individuals. A Buddha attains it, a Jesus, a Mohammed, a Moses, a Zarathustra. But they attain truth when they are absolutely alone in their deep meditative states, when they forget all about the world and the other, when they are no longer obsessed by the other in any possible way, when they are utterly alone drowning in their own consciousness and reaching the very bottom core of it. Then they know what truth is.

But the crowd keeps you away from yourself. The crowd is an escape from your real being. The crowd makes it possible for you to remain interested in others; it never allows you any self-encounter.

If you become part of a group by dropping your individuality, you are committing suicide. And that's what people are doing. People are tired of themselves; they want to commit suicide. They may not be courageous enough to really commit suicide, but these groups give them ways to commit psychological suicide: "Become part of the group."

And a group can have a mind—not a soul. A group can easily have a mind; that's how people are. Catholics have a certain mind, Mohammedans have a certain mind, Hindus have a certain mind. People who have no individuality start having a certain mind—the mob mind. In the army the whole effort is to destroy the individual and give you a uniform, a number. Now, to give you a number is a subtle way of destroying your individuality. A name gives you a uniqueness, "Number 11" takes your individuality from you.

Frank is a totally different matter—if Frank dies, if Robert dies, a person dies; if Number 11 dies, who cares? Frank cannot be replaced by anybody else, but Number 11?—there is no problem. You can fix a number on anybody and he becomes that number. In the army, scientifically, technologically, the individuality is destroyed. Your name disappears and you become a number. Your hair is cut in the same way. You are forced to follow stupid orders year in, year out: left turn, right turn, about turn . . . for what?!

In the army there is no "why." You are simply told to do such a thing and you have to do it. In fact, the more stupid a thing it is, the better—it prepares you for the work of the army. Following orders for years, one day they say, "Shoot this man!" and you shoot the man, robotlike, without asking why—you have forgotten how to ask why. In the army, the group mind arises, not a group soul, remember.

The soul is always individual; the mind is always group. Any mind, watch carefully, and you will find it belongs to some group. If you believe in God, that means you belong to a certain group that believes in God; they have given the idea, the conditioning, to you. What are your beliefs? From where do they come? They come from the social mind—from the church, from the state; you can find the source from where they come. You can watch your mind and you will see that all that you carry in your mind and think is yours is not yours. It has all come from different sources—parents, teachers, priests, politicians—others have given it to you. There is something like a Christian mind and there is something like a Mohammedan mind and something like a Jewish mind and a Buddhist mind—but there is no Buddhist soul, there is no Christian soul.

Minds belong to groups. In the army you will find it absolutely clear that the individual people have lost their minds. Instead, the regiment has the mind. And to a lesser extent the same is the case in the society. But the soul is always individual; it cannot be given to you by anybody. It is already in you: it has to be discovered.

The greatest adventure that can happen to a human being is the movement from mind to no-mind, the movement from personality to individuality. The no-mind has an individuality; the mind is social.

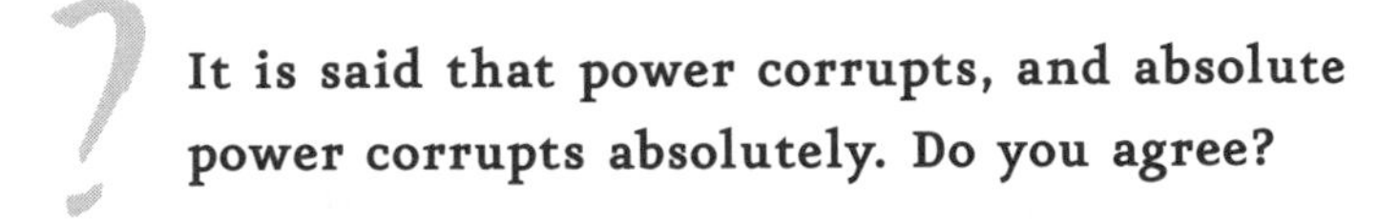

It is said that power corrupts, and absolute power corrupts absolutely. Do you agree?

Lord Acton's famous statement I have thought about from every possible angle, and I have found it always gives some new insight. He says power corrupts, and absolute power corrupts absolutely. I don't think so, because I don't see it happening that way. But Lord Acton was speaking from his whole life's experience; he was a politician himself, so what he was saying was not unfounded.

Still, I dare to disagree with him because my understanding is that power certainly corrupts, but it corrupts only a person who was potentially corruptible. He may not have been known as corrupted before, because he had no opportunity, he had no power. But power itself cannot corrupt a person who has no potential for corruption. So it is not the power that is corrupting the person; in fact the power is simply revealing the person to you. The power is making actual what was before only the potential.

If you look in a mirror and you see an ugly face, are you going to say that the mirror corrupts? The poor mirror simply reflects. If you have an ugly face, what can the mirror do about it?

I have heard about a madwoman who, whenever she came across a mirror, would immediately destroy it. She was ugly, but her belief was that mirrors were the reason for her ugliness. If there were no mirror she would not be ugly. Perfect logic! In a certain way she is not being absolutely illogical. If she were alone on the earth—no mirror, no eyes, because eyes are also mirrors—do you think she would be ugly? Alone on the earth without any mirrors, without any eyes to mirror her, she would be just herself, neither beautiful nor ugly. But she would be the same. The only change that has happened is that now she cannot see her reflection. Nothing has changed, only the reflectors have been removed.

The same is true about Lord Acton's famous dictum, "Power corrupts"—it seems so.

I would like to say that power mirrors. If you are potentially ready to be corrupted, power gives you the chance. And if you have an absolute potential—like an Adolf Hitler, a Joseph Stalin, a Mussolini—then what can power do about it? Power is simply available to you. You can do much with it. If you are a corruptible person, you will do what you always wanted to do but did not have the power to do. But if you are not potentially corruptible, then it is impossible for power to corrupt you. You will use the power, but it will not be corruption, it will be creation. It will not be destructive, it will be a blessing to people. And if you have the potential of being a blessing to people, then absolute power will be an absolute blessing in the world.

But human life has many strange aspects to it. Only the potentially corruptible person moves toward power. The potentially good person has no desire for it. The will-to-power is the need of a corrupted being, because he knows that without power he will not be able to do what he wants to do.

Adolf Hitler first wanted to be an architect, but all the schools of architecture refused him because he had no potential for it. He could barely even draw a straight line. He wanted to become an artist—if not an architect, then an artist—but no school would accept him. If the school of architecture was not going to accept him, then it was clear that art, particularly painting, would need an even greater talent, and he had none. Disappointed everywhere, rejected from everywhere, he started moving towards power.

Adolf Hitler's will-to-power was really strong. A man who was not able to become an architect or a painter became so powerful that the whole destiny of humanity was in his hands. And one of the first things he did after he became powerful, absolutely powerful, was to start designing buildings—architecture. He made designs for many ugly structures, and the government had to build them because, although no architect was ready to accept that these designs were worth even a second look, if they were coming from Adolf Hitler you could not reject them. Their rejection would mean your death or imprisonment, because that was the only language he knew: "Either you are with me or you are no more." But his designs are enough proof that this man simply had no talent to conceive buildings.

After Adolf Hitler became powerful, in his spare moments he was painting; of course, then, everybody had to appreciate his paintings. None of them were worth calling a painting; they were just a waste of canvas and color, without any significance. Not only that, they were ugly—if you had kept his painting in your bedroom, in the night you would have suffered nightmares.

Power brings into actuality what is hidden in you.

But strangely, the good person has no need to be powerful, because good can manifest without power. There is no need for good to have power. Good has its own intrinsic power. Evil needs some outside power to support it.

Kahlil Gibran has written a beautiful story. This one man has written so many beautiful stories that there seems to be no comparison to him in the whole of history. This is a very small story, and that is where Kahlil Gibran's beauty is. He does not write big stories that can be made into films; his stories are composed only of a few lines but penetrate the very depths of the human being.

The story is: God created the world and everything else that was needed. He looked around and he felt that two things were missing: beauty and ugliness. So these two things were the last things he created. Naturally, he gave beautiful clothes to beauty, and to ugliness he gave ugly clothes. He sent them both from heaven to the earth.

It was a long journey, and by the time they reached the earth they were feeling tired and dusty, so the first thing they decided to do was to take a bath. It was early morning, the sun was just rising, and they went to a lake, dropped their clothes on the bank, and both jumped in. It was really refreshing and cool, and they enjoyed it.

Beauty went swimming far into the lake, and when she looked back, she was surprised; ugliness was missing. She came back and found that her clothes were missing, too. Then beauty understood what had happened: Ugliness had taken her clothes and run away. The story ends by saying that since then, ugliness is hidden in the clothes of beauty, and beauty is compulsorily wearing the clothes of ugliness. Beauty is running after ugliness, searching for her, but she has not yet been able to find her.

It is a beautiful story. Ugliness needs something to hide itself behind, to help it pretend—to have a false mask. Beauty had not thought about it at all; the idea had not even occurred to her that it was possible that ugliness would steal her clothes and run away.

When you have a heart throbbing with goodness, with blessings, you feel no need to be a president or the prime minister. You have no time to waste in this ugly game of power politics. You have plenty of energy—that energy comes with goodness. You will create music, you will compose poetry, you will sculpt beauty in marble; you will do something for which power is not needed. All that is needed is already provided for you. That's the beauty of good, that it is intrinsically powerful.

Let it be very clearly understood: You can be certain that anything that needs power from outside is not good. It is something intrinsically impotent; it will live on borrowed life.

So in life this strange situation happens: bad people reach good positions, become respectable or honored, not only in their time but throughout history. It is full of their names.

In history, Gautam Buddha, Mahavira, Lao Tzu, Chuang Tzu, Lieh Tzu—people like these you will not find even in the footnotes. And Alexander the Great, Genghis Khan, Tamerlane, Nadirshah, Napoleon Bonaparte, Adolf Hitler—they make up the major portion of history. In fact, we have to write the whole of history again because all these people have to be completely erased. Even the memory of them should not be carried on, because even their memory may have evil effects on people. A better humanity will not give these names even a place in the footnotes; there is no need. They were nightmares; it is better they are completely forgotten so they don't follow you like shadows.

We have to rediscover people who have lived on this earth and made it in every way beautiful; shared their joy, their dance, their music, shared their ecstasies—but lived anonymously. People have completely forgotten even their names. People don't have any idea how many mystics have lived on this earth and are not known. The reason that you know those few names that are known is not simply that they were mystics—there are some extra reasons. Just think: If Jesus had not been crucified, would you have ever heard his name? So it is not Jesus—not his qualities, not his goodness—but his crucifixion that makes him a historical figure. You know Gautam the Buddha not because he was an enlightened man but because he was the son of a great king. When the son of such a great king renounces his kingdom, of course the whole country far and wide buzzes with his name. And not because he is religious, but because he has renounced such a big kingdom—the same kingdom that you have been aspiring to and dreaming of perhaps for many lives. "This man has some nerve—he just drops the whole kingdom without ever looking back!" That's why history has recorded the existence of Gautam Buddha. Somewhere they had to mention his name because he was a king who renounced his kingdom. If he had been a poor man's son, then nobody would have even heard about him. There have been many whose names are not known at all. Even while they were alive only a few people came to feel that they had a different kind of presence.

Goodness has its own intrinsic power, and it has its own benefit, blessing.

? **Can you talk more about what power means in the spiritual sense? Not as part of politics, but as the energy of goodness and life itself?**

In the spiritual sense, power and force never become one. Power is something that radiates from you; the source is within. Force is violent. Force is interference, a trespass on the freedom of others. Ordinarily, people don't make the distinction between the two words. They use them almost synonymously.

Love is power, but not force. A president has force, but not power. Power never hurts anybody; it is always a healing energy. It showers on you like flowers showering on you. It is a fragrance that reaches to you very silently, not making any noise. It is for you to receive it or not to receive it. It does not force you to receive it.

Power keeps your dignity intact—in fact, it enhances it. It makes you more individual, it allows you more freedom. It makes no conditions on you. Force is totally the opposite of power. Force is violence against the other. But these words became synonymous, and there must be some reason why. It is because in life we experience power changing into force.

For example, you love someone; that is power. But then you get married, you are a husband and she is a wife; it is a social contract, it is business. Now power disappears and force enters in. You will still use the same words, but they don't mean the same. You will still say, "I love you," but you know these are only empty words. Yes, once they were alive, once they had immense content. Once there was juice in them—now everything is just dry. You have to say, "I love you." It is not coming from your heart, it is coming from your head. The space has changed. You will still kiss your wife, but it will be just an exercise of the lips; behind the lips there is nobody. You may be far away, thinking of your secretary. Your wife may be far away, thinking of her boss. Now power, which was a radiance, a field of energy, has disappeared. Instead there is force. Love is gone; law has entered into life.

Because of these changes of power into force, the words have become synonymous—even to the linguists, who should know better.

The difference is very subtle. Force is always that of the sword, and the sword may grow into nuclear weapons. Power is always of love. It can grow only into deeper mysteries, more unknown spaces. Ultimately, it can open doors to both the lovers of something transcendental. It can help them to merge with the universe. In the moments of love when their powers meet, they are two bodies but not two souls. In those moments they start feeling a deep synchronicity with existence itself—with the grass, with the trees, with the birds, with the clouds, with the stars—something only the heart is capable of. It is not a question of reasoning, but of experiencing.

So in that sense, power is spiritual. Force is animal.

Love is the greatest miracle in existence. Naturally, there is no power higher than love. But love is not a force. The very word "force"—the very sound of the word—indicates that you are interfering in somebody's being. You are destroying somebody, reducing somebody to a thing.

So remember, power never becomes force. It becomes bigger and bigger; it can become universal, but it still remains power. It is a benediction, a blessing. Force is ugly. Force is inhuman. Don't be misled by the fact that in the dictionaries they mean the same. Dictionaries are not written by enlightened people; otherwise, words would have different meanings, different connotations, and language would have a purity. But unconscious people go on writing dictionaries and books on linguistics. They have never known anything like power; they have known only force. Naturally, to them the words are synonymous. But to me they are contraries.

Keep them separate; never become attracted towards force. Be full of power—which is yours. And expand it, let others share it.

Lost and Found: In search of ordinariness

Everybody is after being extraordinary. That is the search of the ego: to be someone who is special, to be someone who is unique, incomparable. And this is the paradox: the more you try to be exceptional, the more ordinary you look, because everybody is after extraordinariness. It is such an ordinary desire. If you become ordinary, the very search to be ordinary is extraordinary, because rarely does somebody want to be just nobody, rarely does somebody want to be just a hollow, empty space. This is really extraordinary in a way, because nobody wants it. And when you become ordinary you become extraordinary, and, of course, suddenly you discover that without searching you have become unique.

In fact, everybody is unique. If you can stop your constant running after goals for even a single moment, you will realize that you are unique. Your uniqueness is nothing to be invented, it is already there. It is already the case—to be is to be unique. There is no other way of being. Every leaf on a tree is unique, every pebble on the shore is unique, there is no other way of being. You cannot find two identical pebbles anywhere on the whole of earth.

Two identical things do not exist at all, so there is no need to be "somebody." You just be yourself, and suddenly you are unique, incomparable. That's why I say that this is a paradox: those who search fail, and those who don't bother, suddenly attain.

But don't get confused in words. Let me repeat: The desire to be extraordinary is very ordinary, because everybody has it. And to have the understanding just to be ordinary is very extraordinary, because it rarely happens—a Buddha, a Lao Tzu, a Jesus have it.

To try to be unique is on everybody's mind; and all these people fail and fail utterly. How can you be more unique than you are already? Uniqueness is already there, you have to discover it. You are not to invent it, it is hidden within you; you have to expose it to existence, that's all. This uniqueness is not to be cultivated. It is your treasure, you have been carrying it forever and ever. It is your very being, your very core of being. You have just to close your eyes and look at yourself; you have just to stop for a while and rest and look.

But you are running so fast, you are in such great haste to achieve it, that you will miss it.

It is said by one of Lao Tzu's great disciples, Lieh Tzu, that once an idiot was searching for fire with a candle in his hand. Said Lieh Tzu: "Had he known what fire was, he could have cooked his rice sooner." He remained hungry the whole night because he was searching for fire but couldn't find it—and he had a candle in his hand, because how can you search in the dark without a candle?

You are searching for uniqueness, and you have it in your hand; if you understand, you can cook your rice sooner. I have cooked my rice and I know. You are unnecessarily hungry—the rice is there, the candle is there, the candle is fire. There is no need to take the candle and search. If you take a candle in your hand and you go on searching all over the world, you will not find fire because you don't understand what fire is. Otherwise you could have seen that you were carrying it in your hand.

It happens sometimes to people who wear glasses. They have the glasses on and they are searching for them. They may be in a hurry, and when they are in a hurry they search everywhere—they completely forget that they have the glasses on. One can get in a panic. You may have had certain experiences like this in your life; because of the very search you become so panicky and so worried and so disturbed that your vision is no longer clear, and something that is just in front of you, you cannot see.

This is the case. You need not search for uniqueness, you are unique already. There is no way to make a thing more unique. The words "more unique" are absurd. Unique is enough. There exists nothing like "more unique." It is just like the word "circle." Circles exist; there is no such thing as "more circular." That is absurd. A circle is always perfect, "more" is not needed.

There are no degrees of circularity—a circle is a circle, less and more are useless. Uniqueness is uniqueness, less and more don't apply to it. You are already unique. One realizes this only when one is ready to become ordinary, this is the paradox. But if you understand, there is no problem about it, the paradox is there, and beautiful, and no problem exists. A paradox is not a problem. It looks like a problem if you don't understand; if you understand, it is beautiful, a mystery.

Become ordinary and you will become extraordinary; try to become extraordinary and you will remain ordinary.

? Please speak on the difference between ordinariness and mediocrity.

Mediocrity is the general state of humanity as it is. It is a retardedness of intelligence. Nobody wants you to be intelligent, because the more intelligent you are, the more it is difficult to exploit you. Every vested interest wants you to be mediocre. A mediocre person is just like a tree whose roots have been continuously cut so it cannot grow. The mediocre person never comes to know fruition, flowering, fragrance. But this is the common state. And to keep the mediocre person mediocre, a strange thing has to be put in his mind: that he is extraordinary.

George Gurdjieff used to tell a story:

There was a shepherd who was a magician, and he had many sheep. To take care of them, not to have them wander into the forest and be eaten by wild animals, he managed a strategy. He hypnotized all the sheep and told them, "You are not sheep, you are lions." After that day, the sheep started behaving like lions. The mediocre person will rebel against mediocrity because it is ugly. But the society in so many ways gives people the feeling of being "extraordinary." Hence, it is very difficult to find a person who does not, deep down, believe that he is special, the only begotten son of God. He may not say so, because he knows what happens if you say that you are the only begotten son of God. Then crucifixion is certain, and resurrection—nobody knows whether it really happened or not. So he keeps it inside. This helps him to remain mediocre. If he understands he is mediocre, that very understanding will destroy his mediocrity. To understand that you are mediocre is a great jump into intelligence.

The ordinary person is the natural person. Nature does not produce special people. It produces unique people, but not special. Everybody is unique in his own way.

The big pine tree and the small rosebush—which is higher? Neither the pine tree ever boasts that she is higher, nor the rosebush ever boasts, "You may be higher, but where are the roses? The real height is in the roses and the fragrance, in the flowering. Height itself is not enough to be higher." No, the rose bush and the pine remain together without any quarrel, competition, for the simple reason that both understand they are part of the same nature.

When I talk about ordinariness, I am saying drop the idea of being extraordinary, which is keeping you mediocre. To be ordinary is the most extraordinary thing in the world. Just watch yourself. It hurts very much, it is painful to accept that you are not extraordinary. Then watch what happens when you accept the idea that you are ordinary. A great burden is relieved. Suddenly you are in the open space, natural, just the way you are.

The ordinary person has a uniqueness and simplicity, humbleness. Out of his simplicity, humbleness, uniqueness, he has really become extraordinary, but he has no idea of it.

The people who are humble and just accept that they are ordinary people like everybody else—you will see a light in their eyes. You will see a grace in their actions. You will not see them competing, you will not see them cheating. You will not see them betraying. They will not have double minds. They will not be hypocrites.

If you are an ordinary person, what is the need to be a hypocrite? You can show your heart openly to anybody, because you are not pretending anything. You become secretive when you start pretending. You start feeling very great. You may say it or not, but through your hypocrisy, through your masks, your head goes on becoming more and more swollen. It is a sickness.

And who is the person who believes himself extraordinary?

The person who suffers immensely from an inferiority complex. To cover it up, he projects just the opposite idea. But he is only deceiving himself; nobody else is deceived.

An ordinary person has no need to be a hypocrite, no need to be a pretender. He is just open; he need not be secretive. And there is beauty in openness, simpleness.

Everybody has to look within himself. But people are such deceivers that, deceiving others, slowly they start deceiving themselves. They become so articulate in deceiving. It is dangerous to be a hypocrite, because sooner or later you will start thinking this is your real face.

In my decades of work with people I have come across thousands of people, intimately, and I have been puzzled at how these people have deceived themselves. To deceive others can be understood, but they have deceived themselves. And you cannot take them out of that deception, because that is their only treasure. They know that behind it there is just darkness, hollowness, an inferiority complex. So they cling to the deception.

This is a problem with all mediocre people. They cannot tolerate anybody who is better than them because that destroys their illusion of being extraordinary. But nobody can take away your ordinariness. It is something that is not a projection, but a reality.

The rosebush is ordinary, the pine is ordinary, the deer is ordinary. Why should any human being try to be extraordinary? Only human beings seem to be sick. The whole existence lives in absolute ordinariness and is so joyful, such a blessing, but the human being is sick. The sickness is that he cannot accept himself as he is. He wants to be somebody great: "Alexander the Great." Less than that won't do.

But he forgets what Alexander gained. He lived only thirty-three years, spent his whole life fighting, invading, killing. He had no chance to live, no time to live.

Alexander had met a great sage, a wise man, Diogenes, on his way to invade India. He asked Diogenes if he had any message for him. Diogenes said, "Only one: rather than wasting time, live it. You are not living yourself, and you are not allowing others to live. You are committing immense crimes against life—for what? Just to be called Alexander the Great? Everybody thinks like that. Just inside, you can call yourself Alexander the Great; nobody is preventing you. If you want, you can even put a label on your chest: 'Alexander the Great'—but live! You will look like a buffoon, but that is far better than to *be* a buffoon; at least you will have time to live, love, sing, dance."

Alexander understood the message. He said, "I can see the point. When I come back, I will try to follow it."

Diogenes said, "Remember, nobody comes back from such an ego trip, because this ego trip never ends, it goes on and on. You will end before your ego trip ends." And that's what happened: Alexander never made it back home. On the way back, he died. And when he was dying, he remembered Diogenes' statement that nobody comes back:

"Ego drives you, and there is no end for the ego. It creates more goals, new goals, higher goals." In deep respect for Diogenes, Alexander told the people who were going to carry his body to the grave, "Let my hands hang out of the casket."

His chief minister said, "But this is not the tradition. The hands have to be inside the casket. Hanging them outside will look really odd."

But Alexander said, "I want them to hang out, because I want people to know that I had come empty-handed into the world, empty-handed I lived in the world, and empty-handed I am going from the world."

These empty hands of Alexander the Great represent almost everybody's hands.

If you want to live authentically and sincerely, then just be ordinary. Then nobody can compete with you. You are out of the race of competition, which is destructive.

Suddenly you are free to live. You have time to live. You have time to do what you want to do. You can laugh, you can sing, you can dance. You are an ordinary person. Even if the whole world laughs at it, so what? They are all extraordinary people, they have the right to laugh. You have the right to dance. Their laughter is phony; your dance is real.

But the mediocre mind has no capacity for understanding. It is stuck somewhere near thirteen years in its mental age, or even below it. The person may be forty, fifty, seventy years old—that does not matter, that is the physical age. He has been growing old, but he has not been growing up. You should note the distinction. Growing old, every animal does. Growing up, only a few human beings manage. And the first step is just to accept your simpleness, humbleness.

How can you be an egoist in such a beautiful, immense, vast, infinite universe? What ego can you have? Your ego may be just a soap bubble. Maybe for a few seconds it will remain, rising higher in the air. Perhaps for a few seconds it may reflect a rainbow, but it is only for a few seconds. In this infinite and eternal existence your egos go on bursting every moment.

It is better not to have any attachment to soap bubbles. You can play with them while you are in your bathtub. You can go on bursting those soap bubbles, telling yourself, "This is my ego that I myself am destroying." So when you come out of your bathtub, you are an ordinary person, fresh, humble, clean.

The desire to rule over others, the will to power, is one of the greatest crimes that man has committed. You have to be aware of it. Hence, my insistence on being just ordinary. And it is beautiful, I am saying it out of my experience.

No egoist in the whole history of humanity has said that ego is beautiful, that it has given him great ecstasies. All the egoists have died in frustration, despair, because the ego knows no limits. So you are always frustrated.

I can tell you from my experience of being just an ordinary human being that it is the ultimate ecstasy. It merges you with existence. There is no barrier. It merges you with the stars, and with the sky, and with the earth. You are no longer separate. Ego separates you. And the feeling of oneness with this exquisite existence is what religiousness is, to me.

? **If everybody accepted their ordinariness, would that solve most of the problems of inequality in the world?**

In the past these were the only two alternatives: either everyone is equal—equality of all human beings—or people are unequal. The alternative is to understand that people are unique, incomparable. They cannot be compared, so how can you say who is inferior and who is superior? Is the flower of the marigold inferior to the rose? How can you decide? They are unique in their individualities. The whole existence produces only unique people; it does not believe in carbon copies. So the question of equality or inequality does not arise. This understanding cuts the problem from the very roots.

There is a Greek story: one crazy king had a very beautiful house made only for guests, and he had made a golden bed. When the guest entered the house he could not believe it—those guests were also kings—that he would be receiving such a warm welcome, so much respect and honor: "And people think that this man is crazy! He is not." But soon they were to find that he was. His craziness was that the guest had to fit with the length of the bed. If he was longer, then he had to be made shorter—a little part of his legs would be chopped off. If he was shorter—I think that crazy man was the inventor of traction—the king had big wrestlers who would pull the guest from both ends to make him fit the size of the bed. Whether he died or lived was not important; the size of the bed was important! Mostly the men would die.

This idea of making everybody equal, cutting them to the same size—economically, educationally, in other ways—is absurd, because inequality will show in other dimensions. People are not equally beautiful—then plastic surgery has to make them equally beautiful. Their color is not the same—then someday they have to be injected with pigments to make their color the same.

Everything is unique; you cannot find two persons equal; and communism, for instance, has the idea that the whole of humanity has to be equal. Intellectually you cannot make them equal. The genius of a musician and the genius of a mathematician are totally different worlds. If you want them to be equal, then you will have to destroy the heights, the peaks of genius, and reduce them to the lowest denominator. Then communism will be the greatest massacre that has happened to humanity in the whole of history.

I stand for man's uniqueness. Yes, every person should be given equal opportunity to be his or her self. In other words, every person should be given equal opportunity to be unequal, to be unique. The opportunities can be given, but the mathematician should become a mathematician, and the musician should become a musician.

But no society up to now has allowed the individual his freedom. You think that you are free. You are simply living in an illusion. Humanity will only be free the day there is no inferiority complex produced in children; otherwise, freedom is just hypocrisy. Others are trying to make you a puppet.

The intentions of the parents are not bad, the intentions of the teachers are not bad. I never suspect their intentions, but I suspect their intelligence. I suspect their understanding of human nature, its growth, its possibilities.

If you are clean inside, having no wounds of inferiority, then who cares what people expect of you? You have never fulfilled anybody's expectations. You have been simply living your life according to your own insight, intuition, intelligence. And that's the way it should be. A healthy human being will not have an inferiority complex.

And the other side of the story is: if you don't have an inferiority complex, you will never try to be superior. There is no need to be superior to somebody, dominating somebody, having the upper hand over somebody, controlling somebody; you will never become a politician. Only people who are basically suffering from an inferiority complex are attracted to politics. The very attraction towards politics is proof of what their problem is. Anybody who is attracted towards politics should be immediately treated psychologically. All politicians are sick, without any exception. Unless they are sick, they will not be in politics.

A person who has no desire to have power over others, to prove himself—because there is no need!—he is alive, he is breathing, he is doing his thing; that is enough proof. He has made his mark, and certainly it is his signature, not somebody else's. And remember, if even your thumbprint is unique in the whole world, what about your being? If nature does not create two thumbs alike, look how much care there is! Not even by mistake do two thumbs have the same lines—and there are billions of people on the earth.

Being is so significant that it is irreplaceable. You are just yourself. Do something that comes out of you—not to assert, but to express! Sing your song, dance your dance, rejoice in being whatever nature has chosen you to be.

If we can destroy the inferiority complex, this is very simple: the teachers and the parents just have to be aware not to impose themselves on the helpless children. Within just two decades the new generation will be free of the inferiority complex. And with it will go all politics, all presidents, and all prime ministers. And their going will be such a great relief!

People will express their creativity. There will be musicians, there will be dancers, there will be painters, carpenters. There will be all sorts of creativity around the world. But nobody is competing with anybody else; he is simply doing his best. It is his joy. The joy is not in competing, the joy is not in coming first; the joy is in doing it. It is not outside the act, it is intrinsic to the act. That's my image of the new humanity. We will work, but our work will be our life, our very soul. Whatever we do, it won't matter.

I am reminded of Abraham Lincoln. When he became the president of America, his father was a shoemaker. And, naturally, egoistic people were very much offended that a shoemaker's son should become the president. They were aristocrats, who thought it was their birthright to be in the highest government post. A shoemaker's son? On the first day, as Abraham Lincoln entered to give his inaugural address, just in the middle, one man stood up. He was a very rich aristocrat. He said, "Mr. Lincoln, you should not forget that your father used to make shoes for my family." And the whole Senate laughed; they thought that they had made a fool of Abraham Lincoln.

But Lincoln—and that type of person is made of a totally different mettle—Lincoln looked at the man and said, "Sir, I know that my father used to make shoes in your house for your family, and there will be many others here . . . because the way he made shoes, nobody else can. He was a creator. His shoes were not just shoes, he poured his whole soul in it. I want to ask you, have you any complaint? Because I know how to make shoes myself; if you have any complaint I can make another pair of shoes. But as far as I know, nobody has ever complained about my father's shoes. He was a genius, a great creator, and I am proud of my father!"

The whole Senate was struck dumb. They could not understand what kind of man Abraham Lincoln was. He had made shoemaking an art, a creativity. And he was proud because his father did the job so well that not even a single complaint had ever been heard. And even though he was the president of America, he was ready to make another pair if there was any complaint. The man looked silly. Lincoln insisted, "You have to speak! Why have you become dumb? You wanted to make me a fool, and now, look all around: you have made a fool of yourself."

It does not matter what you do. What matters is how you do it—of your own accord, with your own vision, with your own love. Then whatever you touch becomes gold.

CONSCIENCE VS. CONSCIOUSNESS

Understanding the Freedom of Responsibility

There is no need to develop a conscience at all. What is needed is consciousness, not conscience. Conscience is a pseudo-thing. Conscience is created in you by the society, and it is a subtle method of slavery. Society teaches you what is right and what is wrong. And it starts teaching the child even before the child is aware, before the child can decide on his own what is right and what is wrong, before the child is even conscious of what is happening to him. We are conditioning them according to our ideas—and all these ideas from parents, from priests, teachers, politicians, saints—all these ideas jumble together inside the child and become his "conscience."

Because of this conscience the child will never be able to grow consciousness. The conscience is a false substitute for consciousness, and if you are satisfied with the false you will never even think of the real.

It is deceptive; the way we have been bringing up children is very deceptive and it is ugly, it is a kind of violence against humanity. That's why millions of people live without any consciousness. Before they could have grown into consciousness, we gave them false toys to play with. For their whole lives they think this is all that is needed to live a good life. For their whole lives they believe they will be rewarded if they follow their conscience and will be punished if they don't. They will be punished and rewarded, from the outside and from the inside, too. Whenever you do something that your conscience says is wrong, you feel guilty. You suffer, you feel inner pain; you are afraid, trembling, it creates anxiety. You fear that you may lose the opportunity to go to heaven, that you may fall into hell, and with such great inventiveness your saints have painted the joys of heaven and the miseries of hell!

This is conscience. Conscience is artificial, arbitrary. Rather than making you intelligent, it gives you fixed rules of behavior: "Do this, don't do that."

The day humanity drops this whole nonsense of conscience and starts helping children to grow their consciousness will be the real birth of humanity, a new human being, and a new earth. Then we will help children to become more intelligent, so whenever a problem arises the child has enough intelligence to encounter it, to face it, to respond to it.

And remember, intelligence is not a question of thinking. In fact, you think too much. It is a question of how to stop thinking and to see directly into every situation that you are facing. If there is no thought, there is no barrier, there is no dust in your eyes; you can see clearly.

When this clarity is there, you don't have the alternatives of "good" and "bad." With this clarity there is a choiceless consciousness. You simply do what is good, not that you make any effort to do it. It comes effortlessly to the person of awareness, consciousness, alertness. One simply cannot imagine the bad, the evil. Your whole awareness simply points you towards the good.

The vision of the good is not part of the mind. But if you know only the mind, you don't have clarity. You have hundreds of thoughts moving continuously in your mind; it is a rush hour twenty-four hours a day; a crowd of thoughts goes on, clouds go on moving so fast that you are completely hidden behind the clouds. Your eyes are almost blind. Your inner sensitivity is completely covered by your thoughts.

Through the mind you cannot know what is good and what is bad. You have to depend on others. This dependence is absolutely natural because the mind is a dependent phenomenon; it depends on others; its whole knowledge is borrowed. The mind lives on borrowed knowledge. In every situation it wants somebody to guide it.

Your whole life is being guided by others. From the very beginning you are told what is right and what is wrong by your parents. Then your teachers, then your priests, then your neighbors—not that they know, they too have borrowed from others. This borrowing goes on century after century, generation after generation. Every disease goes on being inherited by the new generation. Each new generation is just a replica of the older generation—a reflection, a shadow, but it does not have its own originality.

It is because of this that you need a God, an ultimate guide. You cannot depend on your parents, because as you grow older you start seeing their falsities, their lies. You start seeing that their advice is not perfect; they are fallible human beings. But the small child believes in the parents as if they are infallible. It is not their fault, it is the small child's innocence; it trusts the father, the mother, who love their children. But finally the child comes to know, as he grows towards a little maturity, that what these people say is not necessarily true. Deep down you are not in agreement with it. Deep down there is doubt.

And deep down you realize that something may be good in one situation and the same thing may be bad in a different situation. Sometimes even poison can be medicine, and sometimes medicine can be poison—you have to understand the changing flux of life.

So thinking cannot decide your actions. It is not a question of deciding as a logical conclusion, it is a question of choiceless awareness. You need a mind without thoughts. In other words, you need a no-mind, just a pure silence, so you can see directly into things. And out of that clarity the choice will come on its own; you are not choosing. You will act just as a buddha acts. Your action will have beauty, your action will have truth, your action will have the fragrance of the divine. There will be no need for you to choose.

You have to look for guidance because you don't know your inner guide is hidden inside you. You have to find the inner guide, and that's what I call your witness. That's what I call your intrinsic buddha. You have to awaken that buddha within, and your life will shower blessings, benediction. Your life will become so radiant with good, with godliness, more than you can possibly conceive.

It is almost like light. Your room is dark, just bring light in. Even a small candle will do, and the whole darkness disappears. And once you have a candle you know where the door is. You don't have to think about it: "Where is the door?" Only blind people think about where the door is. People who have eyes and the light is there, they don't think. Have you ever thought, "Where is the door?" You simply get up and go out. You never give a single thought to where the door is. You don't start groping for the door or hitting your head against the wall. You simply see, and there is not even a flicker of thought. You simply go out.

Exactly the same is the situation when you are beyond mind. When there are no clouds and the sun is bright in the sky, you don't have to think, "Where is the sun?" When there are clouds covering the sun, you have to think about it.

Your own being is covered with thoughts, emotions, feelings, and they are all mind-products. Just put them aside, and then whatever you do is good—not that you follow certain scriptures, not that you follow certain commandments, not that you follow certain spiritual leaders. You are in your own right the guide of your life. And that is the dignity of being human, to be the guide of one's own life. That transforms you into a lion, makes you no longer a sheep always looking for somebody else to defend you.

But this is the problem of almost the whole of humanity. You have been programmed by others as to what is right and what is wrong.

Truth can only arise within you. Nobody else can give it to you. And with truth comes beauty, followed by good. This is the authentic trinity of a truly religious person: truth, beauty, good. These three experiences happen when you enter into your own subjectivity, when you explore the interiority of your being.

You have been living in the porch outside your being; you have never gone in. Once you go in, you will find your buddha, your awareness, your choiceless consciousness. Then you don't have to decide what is right and what is wrong. That choiceless consciousness takes you towards the good without any effort. It is effortless.

You don't need anybody to tell you what is good and what is wrong. All that you need is an awakening within you of a consciousness which allows you to see things as they are. Then there is no question of choice.

Nobody chooses the bad consciously. It is the unconscious, the darkness within you, that chooses the evil. Consciousness brings light to your whole being; you become full of luminosity. You cannot do anything that is harmful to anybody. You cannot do anything that is harmful to your own body. You become suddenly aware that you are one with this whole universe. So your actions become good, beautiful, graceful; your words start having a certain poetry, your silence becomes so deep, so blissful, that your bliss starts overflowing to others.

This overflowing of bliss is the only significant sign of one who is awakened. Just being with that person, just the presence of that person is enough to give you a taste of the beyond.

But it is not according to anybody else, only according to your own awareness.Once you become aware of your inside, you will become aware that, all over, that same consciousness is throbbing, dancing. In the trees, in the rivers, in the mountains, in the oceans, in people's eyes, in their hearts, it is the same song, it is the same dance, and you participate in it. Your participation is good. Your nonparticipation is bad.

Good and Evil: Learning to Live by Your Own Commandments

Every religion has created its own commandments—strange, unnatural—out of fear or out of greed, but they have made this poor humanity that you see around the world.

Even the richest person is poor because he does not have the freedom to act according to his own consciousness. He has to act according to principles given by somebody else, and one does not know whether that somebody else was a con man, a fraud, or just a poet, a dreamer. There is no evidence, because so many people have claimed that they are incarnations of God, that they are messengers of God, that they are prophets of God, and they all bring different messages. Either God is mad or these people are simply lying. Most probably they are lying.

It gives you a great egoistic feeling if you are a prophet, a messiah—somebody special, not just an ordinary human being. Then you can dominate. This is a different kind of politics. Wherever there is domination, there is politics.

The politician is dominating through physical force: through armies, through armaments, through nuclear weapons. The religious prophets, messiahs, saviors, are dominating you spiritually. Their domination is more dangerous, they are far greater politicians. They are dominating your life not only from outside but from inside, too. They have taken over your inside, they have become your morality, they have become your conscience, they have taken over your very spiritual being. From inside they go on dominating you, saying what is right, what is wrong. You have to follow them, otherwise you start feeling guilty, and guilt is one of the worst spiritual diseases. If you follow them you start feeling unnatural, neurotic, perverted, because you are not following your nature. If you follow your nature, you are not following your prophets and your saviors. You are going against the conscience they have implanted in you.

All these religions have created a situation in which we cannot be at ease, we cannot enjoy life, we cannot live it in its totality. So my suggestion is, it is better to let humanity be free from all these old superstitions which have dominated so badly, and distorted human nature so immensely. You can see the humanity that is the result. You say that a tree is known by its fruits. If that *is* true—and that is true—then your whole past of prophets, saviors, God, the devil, should be judged by the humanity that you find today.

This insane humanity—miserable, suffering, full of anger, rage, hate. If this is the result of all your religions, of all your leaders—whether political or religious—then it is better to let God and the devil both die. With God and the devil gone, political leaders and religious leaders will not have any support; they will be the next to go.

I want people to be politically free, religiously free, each individual free in every dimension to function out of his own still small voice, out of his own consciousness. And that will be a beautiful world, a real revolution.

? You say there is no need for conscience. Then how does one develop a guide within that will help one make the right decisions in life?

Conscience is a photo plate and consciousness is a mirror. Both reflect reality, but the mirror never clings to any reflection. It remains empty, and hence it remains capable of reflecting new situations. If it is morning, it reflects the morning. If it is evening, it reflects the evening. The photo plate is a fixed reflection of a reality that is no more; if you exposed it in the morning, then it will always remain morning in the photo, it will never become night.

There is no need to develop a conscience. The need is to drop the conscience and develop consciousness. Drop all that you have been taught by others, and start living on your own and searching and seeking. Yes, in the beginning it will be difficult because you won't have any map. The map is contained by the conscience. You will have to move without the map, you will have to move into the uncharted, with no guidelines. Cowards cannot move without guidelines; cowards cannot move without maps. And when you move with maps and guidelines, you are not really entering new territory, new realms—you are going in circles. You go on moving into the known; you never take a jump into the unknown. It is only courage that can drop conscience.

Conscience means all the knowledge that you have accumulated, and consciousness means being empty, being utterly empty and moving into life with that emptiness, seeing through that emptiness and acting out of that emptiness—then your action has tremendous grace and then whatever you do is right. It is not a question of what is right and what is wrong, because something that is right today may be wrong tomorrow. And borrowed knowledge never helps.

> *Homer and Billy Bob were digging a ditch in the blazing Mississippi sun. Seeing the boss sitting coolly in the shade above them, Homer put down his shovel and said, "How come he is up there and we are down here?"*
>
> *"I dunno," said Billy Bob.*
>
> *Homer went up to the boss and asked him, "How come you boss up here and we work down there?"*
>
> *The boss answered, "Because I am smart."*
>
> *"What is smart?" asked Homer.*
>
> *"Here," said the boss putting his hand on a tree, "I will show you. Try to hit my hand."*
>
> *Homer wound up a mighty swing and let fly. Just as he swung, the boss moved his hand away, and Homer crashed into the tree.*
>
> *"Owwww!!!" he screamed.*
>
> *The boss said coolly, "Now you are smart, too."*
>
> *Homer went back to the ditch. Billy Bob asked what happened and Homer said, "Now I am smart."*
>
> *Billy Bob said, "What do you mean, smart?"*
>
> *Homer said, "I will show you."*
>
> *He looked around for a tree, and not seeing one, he put his hand over his own face. "Here," he said, "try to hit my hand. . . ."*

That's what goes on with your so-called knowledge, conscience—situations change, trees are no longer found, but you have a fixed routine and you cannot do anything else. You go on repeating your routine, and life has no obligation to fit with your routine. You have to fit with life.

The mystics have always known that life follows no logic, that life is basically supralogical, that life follows no reason, that fundamentally it is irrational. Conscience is very arbitrary, artificial. It gives you a fixed pattern, a fixed gestalt, and life goes on changing. Life is very uncertain, it goes zigzag. Unless you are conscious you will not be able to live your life truly; your life will be only a pretension, a false phenomenon. You will always be missing the train.

And always missing the train is what creates anguish in man. Just think of yourself always missing the train: rushing to the station, and whenever you reach it the train is leaving the platform. That's what happens to the person who lives according to the conscience: he never catches the train. He cannot! He has a fixed gestalt, and life is a fluid phenomenon. He has a rocklike thing inside him, and life is more like water.

Be conscious. Don't ask how to develop a conscience. Here we are trying to do just the opposite: we are destroying conscience—the Christian conscience, the Hindu conscience, the Mohammedan conscience, the Jain conscience—we are destroying all kinds of conscience. And consciences come in all shapes and all sizes.

Consciousness is neither Christian nor Hindu nor Mohammedan, it is simply consciousness. Conscience divides people, consciousness unites.

What is the need of carrying a guide with you? Consciousness is enough! Whenever a certain need arises, your consciousness will respond. You have a mirror, you will reflect what is happening, and the response will be spontaneous.

When I was a student at university, my professors were very

worried about me. They loved me, and they were worried because I never prepared for examinations. They were even worried that I might answer in such a way that the examiner might not even be able to see my point. My old professor, Dr. S. K. Saxena, used to come early in the morning to wake me up so that I could study. He would sit in my room, saying, "You do a little preparation." Then he would take me to the examination hall, because he was worried that otherwise I might not even go.

When it came to my final oral examination, he was very worried that I might say something that would offend the examiner. He was also going to be present in the exam because he was the head of the department. And he warned me again and again, "Simply stick to the question! Whatever the examiner asks, you simply answer that. Don't go into any depth about it—just a plain answer, the answer that is given in the books will do. I will be there, and if I see that you are going astray, I will just nudge you with my foot underneath the table. Then come back again and just stick to the question."

The first question was asked and the problem arose. The professor who had come to examine me asked, "What is the difference between Indian philosophy and Western philosophy?" Dr. Saxena became afraid, because he knew that the words "Indian" and "Western" were enough for me to start . . . and that was true. I said, "What do you mean by Indian? Can philosophy be Indian and Western also? If science is not Indian and Western, then why should philosophy be?"

Professor Saxena started nudging me with his foot, and I told him, "Don't do that! You just keep to yourself. This is between me and him; you are not supposed to give me any hints."

Now the old examiner was at a loss: what to do? Whatever he asked, I would answer him with another question. He was at a loss because he was just carrying ready-made answers. I told him,

"It seems that you don't know how to respond. Now, it is such a simple proposition to say that philosophy is philosophy and ask what it has to do with East and West? Say something!" But he was working with a fixed gestalt: something must be Indian, something else must be Western, everything has to be this or that—there are adjectives and adjectives. We can't think of this earth as one. We can't think of humanity as one. Now, what is Indian about Buddha, and what is Jewish about Jesus? Nothing at all. I have tasted both Jesus and Buddha, and the taste is the same. But borrowed knowledge always remains in you as fixed, and whenever you respond out of your fixed ideas your response falls short. It is not a true answer to the reality.

So there is no need to develop a conscience to guide you, there is no need to have any guide! All that is needed is intelligence, awareness, consciousness, so that you can respond whatsoever is the case. Life brings challenges, and you bring consciousness to those challenges.

Meditation is a way of dropping conscience and moving into consciousness. And the miracle is that if you can drop conscience, consciousness arises on its own, because consciousness is a natural phenomenon. You are born with it, only the conscience has become a hard crust around it and is preventing its flow. Conscience has become a rock, and the small spring of consciousness is blocked by this rock. Remove the rock and the spring starts flowing. And with that spring flowing, your life starts moving in a totally different way, a way that you have not even imagined before, you could not have even dreamt of. Everything starts to fall into harmony with existence. And to be in harmony with existence is to be right—not to be in harmony with existence is wrong.

So conscience as such is the root cause of all wrong, because it doesn't allow you to fall in harmony with existence. And consciousness is always right, just as conscience is always wrong.

What about criminals? Many of them seem to have neither conscience nor consciousness. There is sometimes a need, isn't there, for a criminal justice system that can try to prevent people from doing harm to others?

No human being is born as a criminal; every child is born as a sage, innocent. It is a certain kind of nurturing, a certain kind of society, a certain upbringing, that reduces people to criminality.

Once poverty is removed, almost 50 percent of crime will be removed, and along with it 50 percent of judges, 50 percent of courts, 50 percent of law enforcement authorities, and 50 percent of laws—just by removing poverty.

Secondly, now science is certain that there are criminal tendencies that are hereditary. You are unnecessarily punishing a person who needs sympathy, not punishment.

In some aboriginal societies, for example, rape does not exist because young children, the moment they become aware of their sexual energy and the upsurge of sensuality, are not required to live in their parents' houses. They have a hall in the village; all the young people can live in that hall. They come in contact with all kinds of girls and all kinds of boys; they are allowed absolute sexual freedom, with only one condition—which seems to be very significant—that you can be with a girlfriend or a boyfriend for only a few days; then you have to change.

This gives a chance for everybody to experience everybody else, and also it gives an immense opportunity to drop jealousy. It is impossible to be jealous because your girlfriend is now moving with somebody else. There is no fixed relationship; only for a few days can you be together, then you move on, you change. By the time they are of marriageable age, they are so experienced with every girl of the tribe and every boy of the tribe that they can choose the right partner; the one with whom they are in the most harmonious relationship. Strangely enough, in such a licentious society there is no rape and there is no divorce, either. They have found the right person because they have been given the opportunity. Their love goes on growing, their harmony becomes richer and richer each day.

With the pill available, men and women can experiment until they find a person whom they would really love to be with forever. They need not be in a hurry to rush to the church, they can wait. For a year or two they can see how their intimacy goes; whether it goes deeper and becomes richer, or if as time passes it fades away. Before deciding on a life partner, this seems to be simply logical—to experiment, to experience as many people as possible. Adultery will disappear, rape will disappear.

Science will find, as we have already been finding, that there are crimes that a person is committing under biological laws; he has a tendency to commit them by his heredity. Then he needs hospitalization, medical care; or, if he has something wrong with his mind, then he needs a psychiatric hospital. But there is no question of calling him a criminal, and there is no question of giving him any punishment.

All punishment is itself a crime. Just because we have not been able to find the causes, or perhaps we were not willing to find the cause, because to deal with the causes would mean changing the whole social structure, and we were not ready for that great revolution.

The rebellious person is ready for a revolution in every area of life. If injustice disappears there is no question of any justice.

It is very difficult to conceive of a humanity that lives without jealousy, without anger, without competitiveness, without a lust for power, but it is all possible. We have just never thought about how to remove the causes.

Why do people want power? Because whatever they are doing is not respected. A shoemaker is not respected like the president of a country. In reality, he may be better as a shoemaker than the president is as a president. The quality should be praised; if a shoemaker is a better shoemaker, then he need not be interested in being a president. His own art, his own craft, will bring him dignity and the respect of the people.

When everybody is respected as he is, when each profession is respected, whatever it is, you are cutting the very roots of crime, of injustice.

When there is no money as an agency for exchange, nobody can become richer and nobody can become poorer.

The rebel will look at every problem of life from its very roots. He will not repress the symptoms, he will destroy the causes. If all the causes of injustice are destroyed, then justice can be restored for the first time.

Right now, we are all living in unjust circumstances, there is multidimensional injustice. And to keep this injustice in place we have armies, police, we have guards, we have courts and judges. These professions are absolutely useless! All these people should be taught some craft—shoemaking, weaving clothes, carpentry. If they cannot do anything very skillful, then unskilled labor—they can at least carry bricks, participate in the construction of houses and roads. At the very least, all your judges and all your great law experts can become gardeners.

But the whole justice establishment is there to protect the many injustices that are in existence, and the people who are in power want those injustices to continue.

The world of my vision, the world of the new humanity, will remove all causes. Many crimes—murder, rape, even stealing—might be hereditary. You might need your chemistry to be changed, your hormones to be adjusted. A few crimes are committed because you have a wrong psychology; you need a good cleaning of the brain, and more clarity of vision. And none of this should not be considered as punishment. If somebody is suffering from tuberculosis you send him to the hospital, not to jail—and to be in the hospital is not considered to be criminal. Once you are healthy and back in the society, your dignity is not destroyed.

There are many problems that have not even been touched by the old humanity. They have been avoiding them, postponing them. Their greatest fear was that it would be exposed that the powerful people were contributors to the causes of all crimes, that the rich people were a cause of crimes, that the priests were a cause of sexual crimes, sexual perversions. They have never brought those causes to light.

Future humanity will destroy all the causes of injustice. And if something comes from heredity, it is a very simple matter of changing your hormones, changing your chemistry, your physiology. If something is in your mind, that too can be fixed.

With the collaboration of science, psychology, psychoanalysis, and psychiatry, the rebellious spirit will be able to remove all injustice, and the very question will become irrelevant.

? **All that seems a little unrealistic to hope for in the near future. What insights can we bring to the justice system in the meantime?**

I would like to make one point clear: that a person can act in a wrong way; that does not mean that the person becomes wrong. Action is a small thing. A person is a tremendous reality. And the action is already past: the person has a pure future in front of him. If he hides the action he destroys his own future, because that action will go on and on in his mind as guilt. If he confesses it and is willing to take whatever punishment is needed for it, he will clean himself completely. His future will become pure.

Confessing to the court, a person should get the most lenient punishment. And I would ask the courts to understand that no criminal needs punishment; all criminals need treatment.

For centuries criminals have been punished and you have not been able to change anything. The numbers of criminals go on growing; then you grow more courts, more lawyers. It is an unnecessary burden. And the criminals—even if you imprison them, you are doing an absolutely irrational act, because living five years or ten years in jail means living in the university of criminology, where all the real masters of crime are. You will learn more, and you will learn one thing from all great criminals: that to commit a crime is not illegal, but to be caught is illegal. So all that you have to do is not to be caught; you have to be more clever, more cunning. Crime is not the problem. The problem is being caught.

So anybody who is sent to a prison comes out an even bigger criminal. When he went into the prison, perhaps he was just an amateur—that's why he was so easily caught. When he comes out, he comes out as a professional, expert. Now it will be difficult to catch him.

So my suggestion to the courts of the world is that up to now what you have been doing with the criminals is not right. A criminal has something wrong in his psychology. He needs psychiatric treatment. Instead of making prisons, make places where he can be given psychiatric treatment, where he can meditate, study, become more intelligent. And give him all the respect that is due to a human being. His acts do not count; what counts is his being.

Can you say more about how we can nurture our own development of consciousness, so

that at least there is no question of our individual actions harming ourselves or others?

Everything has energy—fear, anger, jealousy, hate. You are unaware of the fact that all these things are wasting your life. Your energy is leaking from so many holes. This way you are going to become, sooner or later, bankrupt. In fact, most people become bankrupt by the age of thirty. After that there is nothing; it is a posthumous life, dragging on somehow towards the grave.

You have to face your fear. And do the same with anger, do the same with jealousy, do the same with hatred. And a significant point to remember is: if you witness anything—fear, anger, hate—if you simply watch them as they arise, without any judgment or condemnation, they will disappear, leaving a tremendous amount of energy that you can use for creativity. You will *have* to use it; the leaks have disappeared and you will be overflowing with energy. But if you witness your love, compassion, kindness, humbleness, they will not disappear. They also have tremendous energy, but the more you witness them the stronger they will become in you; they will overwhelm you.

So this is the criterion to decide what is right and what is wrong. If by witnessing, something disappears, leaving all its energy to you, it was wrong.

I don't give you ready-made, labeled things: "This is wrong and this is right, this you have to do, and this you have not to do." I don't give you ten commandments. I give you the whole secret of spiritual life: witness, watch, be aware. If the thing disappears and leaves a great amount of energy behind it, it was wrong. If by witnessing the phenomenon becomes even bigger, love becomes more Himalayan, that means this is the good you have been searching for. If you become more sensitive to beauty, to poetry, that means your love has blossomed. And all the energy that was being used by fear, anger, and hate will be taken over by your love, your sensitivity, your compassion, your creativity. This is the whole alchemy of changing base metals into gold.

This is what alchemists were really doing, but because of Christianity they could not say it openly. This is one of the sad things about religions, that rather than helping really religious people, they prevent them. So the alchemists in Europe found a device to deceive the pope and his agents. They had small labs in which there were many tubes and bottles, many-colored liquids, and stoves. It gave the appearance that they were doing something material, that they were scientists, that they were not mystics—because the mystic was dangerous to the pope, the mystic was dangerous to organized religion. These people were just trying to change base metals into gold; that was perfectly good. In fact, if they succeeded, then they would be in the service of the Church. So they could work with the blessings of the pope. But this was only a facade. The reality was something else, which was going on behind the scenes. Being scientists was just the superficial mask. They were not doing anything; not a single gram of base metal was changed into gold in hundreds of years. Can't you see? All those bottles and tubes and water with many colors passing from one bottle into another—that was simply to hide behind. And who is not interested in changing base metal into gold? Everybody was interested.

Alchemists were respected for their facade. What they were actually doing was of a different dimension. They were trying to change fear, anger, hatred, into love, compassion, creativity, sensitivity. They were trying to bring a transformation in the soul of man.

So this is the basic alchemy: you watch, witness without any judgment. There is no need of any judgment. That which is wrong will disappear, leaving a great energy behind. And that which is good will become bigger and will start absorbing the energies that have been left; only a great fragrance of love, light, and laughter remains behind.

Rules and Responsibilities: Walking the Tightrope of Freedom

I am not against rules, but the rules should arise out of your understanding. They should not be imposed from the outside. I am not against discipline! but discipline should not be slavery. All true discipline is self-discipline. And self-discipline is never against freedom—in fact, it is the ladder to freedom. Only disciplined people become free, but their discipline is not obedience to others: their discipline is obedience to their own inner voice. And they are ready to risk anything for it.

Let your own awareness decide your lifestyle, life pattern. Don't allow anybody else to decide it. *That* is a sin, to allow anybody else to decide it. Why is it a sin? Because you will never be in your life. It will remain superficial, it will be hypocrisy.

A person of awareness is not controlled either by past or by future. You have nobody to force you to behave in a certain way. The Vedas are no longer on your head, Mahavira and Mohammed and Christ no longer force you to move anywhere. You are free. That's why in India we call such a person a *mukta*. A *mukta* means one who is totally free. One *is* freedom.

In *this* moment, whatever the situation, one responds with full awareness. That is your responsibility. You are capable of response. Your responsibility is not an obligation, it is a sensitivity to the present moment. The meaning of responsibility changes. It is not responsibility as an obligation, as a duty, as a burden, as something which has to be done. No, responsibility is just a sensitivity, a mirrorlike phenomenon. You come before the mirror, and the mirror reflects, responds. Whatever happens, a man of awareness responds with his totality. He does not hold anything back; that's why he never regrets, that's why he never feels guilty; whatever could be done, he has done, he is finished with it. He lives each moment totally and completely.

In your ignorance everything is incomplete. You have not completed anything. Millions of experiences are inside you, waiting for their completion. You wanted to laugh, but the society wouldn't allow it. You suppressed it. That laughter is waiting there as a wound. What a miserable state—even laughter becomes a wound! When you don't allow laughter, it becomes a wound, an incomplete thing inside you waiting and waiting someday to be completed.

You loved somebody, but you could not love totally, your character prohibited it, your conscience wouldn't allow it. Even when you are with your beloved in the dark night, alone in your room, society is present. The constable is standing there and watching. You are not alone. You have a conscience, your beloved has a conscience: how can you be alone? The whole society is there, the whole marketplace is standing all around. And God, looking down from above, watching you, looking at what you are doing, God seems to be the universal Peeping Tom—he goes on looking at people. The society has used God's eyes to control you, to make you a slave. You cannot even love totally, you cannot hate totally, you cannot be angry totally. You cannot be total in anything.

You eat halfheartedly, you walk halfheartedly, you laugh halfheartedly. You cannot cry—you are holding thousands of tears in your eyes. Everything is a burdened thing, loaded; the whole past you are carrying unnecessarily. And this is your character.

A buddha has no character because he is fluid, because he is flexible. A character means inflexibility. It is armorlike. It protects you from certain things, but then it kills you, too.

?

Don't we need some kind of inner control, though? I'm afraid my life might just degenerate into chaos if I don't make any effort to discipline myself.

Once you become too controlled, you don't allow life to happen to you. You have too many conditions, and life cannot fulfill those conditions.

Life happens to you only when you are unconditionally accepting it; when you are ready to welcome it whatever shape it comes in, in whatever form it takes. But a person who has too much control is always asking life to come in a certain form, fulfilling certain conditions, and life doesn't bother; it just passes these people by. They remain almost dead, vegetating.

The sooner you break out of the confinements of control the better, because all control is from the mind. And you are greater than the mind—so a small part is trying to dominate you, trying to dictate what happens to you. Life goes on moving and you are left far behind, and then you are frustrated.

The logic of the mind is such that it says, "Look, you didn't control things well, that's why you missed, so control more." The truth is just the opposite: people miss because of too much control.

Be like a wild river, and much that you cannot even dream of, cannot even imagine, cannot even hope for, is available just around the corner, just within reach. But you have to open your hand; don't go on living the life of a fist, because that is the life of control.

Live a life of an open hand. The whole sky is available, don't settle for less. Never settle for less. The whole sky is our birthright—to fly to the farthest corners of existence and to enjoy and delight in and celebrate all that life has given.

? Is there a difference between control and discipline? I have always been hard on myself, and I feel that because of this I have missed much of the joy of life.

There is not only a difference, there is a vast difference: discipline and control are polar opposites. Control is from the ego, discipline is from the non-ego; to control is to manipulate yourself, to discipline is to understand yourself. Discipline is a natural phenomenon, control is unnatural; discipline is spontaneous, control is a sort of suppression. Discipline needs only understanding—you understand and you act according to your understanding. Discipline has no ideal to follow, discipline has no dogma to follow, discipline is not perfectionistic, discipline leads you by and by toward wholeness.

Control is perfectionistic, it has an ideal to be achieved; you have an idea in the mind about how you should be. Control has many shoulds and many should-nots, discipline has none. Discipline is a natural understanding, a flowering.

The very word "discipline" comes from a root which means "to learn"; it comes from the same root as the word "disciple." A disciple is one who is ready to learn, and discipline is that capacity of openness which helps you to learn.

Discipline has nothing to do with control. In fact, a disciplined mind is never a mind which thinks in terms of control, there is no need for it. A disciplined mind needs no control, a disciplined mind is absolutely free.

An undisciplined mind needs control because an undisciplined mind feels that without control there is danger. An undisciplined mind cannot trust itself, hence the control. For example, if you don't control yourself you may kill somebody; in anger, in rage, you can be a murderer. You need control, because you are afraid of yourself.

A man of understanding, a man who understands himself and others, always feels compassion. Even if somebody is an enemy, you have compassion toward him because a man of understanding can understand the viewpoint of the other also. He knows why the other feels as he feels, he knows why the other is angry, because he knows his own self, and in knowing that, he has known all others. He has compassion, he understands, and he follows understanding. When I say this don't misunderstand me—understanding in fact need not be followed. The very word "following" gives the idea of having to do something: you understand, then you have to do something, you have to follow the understanding. No, understand, and everything settles by itself. You need not follow, it simply starts happening.

So it is important to understand the difference between control and discipline. Control is a false coin, invented by society as a substitute for discipline. It looks exactly like discipline: every false coin looks that way, otherwise it could not circulate in the market. There are many false coins about the inner life. Control is a false coin for the real coin of discipline.

Never try to control yourself. Who will control, really? If you understand, there is no need to control; if you don't understand, then who will control? This is the crux of the whole problem.

If you understand, what is the need to control? You understand, so you do whatsoever is right. Not that you have to do it, you simply do it because how can you do the wrong? If you are hungry, you don't start eating stones—you understand that stones cannot be eaten, finished! There is no need to give you a commandment, "Never eat stones when you are hungry." It will be simply foolish to say it. When you are thirsty you drink water. What is the need to make any "should" or "should-not" about it?

Life is simple when you understand. There are no regulations or rules around it, there is no need, because your very understanding is the rule of all rules. There is only one golden rule, and that is understanding; all other rules are useless, they can be thrown away. If you understand, you can drop all controls, you can be free because whatever you do, you will do through understanding.

If you ask me the definition of what is right, I will say that which is done through understanding. Right and wrong have no objective values; there is nothing like a right action and a wrong action, there are only actions done through understanding and actions done through nonunderstanding. So sometimes it is possible that one action may be wrong this moment and right the next moment because the situation has changed and now the understanding says something else. Understanding is to live moment to moment, with a sensitive response to life.

You don't have a fixed dogma of how to act; you look around, you feel, you see, and then you act out of that feeling, seeing, knowing—the action comes.

A man of control has no vision of life, he has no sensitivity to life. When the road is right in front of him, open, he consults a map; when the door is just in front of him he asks others: Where is the door? He is blind. Then he has to control himself because the location of the door is changing every moment. Life is not a dead, static thing—it is not. It is dynamic.

So the same rule that was good for yesterday will not be good for today and cannot be good for tomorrow. But one who lives through control has a fixed ideology and follows the map. Roads go on being changed every day, life goes on moving into new dimensions, but he goes on carrying his old, rubbishy ideology. He looks at his idea, then he follows it, and then he is always in the wrong situation.

That's why you feel that you have missed many joys in life. You have to miss, because the only joy that life can give is a response of understanding. Then you feel many joys, but then you don't have any rules, any ideas, any ideals, then you are not here to follow certain codes; you are here to live and discover your own code of life.

When you become aware of your own code of life, you will see that it is not a fixed thing. It is as dynamic as life itself.

If you try to control, it is the ego; it is the ego manipulating you in many ways. Through the ego, society manipulates you, and through society, the dead, all those who are dead now, manipulate you. Every living being, if he follows a dead ideology, is following dead people.

Zarathustra is beautiful, Buddha is beautiful, Lao Tzu is beautiful, Jesus is beautiful—but they are no longer applicable. They lived their lives, they flowered beautifully. Learn through them but don't be a stupid follower. Be a disciple but don't be a student.

A student learns the word, the dead word; a disciple just learns the secrets of understanding, and when he has his own understanding, he goes on his own way. He pays his respect to Lao Tzu and says, "Now I'm ready, I'm grateful, I go my own way." He will always be grateful to Lao Tzu, and this is the paradox: people who have been dedicated to following Jesus, Buddha, or Mohammed can never forgive them. If you miss the joys of life because of these people how can you forgive them? How can you really be in gratitude? In fact you are deeply in anger. If you come across them you will kill them, you will murder them, because these are the people who have forced you into a controlled life; these are the people who didn't allow you to live as you would have liked to live; these are the people, Moses and Mohammed, who have given you commandments about how to live. You cannot forgive them. Your gratitude is false. You are so miserable, how can you be grateful? For what? For your misery can you be grateful? No, you can be grateful only when you are blissful.

Gratitude follows like a shadow when you have an inner blessing, a feeling of constant benediction.

Be a person of discipline but never be a person of control. Drop all rules and regulations and live life with a deeper alertness, that's all. Understanding should be the only law. If you understand you will love, if you love you will not commit any harm to anybody. If you understand you will be happy, if you are happy you will share. If you understand you will become so blissful that from your whole being, as a continuum, like a river, a thankfulness towards existence will arise.

Try to understand life, don't force, and remain always free from the past; because if the past is there and you are controlling, you cannot understand life. And life is so fleeting, it doesn't wait.

But why do people try to make rules? Why do they fall into the trap at all? They fall into the trap because a life of understanding is a life of danger. You have to rely upon yourself. The life of control is comfortable and secure, you need not rely on yourself: Moses will do, the Bible will do, the Koran will do, the Gita will do—you need not bother about the problems, you can escape from them. You take shelter in old words, disciplines, thoughts, you cling to them. This is how you can make a comfortable life, a life of convenience—but a life of convenience is not a life of bliss. Then you miss joy because joy is possible only when you live dangerously. There is no other way to live.

Live dangerously, and when I say "Live dangerously," I mean live according to your own self, whatever the cost. Whatever is at stake, live according to your own consciousness, according to your own heart and feeling. If all security is lost, all comfort and convenience is lost, then, too, you will be happy. You may be a beggar, you may not be a king, you may be on the streets in rags, but no emperor can compete with you. Even emperors will feel jealous of you because you will have a richness, not of things, but a richness of consciousness. You will have a subtle light around you and you will have a feeling of blissfulness. Even others can touch that feeling. It is so visible, so substantial, others will be affected by it, it will become a magnet. You may outwardly be a beggar, but inwardly you have become a king.

But if you live a life of convenience and security and comfort, you will avoid danger, you will avoid many difficulties and sufferings; but by avoiding those difficulties and sufferings you will avoid all the bliss that is possible in life. When you avoid suffering you avoid bliss, remember that. When you try to escape a problem you are escaping the solution also. When you don't want to face a situation you are crippling your own life. Never live a controlled life—that is the life of an escapist—but be disciplined. Disciplined not according to me, not according to anybody, but according to your own light. "Be a light unto yourself." That was Buddha's last saying before he died; the last thing that he uttered. That is discipline.

Reaction and Response: The knack of rolling with the punches

The word "responsibility" has been used in a wrong way. It gives a feeling of burden. You have to do it, it is a duty; if you don't do it you will feel guilty. I want to remind you that the word "responsibility" has none of those connotations. Break the word in two—response-ability—and you enter a totally different meaning of the word, in a different direction. Response-ability is not a burden. It is not a duty; it is not something you have to do in spite of yourself.

Response-ability simply means spontaneous response. Whatever situation arises, joyously you respond to it, with your totality, with your intensity. And this response will not only change the situation, it will also change you.

There are two words to be remembered: one is "reaction" and one is "response-ability." Most people react, they don't respond. Reaction comes from your memory, from your past experiences, from your knowledge; it is always inadequate in a fresh, new situation. And existence is continuously fresh. So if you act according to your past, that is reaction. But that reaction is not going to change the situation, it is not going to change you, and you will be in utter failure.

Response is moment to moment. It has nothing to do with memory, it has something to do with your awareness. You see the situation with clarity; you are clean, silent, serene. Out of this serenity, spontaneously you act. It is not reaction, it is action. You have never done it before, but the beauty of it is that it will suit the situation, and it will be a joy to you to know that you are capable of being spontaneous.

There are very few joys in life greater than spontaneity. Spontaneity means to be in the moment; it means acting out of your awareness, not acting according to your old conditionings. Those days are gone—those conditions, conceptions are absolutely invalid.

You don't have to learn response; you don't have to be taught it; it comes out of your silence, your serenity, of its own accord. Many of your acts are not actions, because they are coming from the memory—they are re-actions. The authentic act comes from your consciousness.

I am response-able, not responsible. I will act out of my love, not because of any sense of duty or obligation. And I will act in the moment, without referring to my memory system, because the memory is always of the past and existence is always new—they never meet.

So the first thing I want you to understand is, don't make the whole word "responsibility"; break it into two: response-hyphen-ability. It changes the whole color.

A rebel is renouncing the past. He is not going to repeat the past; he is bringing something new into the world. Those who have escaped from the world and society are escapists. They have really renounced responsibilities, but without understanding that the moment you renounce responsibilities, you also renounce freedom. These are the complexities of life: freedom and responsibilities go away together, or remain together.

The more you are a lover of freedom, the more you will be ready to accept responsibilities. But outside of the world, outside the society, there is no possibility of any responsibility. And it has to be remembered that all that we learn, we learn through being responsible.

You can act in two ways: one is reaction, another is response. Reaction comes out of your past conditionings; it is mechanical. Response comes out of your presence, awareness, consciousness; it is nonmechanical. And the ability to respond is one of the greatest principles of growth. You are not following any order, any commandment, you are simply following your awareness. You are functioning like a mirror, reflecting the situation and responding to it—not out of your memory, from past experiences of similar situations; not repeating your past actions; but acting fresh, new, in this very moment. Neither is the situation old nor is your response—both are new. This ability is one of the qualities of the rebel.

Renouncing the world, escaping to the forest and the mountains, you are simply escaping from a learning situation. In a cave in the Himalayas you won't have any responsibility, but remember, without responsibility you cannot grow; your consciousness will remain stuck. For growth it needs to face, to encounter, to accept the challenges of responsibilities.

Escapists are cowards; they are not rebels, although that's what has been thought up to now, that they are rebellious spirits.

They are not, they are simply cowards. They could not cope with life. They knew their weaknesses, their frailties, and they thought it was better to escape, because then you will never have to face your weakness, your frailty, you will never come to know any challenge. But without challenges how are you going to grow?

? Is what you call "response-ability" similar to Jesus' saying that if someone hits you, you should turn the other cheek?

I will not say to you that "response-ability" means to turn your other cheek if somebody hits you, no. I can only say one thing: let that moment decide. Sometimes perhaps you have to turn the other cheek. Sometimes perhaps you have to hit the person harder than he has hit you. Sometimes perhaps you have to hit him on *both* cheeks, but nothing can be given to you as a ready-made formula. It will depend on you, the person, the situation.

But act with awareness, then whatever you do is right. I don't label acts as right and wrong. To me, the quality of your awareness is decisive. If you can respond with awareness, then whatever your response is, I declare it right. If you lose your awareness and react, then whatever you do—you may be turning the other cheek—it is wrong. Do you see that I have used two different words? With awareness I used the word "response"; with unawareness I used the word "reaction."

Response comes from yourself. Reaction is created by the other person. He has hit you. He is the master of the situation, and you are simply a puppet. You are reacting. His action is decisive, and because he has done something, now you are doing something in reaction. This is unconscious behavior. That's why an unconscious person's behavior can be manipulated very easily. You smile, she will smile. You be angry, he will be angry.

It is because of this that people like Dale Carnegie can write books like *How to Win Friends and Influence People*. All that you have to know is simple reactions.

Carnegie himself describes a situation. He was working as an insurance agent, and there was a rich woman, the richest in the town, a widow, who was very much against insurance and insurance agents; so much so that nobody could even make an appointment to see her—just at the gate they would be turned away. Her orders to her gatekeeper were "Throw them out!" No question of getting in to see her.

And when Dale Carnegie joined the company, all the other agents said to him, "You are writing this book about winning friends and influencing people. Now, if you can sell insurance to this old lady, we will think you have something to say; otherwise, it is all hocus-pocus." And he managed to insure the woman. How did he do it? A simple method.

Early in the morning he went around the woman's house. She was in the garden. Standing outside the fence, he said, "I have never seen such beautiful flowers."

The old woman asked, "Are you interested in roses?"

He said, "How did you know? I am mad about roses; the only flower that really attracts me is the rose."

The woman said, "Why are you standing outside? Come in, I will show you my roses. I am also mad about roses, and you will not come across such big rose flowers as I have grown here in my garden." And he was invited in. They went around her big garden, full of beautiful roses, and he was all praise and poetry. The woman was so impressed that she said, "You seem to be such an intelligent man, I want to ask you one question. What do you think about insurance?"—because she was tortured by these insurance agents continually, and they were always trying to visit and being thrown out.

He said, "For that I will have to come back again, because I have to think it over and do a little research on it. I never advise anybody unless I am certain."

The woman said, "That's right. You are the first man who is not too eager to advise me. That is the sure sign of a fool: too eager to advise others."

He said, "No, I will have to look at the whole matter. Perhaps it will take a few days." And during those few days he used to stop by every morning and stand outside the fence.

The woman said, "There is no need to be standing out there. I have told all the servants that for you my doors are open any time of day. Whenever you want to come into the garden, you can come. If you want to come into the house, you can. It is your house, don't be shy." Within a few days he had gone to her with all the forms, the files, and everything. He said, "I have worked out the whole thing. In fact, I had to become an agent of an insurance company to find out absolutely all the details, the inside story, because from the outside you cannot know much. Now I am absolutely certain that this is the thing for you."

Now, this is the way the whole of humanity functions, through reaction. You just do something that you know how the other unconscious being is going to react to. And it is very rare that an insurance agent will meet an awakened person, a rare possibility. In the first place, the awakened person will not have anything to be insured. Only with the awakened person will Dale Carnegie fail, because that person will not react but respond. And response you cannot predict.

The man of awareness is unpredictable because he never reacts. You cannot figure out beforehand what he is going to do. And each moment he is new. He may have acted in a certain way in a certain moment. The next moment he may not act in the same way because in the next moment everything has changed. Every moment life is continuously changing; it is a moving river; nothing is static except your unconsciousness and its reactions.

Unconscious people are predictable. You can manage them easily. You can make them do things, say things, even things that they never wanted to do or never wanted to say, because they react.

But a person of awareness, one who is authentically religious, only responds. He is not in your hands; you cannot pull him down, you cannot make him do anything. You cannot manage to draw out even a single sentence from him. He will do only that which in that moment he finds—through his awareness—is appropriate.

? **As I understand it, an unconscious person reacts while a wise person is able to simply watch his emotions as they arise rather than acting on them mechanically. But what about spontaneity? Is spontaneity really compatible with watching?**

When you have learned how to watch, when you have learned how to be utterly silent, unmoving, undisturbed, when you know how to just sit, sitting silently, doing nothing, then it's true, as the Zen saying goes, that the spring comes and the grass grows by itself. But the grass grows, remember!

Action does not disappear, the grass grows by itself. Becoming watchful does not mean that you become inactive; action happens through you, although there is no doer anymore. The doer disappears, but the doing continues. And when there is no doer, the doing is spontaneous; it cannot be otherwise. It is the doer that does not allow spontaneity.

The doer means the ego, the ego means the past. When you act, you are always acting through the past, you are acting out of experience that you have accumulated, you are acting out of the conclusions that you have arrived at in the past. How can you be spontaneous? The past dominates, and because of the past you cannot even see the present. Your eyes are so full of the past, the smoke of the past is so thick, that seeing is impossible. You cannot see! You are almost completely blind—blind because of the smoke, because of the past conclusions, because of your knowledge. The knowledgeable person is the most blind person in the world. Because he functions out of his knowledge, he does not see what the case is. He simply goes on functioning mechanically. He has learned something and it has become a ready-made mechanism in him, he acts out of it.

But life has no obligation to fit with your conclusions. That's why life is very confusing to the knowledgeable person. He has all ready-made answers, he has everything crammed. But life never raises the same question again; hence, the knowledgeable person always falls short.

Certainly, one has to know how to sit silently. That does not mean that one goes on sitting silently forever. It is not that you have to become inactive; on the contrary, it is only out of silence that a real response, a real action arises. If you are not silent, if you don't know how to sit silently in deep meditation, whatever you go on doing is reaction, not action. You react.

Somebody insults you, pushes a button, and you react. You are angry, you jump on the person—and you call it action? It is not action, it is reaction. The other person is the manipulator and you are the manipulated. The other person has pushed a button and you have functioned like a machine. Just like you push a button and the light goes on, and you push the button and the light goes off, that's what people are doing to you: they switch you on, they switch you off. Somebody comes and praises you and puffs up your ego, and you feel so great; and then somebody comes and punctures your ego and you are simply flat on the ground. You are not your own master. Anybody can insult you and make you sad, angry, irritated, annoyed, violent, mad. And anybody can praise you and make you feel you are at the heights, you are the greatest, Alexander the Great was nothing compared to you.

You act according to others' manipulations. This is not real action.

Buddha was passing through a village and the people came and they insulted him. They used all the four-letter words that they knew. Buddha stood there, listened silently, very attentively, and then said, "Thank you for coming to me, but I am in a hurry. I have to reach the next village, people will be waiting for me there. I cannot devote more time to you today, but tomorrow coming back I will have more time. You can gather again, and tomorrow if something is left that you wanted to say and have not been able to, you can say it. But today, please excuse me."

Those people could not believe their ears: this man has remained utterly unaffected, undistracted. One of them asked, "Have you not heard us? We have been abusing you like anything, and you have not even answered!"

Buddha said, "If you wanted an answer, then you have come too late. You should have come ten years ago, then I would have answered you. But for these ten years I have stopped being manipulated by others. I am no longer a slave, I am my own master. I act according to myself, not according to anybody else. I act according to my inner need. You cannot force me to do anything. It's perfectly good: you wanted to abuse me, you abused me! Feel fulfilled. You have done your work perfectly well. But as far as I am concerned, I don't take your insults, and unless I take them, they are meaningless."

When somebody insults you, you have to become a receiver, you have to accept what he says; only then can you react. But if you don't accept, if you simply remain detached, if you keep the distance, if you remain cool, what can he do?

Buddha said, "Somebody can throw a burning torch into the river. It will remain alight till it reaches the river. The moment it falls into the river, all fire is gone; the river cools it. I have become a river. You throw abuses at me. They are fire when you throw them, but the moment they reach me, in my coolness, their fire is lost. They no longer hurt. You throw thorns, falling in my silence they become flowers. I act out of my own intrinsic nature."

This is spontaneity. The person of awareness, understanding, acts. The one who is unaware—unconscious, mechanical, robot-like—reacts.

You say, "The unconscious person reacts while the wise person watches." It is not that you simply watch, watching is one aspect of your being. The wise person does not act without watching, but don't misunderstand. Your intelligence becomes sharpened only when you act. And when you act moment to moment out of your awareness and watchfulness, great intelligence arises. You start shining, glowing, you become luminous. But it happens through two things: watching, and the action that arises out of that watching. If your watching becomes inaction, you are committing suicide. Watching should lead you into action, a new kind of action. A new quality is brought to action.

You watch, you are utterly quiet and silent; you see what the situation is, and out of that seeing you respond. The man of awareness responds, he is "responsible"—literally! He is responsive, he does not react. His action is born out of his awareness, not out of your manipulation; that is the difference.

Hence, there is no question of any incompatibility between watching and spontaneity. Watching is the beginning of spontaneity; spontaneity is the fulfillment of watching.

The man of understanding acts, acts tremendously, acts totally, but acts in the moment, out of his consciousness. The watchful mind, the meditative mind, functions like a mirror. It catches no impression; it remains utterly empty, always empty. So whatever comes in front of the mirror, it is reflected. If you are standing before the mirror, it reflects you. If you are gone, don't say that the mirror has betrayed you. The mirror is simply a mirror. When you are gone, it no longer reflects you; it has no obligation to reflect you anymore. Now somebody else is facing it, it reflects somebody else. If nobody is there, it reflects nothing. It is always true to life.

Learn sitting silently—become a mirror. Silence makes a mirror out of your consciousness, and then you function moment to moment. You reflect life. You don't carry an album full of old pictures within your head. Then your eyes are clear and innocent, you have clarity, you have vision, and you are never untrue to life.

This is authentic living.

MEANING AND SIGNIFICANCE

From the Known to the Unknown to the Unknowable

People wonder why there seems to be no meaning in life. Meaning does not exist a priori. There is no meaning existing in life; one has to create it. Only if you create it will you discover it. It has to be invented first. It is not lying there like a rock, it has to be created like a song. It is not a thing, it is a significance that you bring through your consciousness.

Truth cannot be given to you, but you can smell the perfume of it. And then you can start searching for it in your own innermost core, in your own being. It has to evolve. It is a growth. Meaning is a growth. You will have to devote your whole life to it.

And the modern mind is feeling more meaningless than ever has been the case, because of the past centuries lived in a kind of stupor, sleep. Orthodoxy was prevalent, convention was heavy and strong. The citadel of religion was very powerful, dictatorial. People have lived for centuries in belief. Now, during this century, more and more people have dared to drop beliefs. Those beliefs served to give people a feeling that there was meaning in life; now those beliefs have disappeared. This is good—as far as it goes it is good that beliefs have disappeared. This is the first age of agnosticism. For the first time, more and more people have become mature, mature in the sense that they do not rely on beliefs, on superstitions. They have dropped all those superstitious beliefs.

But a kind of vacuum has come into existence. The beliefs have disappeared, and with the beliefs, the false sense of meaning they had given you has also disappeared. An emptiness has settled in. The negative part has been done, we have demolished the old building, now the positive part has to be done. We have to erect a new building. The old temple is no more, but where is the new one? Belief has been destroyed, but where is trust? Belief has gone—this is good, but this is not enough. It is necessary but not enough. In this age, belief has disappeared but nothing has appeared in its place. Now you will have to grow into trust.

You must have heard about a German thinker, Ludwig Feuerbach. He seems to be the herald of the contemporary mind. Feuerbach explained God away in terms of the infinite desire of the human heart. He said there is no God; God does not exist as an objective reality. It is only a wish fulfillment. Man wants to become omnipotent, omnipresent, omniscient. Man wants to become God—this is the desire, to become infinite. It is a desire to become immortal, a desire to become absolutely powerful.

This statement by Feuerbach was one of the first hammerings on the belief in God. He said that God is not objective; there is no God. God is just a projection in the human mind; God has no ontology, he is only a psychological dream. We think in terms of God because we feel ourselves to be impotent. We need something to make ourselves complete. We need an idea that gives us a feeling that we are not strangers here, that in this world there is somebody who looks after us. God is nothing but a projected father. We want to lean upon something. It is just a pure desire, it has no reality.

Then came Karl Marx. Marx saw God as an ideological attempt to rise above the given reality. Marx said that because people are poor, suffering, in misery, they need a dream, a dream that can give them hope. People are living in such hopelessness, in such utter misery, that if they cannot dream that somewhere in the future everything will be perfect, they will not be able to tolerate this intolerable reality. So God is the opium, religion is opium for the masses. It is a drug. It helps people, consoles them. It is a kind of tranquilizer. You are in such pain that you need a painkiller; today, yes, today is miserable, but tomorrow everything is going to be good.

Marx says that's why Jesus' Beatitudes have become so important: "Blessed are the poor." Why? Why are the poor "blessed"? Because "they shall inherit the kingdom of God." Now the poor person can hope. Here he is poor, but there he will inherit the kingdom of God. Not only that, Jesus says, "Those who are the first here will be the last there, and those who are the last here will be the first." Now the poor person feels really happy. He forgets his poverty. He is going to be the first in the kingdom of God. Marx thinks these statements are just drugs.

His point of view also looks very logical. When people are in misery, they have only one way to tolerate it: to pass time away, they can imagine a better future. You are in the hospital; you can imagine that tomorrow you will be getting out of the hospital, going home, and everything will be okay. It is only a question of a few hours more. You can tolerate it.

This world is a question of only a few years, don't be worried about it. Soon paradise is waiting for you. The poorer you are, the higher you are going to be in paradise. And all that you are missing here is abundantly supplied there. You don't have a beautiful woman? Don't be worried. In paradise everybody will have as many as they want, and the most beautiful women you can conceive of. Here you aren't allowed to drink alcohol? In paradise there are streams of wine, alcohol of all kinds. You can drink as much as you want, you can absolutely soak yourself in it.

These dreams are just consolations for those who are downtrodden, oppressed. So Marx says that religion is just a trick to exploit people, a trick to keep them under your rule, a trick so that they cannot rebel. He hammered very hard on the old beliefs.

And then the third hammer came with Friedrich Nietzsche. He said, "God is nothing but a weakening of the will to live." When a person becomes old or a society becomes old, rotten, dull, and dying, it starts thinking of God. Why? Because death is coming close and one has to somehow accept death. Life is slipping out of one's hands, one cannot do anything about it—but at least one can accept death. God is a trick to accept death. And Nietzsche says that death is accepted by only those who have become weak.

He used to say that the very idea of God comes out of the feminine mind; he used to say that Buddha and Christ are both effeminate, they are not really masculine. They are too soft. They are people who have accepted the defeat and are no longer fighting for survival. When a person stops fighting for survival, he becomes religious. When the will to power is no longer functioning, one starts shrinking and dying and starts thinking of God. God is against life, life is the will to power. Life is constant struggle; life is conflict and one has to win. When people become too weak and cannot win, those defeated minds start becoming religious. Religion is defeatism.

Feuerbach, Marx, Nietzsche—these three together created the atmosphere where it could be declared that God is dead and man is free.

This is the situation into which you have been born. If you are contemporary at all, this is the situation. You are more in tune with Feuerbach, Marx, and Nietzsche than you are in tune with the founders and prophets of the religions. They are far away; we don't belong to them, they don't belong to us. The distance is too great. Our real prophets are Feuerbach, Marx, Nietzsche, Freud, Darwin—and these people have destroyed the whole fabric, the whole structure, the whole pattern of belief.

I would like to tell you that they have done a great service to humanity. But don't misunderstand me. They have cleaned human consciousness completely of belief, but this is only half the job. Now something else is needed. It is as if you are preparing for a garden and you prepare the ground, you pull up all the weeds, and you throw away all the stones. Now the ground is ready, but then you simply wait and you don't bring in the rose bushes, you don't sow new seeds.

These people have done a great service to humanity. They have uprooted all the weeds. But just by uprooting the weeds the garden cannot be ready. It is part of preparing a garden to uproot the weeds, but this is not the garden itself. Now you have to bring the roses. Those roses are missing, hence meaning is missing.

People are stuck. They think this clean patch of ground where no belief grows, where no desire springs up about the unknown and the beyond, is the garden. And when they start looking all around, they see that it is nothing. It is a desert. Those people have cleaned the ground, but now only a desert is there. So man has become very anxious. Anxiety has been repressed for centuries so that people could conform to the party, to the religion, to the sect, to the society. For thousands of years the anxiety has remained locked up and man has functioned as a slave. Now the lock has been broken, man is no longer a slave, and the whole repression of thousands of years has broken loose. Man is going mad.

What these people have done can turn into a great liberation or it can become just a loss. It depends. If you use this situation rightly and you start growing roses in your heart, soon you will have a great thankfulness toward Feuerbach, Marx, Nietzsche, Freud, and all the people who have destroyed belief, who have destroyed the old religion. They have prepared the way for a new kind of religiousness—more mature, more adult, more grown-up.

I am all for them, but I don't stop with them. If you stop, meaninglessness will be your destiny. Yes, it is good that there exists no God, but then start finding out what exists in your inner being.

They have created a situation in which you can say "Don't know"—that's what agnosticism is. Now use this as a jumping board to go into the unknown. You are ready to go into the unknown. Knowledge is not binding you, nobody is shackling your feet. You are free for the first time. But what are you doing standing there? You had been standing there because you were chained, and now you are still standing there even though the chains have been removed. Move forward. Now explore! The whole existence is yours. Explore it with no concept, with no prejudice, with no a priori philosophy.

Knowledge has been destroyed and that's good. These people—Feuerbach, Marx, Nietzsche, and others—have done a good job of clearing away the whole nonsense of centuries, but remember, even they were not benefited by it. Nietzsche died in a madhouse, and if you are stuck with Nietzsche, you are waiting for madness and nothing else. He did a great service, he was a martyr, but he got stuck with his own negativity. He destroyed the belief, but then he never went to explore. Without belief, what is there? With no belief, what is there? There *is* something. You cannot say there is nothing, there is something. What is it? He never went into meditation. Thinking, logical thinking, can do one thing: it can destroy belief. But it cannot lead you into truth.

We have to create meaning now. The meaning is no longer given by the society, is no longer given by anybody else. Martin Heidegger says that once one has become aware of the meaninglessness of life and existence, there arises great anxiety, angst, anguish. He says: "This happens through unlocking that which subjection to conformity and conditioning of centuries had locked. Once this liberation has happened one can act, but not according to norms given by anybody or anything. One has to fall upon oneself."

Heidegger is right. You have to fall upon yourself. Now you cannot lean on anybody. No scripture will help, prophets are gone, messengers are no longer there. You will have to lean upon yourself. You will have to stand on your own feet. You will have to become independent. Heidegger calls it "resolve." You will have to come to a resolve, a resolution. You are alone and no help is coming from anywhere. Now what are you going to do? And you don't know anything. No belief exists to give you a map. No chart exists, and the uncharted is all around. The whole existence has again become a mystery.

It is a great joy for those who have courage because now exploration is possible.

This is what Martin Heidegger calls resolve, because through it the individual becomes resolute, the individual becomes individual. No God, no conventions, no laws, no commandments, no norms, no principles—one must be oneself and one must decide where to go, what to do, and who to be. This is the meaning of the famous existentialist maxim that existence precedes essence; that is, there is no essential human nature. Man creates what he is, man creates himself. The meaning has to be created. You have to sing your meaning, you have to dance your meaning, you have to paint your meaning, you have to live it. Through living, it will arise; through dancing, it will start penetrating your being. Through singing, it will come to you. It is not like a rock just lying there to be found, it has to bloom in your being.

Energy and Understanding: The journey from lust to loving

Energy is understanding, they are not two things. What kind of energy is understanding? When the energy is unoccupied, it becomes understanding. When energy is occupied, it remains ignorance, it remains unconsciousness.

For example, your sex energy is occupied with a woman or with a man. It will remain ignorance because the energy is focused on the object; it is going outward, it is extroverted. If the energy is freed from the object, where will it go? It will start falling into the subject, into your inner source. And energy falling back into the source becomes understanding, becomes awareness.

And I am not saying be against sex, no. But let sex be more a subjective phenomenon than an objective phenomenon. And that is the difference between sex and love. Love is subjective, sex is objective.

You become interested in a woman or in a man as an object, and sooner or later the interest will be finished because once you have explored the object, nothing is left. Then you are ready to move to somebody else. Yes, the woman looks beautiful, but how long can she look beautiful? An object is an object. She is not yet a person to you, she is just a beautiful object. It is insulting. You are reducing a soul into an object, a subjectivity into an object. You are trying to exploit. You are turning her into a means. Your energy will remain ignorant. And you will go on moving from one woman to another, and your energy will go on running in circles. It will never come back home.

Love means you are not interested in the woman or the man as an object. In fact, you are not there to exploit the other, you are not there to get something from the other. On the contrary, you are so full of energy, you would like to give some energy to the person. Love gives. Sex only wants to get.

And when love gives, it remains subjective, it remains rooted in oneself. Lovers help each other to be more and more themselves. Lovers help each other to become authentically individual. Lovers help each other to be centered. Love is respect, reverence, worship. It is not exploitation. Love is understanding. Because energy is unoccupied with the object, it remains free, untethered to anything. And that brings the transformation. It accumulates inside you.

And remember: just as it happens in the world of physics, so it happens in the world of metaphysics. After a certain quantity of energy, a qualitative change happens. The qualitative change is nothing but the outcome of the quantitative change.

For example, if you heat water to the boiling point, it evaporates. Up to the boiling point, it has not evaporated; it is still water—hot, but still water. But beyond the temperature at which it boils, it evaporates—it is no longer water. It has changed its form. The transformation has happened.

Just like that, when your energy accumulates, don't go on wasting it on objects—and people *are* wasting it on objects. Somebody is interested in money; he puts his whole energy into it. Of course, he accumulates a lot of money, but in accumulating it he dies, dissipates, becomes empty, becomes a beggar. Money goes on accumulating, and he goes on becoming more and more beggarly. Somebody puts his energy into politics, into power. He becomes a prime minister, but deep down he is a beggar. He may be the most important beggar in the country, but still he is a beggar.

If you put your energy into objects, you will live a life of nonunderstanding, unawareness. Don't put your energy into objects.

Let energy fall back into your being. Let it accumulate. Let your life become a great reservoir. Let your energy just be there without any occupation. And at a certain point—the jump, the quantum leap, the transformation. Energy becomes luminous, turns into awareness, becomes understanding.

It is energy that becomes understanding. So when you are depleted of energy, you start losing your understanding. When you are tired, your intelligence is less. You have observed it. In the morning your intelligence is fresher than in the evening. In the morning you are more understanding, more compassionate, more loving, than in the evening.

Have you observed it? Beggars come in the morning to beg. They understand the psychology. In the evening, who is going to give to them? People are so angry by that time, so frustrated with life. In the morning they have rested the whole night, a deep sleep, their energy is fresh, they have accumulated eight hours of energy. They are more understanding, have more compassion, more love, more sympathy. It is possible to persuade them to give something to you. They have something, so they can give. By the evening, they don't have anything; they have lost all they had in the morning, they are dead tired.

Children are more understanding—have you observed it or not?—than old people. Old people become hard, cruel, cunning. Their whole life they have remained occupied with objects. Most old people become Machiavellian. Young children are innocent, trusting, closer to buddhas. Why? Their energy is overflowing.

Young children learn things so fast. Why? The energy is there, hence the intelligence. The older you become, the more difficult it becomes to learn a thing. They say it is difficult to teach an old dog new tricks. Why? It should not be so, because the dog knows so many tricks already, he can learn a few more. It should be easier for him because he has practiced learning so much that he can learn a few more easily. But it is not so.

Children learn fast. If a child is born in a town where five languages are spoken, he starts learning all five; he becomes efficient in all five. They all become his mother tongue. A child has infinite capacity to learn, and the reason is only one: his energy is still overflowing. Soon it will be dissipated in life.

The man of meditation becomes the man of understanding because his energy accumulates. He is not wasting it. He is not interested in trivia; he does not put any energy at all into petty things. So whenever the time arises to give, he has it to give.

Energy is understanding. Be conscious of it and use your energy very consciously, and use your energy in such a way that you don't simply go on wasting it.

? **Would you talk to us about using our sexual energy for growth, as it seems to be one of our main preoccupations in the West?**

Sex is *the* energy. So I will not say sexual energy because there is no other energy. Sex is the only energy you have. The energy can be transformed, it can become a higher energy. The higher it moves, the less and less sexuality remains in it. And there is an end peak where it becomes simply love and compassion. The ultimate flowering we can call divine energy, but the base, the seat, remains sex. So sex is the first, bottom layer of energy and godliness is the top layer. But the same energy moves.

The first thing to be understood is not to divide your energies. Once you divide, then a dualism is created. Once you divide, then conflict and struggle are created. Once you divide your energies, you are divided—then you will be for or against sex.

I am neither for nor against, because I don't divide. I say sex is the energy, the name of the energy; call that energy *x*. Sex is the name of that *x* energy, the unknown energy, when you are using it only as a biological reproduction force. It becomes divine once it is freed from biological bondage, once it becomes nonphysical; then it is the love Jesus talks about or the compassion of Buddha.

People are obsessed today because of Christianity. Two thousand years of Christian suppression of sex energy have made the Western mind too obsessed with it.

First, for two thousand years the obsession was with how to kill it. You cannot kill your sex energy. No energy can be killed, energy can only be transformed. There is no way to destroy energy. Nothing can be destroyed in this world, it can only be transformed, changed, moved into a new realm and dimension. Destruction is impossible.

You cannot create a new energy, and you cannot destroy an old energy. Creation and destruction are both beyond you. They cannot be done. Now, scientists agree, not even a single atom can be destroyed.

For two thousand years, Christianity was trying to destroy sex energy. Their idea has been that religion consists of becoming absolutely without sex. That created a madness. The more you fight, the more you suppress, the more sexual you become. And then sex moves deeper into the unconscious. It poisons your whole being.

So if you read the lives of Christian saints, you will see they are obsessed with sex. They cannot pray, they cannot meditate. Whatsoever they do, sex comes in. And they think that the devil is playing tricks. Nobody is playing tricks. If you suppress, *you* are the devil.

After two thousand years of continuous sex repression, the West became fed up with it. It was too much and the whole wheel turned. Then, instead of repression, indulgence became the new obsession. From one pole the mind moved to the other pole. The disease remained the same. Once it was repression, now it is to indulge more and more in it. Both are sick attitudes.

Sex has to be transformed, neither repressed nor indulged.

And the only possible way to transform sex is to be sexual with deep meditative awareness.

Move into sex, but with an alert, conscious, mindful being. Don't allow it to become an unconscious force. Don't be pulled and pushed by it. Move knowingly, understandingly, lovingly. But make sexual experience a meditative experience. Meditate in it. This is what the East has done through Tantra.

And once you are meditative in sexual experience, the quality of it starts changing. The same energy which is moving into sexual experience starts moving towards consciousness.

You can become so alert in a peak sexual orgasm as you can otherwise never become, because no other experience is so deep, no other experience is so absorbing, no other experience is so total. In a sexual orgasm, you are totally absorbed, root and all—your whole being vibrating, your whole being in it. Body, mind—both are in it. And thinking stops completely. Even for a single second, when the orgasm reaches its peak, thinking stops completely, because you are so total you cannot think.

In a sexual orgasm you *are*. Being is there without any thinking. In this moment, if you can become alert, conscious, then sex can become the door to the divine. And if in this moment you can become alert, that alertness can be carried in other moments also, in other experiences also. It can become a part of you. Then eating, walking, doing some work, you can carry that alertness. Through sex, the alertness has touched your deepest core. It has penetrated you. Now you can carry it.

And, if you become meditative, you will come to realize a new fact. That fact is that it is not sex that gives you bliss, it is not sex that gives you the ecstasy. Rather, it is a thoughtless state of the mind and total involvement in the act that gives you a blissful feeling.

Once you understand this, then sex will be needed less and

less, because that thoughtless state of mind can be created without it; that's what meditation means. And that totality of being can be created without sex. Once you know that the same phenomenon can happen without sex, sex will be needed less and less. A moment will come when sex will not be needed at all.

Remember, sex is always dependent on the other. So in sex, a certain bondage remains. Once you can create this total orgasmic phenomenon without any dependence on anybody else, when it has become an inner source, you are independent, you are free.

That's what is meant when the mystics have said that only a truly celibate person can be free, because now he is not dependent on anybody else, his ecstasy is his own.

Sex disappears through meditation, but this is not destroying the energy. Energy is never destroyed; only the form of the energy changes. Now it is no longer sexual, and when the form is no longer sexual, then you become loving.

Really, a person who is sexual cannot love. His love can only be a show, his love is just a means towards sex. A person who is sexual uses love just as a technique towards sex. It is a means. A sexual person cannot really love, he can only exploit the other; and love becomes just a way to approach the other.

A person who has become nonsexual, and the energy is moving within, has become auto-ecstatic. His ecstasy is his own. Such a person will be loving for the first time. His love will be a constant showering, a constant sharing, a constant giving. But to achieve this, you should not be antisex. To achieve this, you have to accept sex as part of life, of natural life. Move with it, only move with more consciousness.

? All this talk about transforming sex is great, but when I look deeply at myself, I find that basically I'm bored with my wife, and I'm afraid of women, and I probably need to deal with that first. What's at the root of this fear?

All men are afraid of women, and all women are afraid of men. They have good reasons to mistrust each other, since they have been trained from early years to be enemies of each other. They are not born to be enemies, but they achieve enmity. And after about twenty years of such training in being afraid of each other they are supposed to marry one day and find complete trust in each other. Twenty years' training of being afraid of each other in a seventy-, eighty-year life, and the most delicate and sensitive part of your life!

Psychologists say we learn 50 percent of our whole life's learning by the time we are seven. In the remaining years we will learn only 50 percent more. Fifty percent is learned by the time we are seven. By the time you are twenty, almost 80 percent is learned. You have become fixed, hard. Distrust has been taught to you. The boys have been told, "Avoid girls, they are dangerous." The girls have been told, "Avoid boys, they are nasty, they will do something evil to you." And then after this complete conditioning of twenty years—just think, twenty years of constantly being taught by the parents, by the school, by the college, by the university, by the church, by the priest—one day suddenly how can you drop this twenty years of conditioning?

The question arises again and again: so many men tell me that they are afraid of women; women tell me they are afraid of men. You were not born afraid; you were not afraid in your beginnings. A child is born simply unafraid. Then we teach him fear and we condition his mind.

This has to be dropped, this has driven people almost neurotic. Then people fight—husbands and wives constantly fighting, and they are wondering why they go on fighting and why all relationships turn sour. Why does it happen? You have been poisoned, and you have to consciously drop that conditioning. Otherwise you will remain afraid.

There is nothing to be afraid of in a man or a woman. They are just like you, just as much in need of love as you are, hankering just as much to join hands with you as you are hankering. They want to participate in your life and they want others to participate in their lives, because the more people participate in each other's lives, the more joy arises. People are looking very sad. They have become very lonely. Even in crowds people are lonely because everybody is afraid of everybody else. Even if people are sitting close to each other, they are holding themselves back, so much so that their whole being becomes hard. A hard crust surrounds them, an armor rises around their being, so even when they meet there is no real meeting. People hold hands, but those hands are cold, no love is flowing. They hug each other, yes, bones clash with each other, but the heart remains far away.

People have to love—love is a great need, just as food is a need. Food is a lower need, love is a higher need, a much higher-order value.

Psychologists have been doing research on children who were brought up in orphanages without any love. Many children can die if they are brought up without love; within two years they die. They are given good food, nourishment, every scientific care, but just mechanically. The nurse comes, gives them a bath, feeds them; every care is taken, but no human love. The nurse will not hug them close to her heart, will not give her warm body to the child; warmth is not given. Within two years many of those children die and there is no visible reason why they die. They were perfectly healthy physically, the body was going perfectly well;

they were not ill or anything, but suddenly, for no apparent reason at all, they start dying. And the remaining children are in more trouble than those who die. Those who die are in a way more intelligent. Those who survive become neurotic, schizophrenic, psychotic, because no love has been showered on them. Love makes you one piece. It is like glue—it glues you together. They start falling into fragments. There is nothing to hold them together, no vision of life, no experience of love—nothing to hold them together. Their lives seem meaningless, so many of them turn neurotic, many of them become criminals.

Love makes a person creative; if love is missing, then a person becomes destructive. Had Adolf Hitler's mother loved him more, the world might have been totally different.

If there is no love, the person forgets the language of creativity, becomes destructive; so criminals, politicians are born. They are the same types of people—there is no difference in them, no qualitative difference. Their faces differ, their masks are different, but deep down they are all criminals. In fact, you have been reading the history of human crimes and nothing else. You have not yet been taught the real history of humanity, because the real history consists of Buddhas, Christs, Lao Tzus. A totally different human history exists, which has been kept out of the schools. History takes note only of crimes, history takes note only of destruction. If you kill somebody on the streets, you will be in the newspapers, and if you give a rose flower to somebody, you will never be heard of again. Nobody will know about it.

If love is missing in childhood, the person will become either a politician or a criminal, or will go mad, or will find some destructive path, because he will not know how to create. His life will be meaningless, he will not feel any significance. He will feel condemned, because unless you have been loved you cannot feel your worth. The moment somebody loves you, you become worthy. You start feeling you are needed, existence would be a little less without you. When a woman loves you, you know that if you are gone, somebody is going to be sad. When a man loves you, you know that you are making somebody's life happy, and because you are making somebody's life happy, great joy arises in you.

Joy arises only in creating joy for others; there is no other way. The more people you can make happy, the more you will feel happy. This is the real meaning of service. This is the real meaning of being religious: help people to become happy, help people to become warm, help people to become loving. Create a little beauty in the world, create a little joy, create a little corner where people can celebrate and sing and dance and be, and you will be happy. Immense will be your reward. But the one who has never been loved does not know it.

So the children who survive without any love prove to be very dangerous people. Love is such a basic need; it is exactly the food for the soul. The body needs food and the soul also needs food. The body lives on material food, the soul lives on spiritual food. Love is spiritual food, spiritual nourishment.

In my vision of a better world children will be taught to love each other. Boys and girls will not be kept apart. No division, no disgust with each other should be created. But why has this disgust been created? Because there has been a great fear of sex. Sex is not accepted, that is the problem, because sex is not accepted the children have to be kept apart. Humanity is going to continue to suffer unless it accepts sex as a natural phenomenon. This whole problem of man/woman arises because sex is condemned.

This condemnation has to go, and now it can go. In the past I can understand there were reasons for it. For example, if a girl became pregnant, then there would have been problems. Parents were very much afraid, the society was very much afraid, people lived in fear. The boys and girls had to be kept apart, great walls had to be raised between them. And then one day, after twenty years, suddenly you open the door and you say, "She is not your enemy, she is your wife. Love her! He is not your enemy, he is your husband. Love him!" What about those twenty years when he was the enemy to be feared? Can you suddenly drop those years so easily? You cannot drop them. They linger on, they hang around you for your whole life.

But now there is no need. In my understanding, the greatest revolution in the world has been that which is created by the pill. Lenin and Mao Tse-tung are nothing compared to the pill; the pill is the greatest revolutionary. This can create a totally different world because fear can be dropped; now there is no need to be afraid. The fear of pregnancy has been the reason behind condemning sex. Now there is no need to condemn it at all, it can be accepted.

In the past, I understand; the fear was there. I can forgive those people in the past, because they were helpless. But now you cannot be forgiven if you teach your children to be separate and antagonize them against each other. There is no need. Now boys and girls can mix and meet and be together, and all fear about sex can be dropped.

And the beauty is that it is because of the fear and condemnation, because of the denial, that sex has become so important; otherwise it is not so important. Try to understand a simple psychological law: if you deny something too much, it becomes very important. The very denial makes it important. You become obsessed with it. Now, if boys and girls are kept apart for eighteen years, twenty years, they become obsessed with each other. They only think of the other, they cannot think of anything else. The mind becomes preoccupied. All those years of antisexual teachings make the mind preoccupied, and all kinds of perversions arise. People start living in fantasies, pornography arises, and this whole thing goes on because of the nonsense that you have created by condemning sex.

Now you want pornography to stop? It cannot stop. You are

creating the situation for it. If boys and girls could be together, who would bother to look at a nude picture?

Go and visit some aboriginal tribe of people who live naked, and show them your *Playboy* magazine and they will all laugh! I have lived with such people, and I have talked with them, and they all laugh. They cannot believe it: "What is this nonsense?" They live naked, so they know what a woman looks like and they know what a man looks like.

Pornography is created by your priests; they are the foundation of it, and then all kinds of perversions arise because when you cannot actually meet the other pole, for which the attraction is natural, you start fantasizing. Then a greater problem arises: years of fantasies and dreams, and then you meet a real woman and she falls very low in relation to your expectations—because of all those fantasies! You were only free to fantasize; now, no real woman is going to satisfy you. Because of your fantasies and dreams you have created such ideas about a woman, which no woman can fulfill. You have created such ideas about men, which no man can fulfill. Hence the frustration. Hence the bitterness that arises between couples. The man feels cheated: "This is not the woman I was hoping for." He was thinking, dreaming, and he was free to create whatever he wanted in his dream, and this woman looks very poor compared to his fantasy.

In your fantasy women don't perspire—or do they?—and they don't quarrel with you, they don't nag you. They are just golden, just sweet flowers, and they always remain young. They never become old, and they don't get grumpy. Because they are your creations, if you want them laughing, they laugh. Their bodies are made not of this world.

But when you meet a real woman she perspires, her breath smells, and sometimes it is natural to be grumpy. And she nags, and she fights, and she throws pillows and breaks things, and she won't allow you a thousand and one things. She starts curbing your freedom. Your fantasy women never curbed your freedom. Now this woman seems to be like a trap. And she is not as beautiful as you had been thinking; she is not a Cleopatra. She is an ordinary woman, just as you are an ordinary man. Neither you are fulfilling her desire nor she is fulfilling your desire. Nobody has the obligation to fulfill your fantasies! People are real people. And because these years of starvation have created a fantasy, it creates trouble for your future life.

You will have to drop your fantasies. You will have to learn to live with reality. You will have to learn to see the extraordinary in the ordinary, and that is a great art. A woman is not just her skin, not just her face, not just her body proportion. A woman is a soul! You have to be intimate with her, you have to get involved in her life, in her inner life. You have to merge and meet with her energies. People don't know how to meet and how to merge; they have never been taught. The art of love has not been taught to you, and everybody thinks that they know what love is. You don't know. You come only with the potential of love but not with the art of it.

You are born with a capacity to learn language, but you have to be taught the language itself. Exactly like this, you are born with the capacity to love, but you are not born with the art of love. That art of love has to be taught, has to be imbibed.

But just the opposite is happening: you have been taught the art of fear, not of love. You have been taught how to hate people. Christians have been taught to hate the Mohammedans, Mohammedans have been taught to hate the Jews, Indians have been taught to hate the Pakistanis. Hate has been taught in so many ways. The man has been taught to fear the woman, the woman has been taught to fear the man, and now suddenly one day you decide to get married—and you get married to your enemy! Then the whole turmoil starts; then life becomes just a nightmare.

If you are bored with your wife, it is because you don't know how to enter into her soul. You may be able to enter her body, but that is going to become boring very soon because that will be repetition. The body is a very superficial thing. You can make love to the body once, twice, thrice, and then you become perfectly acquainted with the body and its contours. Then there is nothing new. Then you start becoming interested in other women: you think they must have something different from your wife, at least behind the clothes you can imagine they must have something different. You can still fantasize about them.

Clothes have been invented to support your sexual desire. A naked woman leaves nothing to your fantasy. That's why naked women are not so attractive; neither are naked men. But when a woman or a man is hidden behind some clothes, they leave much to your fantasy. You can fantasize about what is behind the clothes, you can imagine again.

Now you cannot fantasize about your wife; that is the trouble. You can fantasize about your neighbor's wife, she looks attractive.

People feel bored with their wives and with their husbands, and the reason is that they have not been able to contact the other's real soul. They have been able to contact the body, but they have missed the contact that happens heart to heart, center to center, soul to soul. Once you know how to contact the other person soul to soul, when you have become soul mates, then there is no boredom at all. Then there is always something to discover in the other because each human being is an infinity, and there is no end to exploring.

That's why I say Tantra should become a required part of the education of all human beings. Each school, each college, each university, should teach Tantra. Tantra is the science of contacting souls, of going to the deepest core of the other. Only in a world which knows the art of Tantra will this boredom disappear; otherwise it cannot disappear. You can tolerate it, you can suffer it, you can be a martyr to it. That's how people have been in the past—martyrs. They say, "What to do? This is fate. Maybe next life we will choose some other woman or some other man, but in this life the opportunity is gone and nothing can be done. The children are there, and a thousand and one problems, the prestige, and the society, and the respectability . . ." So they have suffered and they have remained martyrs.

Now people are no longer ready to suffer, so they have moved to the other extreme. Now they are indulging in all kinds of sex and changing partners, but that too is not giving any contentment. Nobody is contented, because the basic thing is that unless you become capable of decoding the inner mystery of your woman or your man, you will sooner or later get fed up, bored. Then either you become a martyr—remain with it, suffer it, wait for death to deliver you—or you start indulging with other partners. But whatever you have done with this woman or with this man will be done with the next, and you will get fed up with the next, and with the next, and your whole life will be just changing partners. That is not going to satisfy you, either.

Unless you learn the secret art of Tantra. Tantra is one of the most important secrets ever discovered. But it is very delicate because it is the greatest art. To paint is easy, to create poetry is easy, but to create a communion with the energy of the other, a dancing communion, is the greatest and the most difficult art to learn.

Tantra can teach people how to love, how to love so deeply that love itself becomes your religion—your woman one day disappears and you find God there; your man one day disappears and you find God there; one day, in deep communion, in deep orgasmic experience, in that ecstasy for a moment you both disappear and there is only God and nothing else.

You have been taught down the ages to be against sex, and that has made you very sexual. Now this paradox has to be understood. If you want to understand, this paradox has to be understood very deeply, clearly: you have been made sexual by all the condemnation of sex.

I have heard about a visit of J. P. Morgan to the home of Dwight Morrow. The great American financier was noted, among other things, for a bulbous red nose of unsurpassed ugliness.

"Remember, Anne," Mrs. Morrow kept saying to her daughter, "you must not say one word about Mr. Morgan's red nose. You must not even look at it very much."

Anne promised, but when Morgan arrived, her mother watched and waited tensely. Anne was as good as gold, but Mrs. Morrow dared not relax. Turning to the financier with a gracious smile, she prepared to pour tea and said, "Mr. Morgan, will you have one or two lumps in your nose?"

That's what has happened to the whole of humanity: repressed sex has become an obsession.

People think I am teaching sexuality—I am teaching transcendence. The interest in sex is a pathological interest that has been created by repression. Once repression is taken away that interest will disappear. Then there is a natural feel, which is not obsessive, not pathological. Whatever is natural is good; this interest in sex is unnatural. And the problem is that this unnatural interest is being created by the priest, by the politician, by the so-called moralists. They are the culprits. They go on creating it, and they think they are helping humanity to go beyond their interest in sex. They are not! They are throwing humanity into this whole mess.

If you understand rightly, then you will be surprised by the experience that you will go through. Soon you will find that sex has become a natural phenomenon. And finally, as your meditations deepen, as you start meeting with each other's souls more and more, the body contact will become less and less. A moment comes when there is no need for sexuality to be there, it has taken a new turn. The energy has started moving upwards. It is the same energy; at the lowest rung it is sex, at the highest rung it is *samadhi*, it is superconsciousness.

Camel, Lion, and Child: The journey of becoming human

Man is not born perfect. He is born incomplete, he is born as a process. He is born on the way, as a pilgrim. That is his agony and his ecstasy, too; agony because he cannot rest, he has to go ahead, he has always to go ahead. He has to seek and search and explore. He has to become, because his being arises only through becoming. Becoming is his being. He can only be if he is on the move.

Evolution is intrinsic to man's nature, evolution is his very soul. And those who take themselves for granted remain unfulfilled. Those who think they are born complete remain unevolved. Then the seed remains the seed. It never becomes a tree and never knows the joys of spring and the sunshine and the rain, and the ecstasy of bursting into millions of flowers.

That explosion is the fulfillment, that explosion is what existence is all about—exploding into millions of flowers. When the potential becomes the actual, only then is man fulfilled. The human being is born as a potential; that is unique to humanity. All other animals are born complete, they are born as they are going to die. There is no evolution between their birth and their death. They move on the same plane, they never go through any transformation. No radical change in their life ever happens. They move horizontally, the vertical never penetrates them.

If the human being also moves horizontally, he will miss his beinghood, he will not become a soul. When the vertical penetrates you, you become a soul. Having a soul means the vertical has penetrated into the horizontal. Or, as an example, you can think of a caterpillar, the cocoon, and the butterfly.

Man is born as a larva. Unfortunately, many die also as larvae, very few become caterpillars. A larva is static, it knows no movement. It remains stuck at one space, at one place, at one stage. Very few people grow into caterpillars. The caterpillar starts moving;

dynamism enters. The larva is static, the caterpillar moves. With movement life is stirred. Again, many remain caterpillars: they go on moving horizontally, on the same plane, in one dimension. Rarely, a man like Buddha—or Rumi or Jesus or Kabir—takes the final quantum leap and becomes a butterfly. Then the vertical enters in.

The larva is static; the caterpillar moves, knows movement; the butterfly flies, knows heights, starts moving upward. The butterfly grows wings; those wings are the goal. Unless you grow wings and you become a winged phenomenon, you will not have a soul.

Truth is realized through three states: assimilation, independence, and creativity. Remember these three words, they are very seminal. Assimilation—that is the function of the larva. It simply assimilates food; it is getting ready to become a caterpillar. It is arranging, it is a reservoir. When the energy is ready it will become a caterpillar. Before the movement, you will need a great energy to move. The caterpillar is assimilation, complete; the work done.

Then the second thing starts: independence. The larva is dropped. Now there is no need to stay in one place. The time has come to explore, the time has come for the adventure. Real life starts with movement, independence. The larva remains dependent, a prisoner, in chains. The caterpillar has broken the chains, starts moving. The ice has melted, it is no longer frozen. The larva is a frozen state; the caterpillar is movement, riverlike.

Then comes the third stage, of creativity. Independence in itself does not mean much. Just by being independent you will not be fulfilled. It is good to be out of the prison, but for what? Independence for what? Freedom for what?

Remember, freedom has two aspects: first, freedom from, and second, freedom for. Many people attain only the first kind of freedom, freedom from—free from the parents, free from the Church, free from the organization; free from this and that, free from all kinds of prisons. But for what? Freedom from is a negative freedom. If you know only freedom from, you have not known real freedom; you have known only the negative aspect. The positive has to be known—freedom to create, freedom to be, freedom to express, to sing your song, to dance your dance. That is the third state: creativity.

Then the caterpillar becomes a winged phenomenon, a honey-taster, searches, discovers, explores, creates. Hence, the beauty of the butterfly. Only creative people are beautiful because only creative people know the splendor of life—they have eyes to see and ears to hear and hearts to feel. They are fully alive, they live at the maximum. They burn their torch from both ends. They live in intensity, they live in totality.

Or we can use the metaphors used by Friedrich Nietzsche. He says that man's life can be divided into three successive metamorphoses of the spirit. The first he calls the camel, the second he calls the lion, and the third he calls the child. Very pregnant metaphors—the camel, the lion, and the child.

Each human being has to assimilate the heritage of his society—his culture, his religion, his people. He has to assimilate all that the past makes available. He has to assimilate the past; this is what Nietzsche calls the camel stage. The camel has the power of storing up in his body enormous amounts of food and water for his arduous journey across the desert.

The situation of the human being is the same: you have to pass across a desert, you have to assimilate the whole past. And remember, just memorizing it is not going to help; it needs assimilation. Also remember that the person who memorizes the past memorizes only because he *cannot* assimilate. If you assimilate the past you are free from it. You can use it, but it cannot use you. You possess it, but it does not possess you.

When you have assimilated food you need not remember it. It does not exist separate from you: it has become your blood, your bone, your marrow; it has become you. The past has to be digested. Nothing is wrong with the past. It is your past. You need not begin from ABC, because if each individual had to begin from ABC, there would not be much evolution. That's why animals have not evolved. The dog is basically the same as it was millions of years ago. Only the human being is an evolving animal. From where does this evolution come? It comes because man is the only animal who can assimilate the past. Once the past is assimilated you are free from it. You can move in freedom and you can use your past.

You can stand on the shoulders of your fathers and forefathers and their fathers and their forefathers. Each generation goes on standing upon the previous generation's shoulders, hence the height that the human being achieves. Dogs cannot achieve that, wolves cannot achieve that; they depend on themselves. Their height is their height. In your height, Buddha is assimilated, Christ is assimilated, Patanjali, Moses, Lao Tzu are assimilated. The greater the assimilation, the higher you stand. You can look from the peak of a mountain, your vision is vast.

Assimilate more. There is no need to be confined by your own people. Assimilate the whole past of all the peoples of the earth; be a citizen of the planet Earth. There is no need to be confined by the Christian and the Hindu and the Mohammedan. Assimilate all! The Koran is yours, the Bible is yours, so is the Talmud, and so are the Vedas and the Tao Te Ching—all is yours. Assimilate all, and the more you assimilate, the higher will be the peak on which you can stand and look far away; distant lands and distant views become yours.

This Nietzsche calls the camel stage. But don't be stuck there. One has to move. The camel is the larva, the camel is a hoarder. If you are stuck at that stage and always remain a camel, then you will not know the beauties and the benedictions of life. Then you will never know the divine. You will remain stuck with the past.

The camel can assimilate the past but cannot use it. The time comes when the camel has to become the lion. Nietzsche says, "The lion proceeds to tear apart the huge monster known as *thou shalt not*." The lion in you roars against all authority.

The lion is a reaction, a rebellion against the camel. Now you begin to discover your own inner light as the ultimate source of all authentic values. You become aware of your primary obligation to your own inner creativity, to your innermost hidden potential.

A few remain stuck at the stage of the lion: they go on roaring and roaring and become exhausted in their roaring. It is good to become a lion, but one has still to take one more jump, and that jump is to become the child.

Now, each of you has been a child. But those who know, they say the first childhood is a false childhood. It is like the first teeth: they look like teeth, but ultimately they are of no use, they have to fall out. Then the real teeth are born. The first childhood is a false childhood; the second childhood is the real childhood. That second childhood is called the stage of the child, or the stage of the sage; it means the same. Unless you become utterly innocent, free from past, so free that you are not even against the past . . . Remember it, the person who is still against the past is not really free. He still has some grudges, some complaints, some wounds. The camel still haunts him; the shadow of the camel still follows him. The lion is there, but still afraid somehow of the camel, fearful that it may come back. When the fear of the camel is completely gone, the roaring of the lion stops. Then the song of the child is born.

The state of the camel is the state of assimilation. The camel does not know how to say no. Obedience, belief—these are the characteristics of the stage called the camel. Adam was in this state before he ate the fruit of the Tree of Knowledge, and each human being passes through this state.

This is a state that is premind and preself. There is no mind yet. The mind is growing but is not a complete phenomenon; it is very vague, ambiguous, dark, nebulous. The self is on the way, but still it is only on the way; there are no clear-cut definitions of it. The child does not know himself as separate yet. Adam, before he ate the fruit, was part of the divine. He was in the womb, he was obedient, a yea-sayer, but he was not independent. Independence enters only through the door of no; through the door of yes, only dependence. So in this stage of the camel, there is dependence, helplessness. The other is more important than your own being: God is more important, the father is more important, the mother is more important, society is more important. The priest is more important, the politician is more important. Except you, everybody is important; the other is important; you are still not there. It is a very unconscious state. The majority of people are stuck there; they remain camels. Almost 99 percent of people remain camels.

This is a very sad state of affairs, that 99 percent of human beings remain camels, larvae. That's why there is so much misery and no joy. You can go on searching for joy but you will not find it, because joy is not given to you from outside. Unless you become a child—unless the third stage is attained—unless you become a butterfly, you will not be able to know joy. Joy is not something given from outside; it is a vision that grows inside you. It is possible only in the third stage.

The first stage is of misery and the third stage is of bliss, and between the two is the state of the lion, which is sometimes miserable and sometimes blissful, sometimes painful and sometimes pleasurable.

At the stage of the camel you are parrots. You are just memories and nothing else. Your whole understanding consists of beliefs given to you by others. This is where you will find the Christians and the Mohammedans and the Hindus and the Jains and the Buddhists. Go into the churches and temples and mosques, and you will find great gatherings of camels. You will not find a single human being. They go on repeating, parrotlike. They are not yet out of unconsciousness, out of their sleep.

And remember, I am not saying that this stage is not necessary; it is, but once it is complete, one has to jump out of it. One is not here to remain a camel forever.

And don't be angry with your parents, or the teachers, or the priests, or the society, because they have to create a kind of obedience in you; only through obedience will you be able to assimilate. The father has to teach, the mother has to teach, and the child has to simply absorb. If doubt arises prematurely, the process of assimilation will be stopped.

Just think of a child in the mother's womb who becomes doubtful; he will die! He becomes doubtful about whether to partake of food from this woman or not, whether the food is really nourishing: "Who knows, it may be poisonous?" He doesn't know whether to sleep for twenty-four hours or not, because this is too much, sleeping continuously for twenty-four hours a day, for nine months. If the child becomes a little bit doubtful, in that very doubt the child will die.

Still, a day comes when doubt has to be imbibed, learned. Each thing has its own season. In the first stage everybody has to be a camel, yea-saying, believing whatever is given—assimilating, digesting. But this is only the beginning of the journey, this is not the end.

The second stage is difficult. The first stage the society gives you; that's why there are millions of camels and very few lions. The society leaves you when you have become a perfect camel. Beyond that, the society cannot do anything more for you. It is there that the work of the society—and the school, the college, the university—ends. It leaves you a perfect camel . . . with a certificate!

A lion you have to become on your own, remember it. If you don't decide to become a lion, you will never become a lion. That risk has to be taken by the individual. That is a gamble. That is very dangerous too, because by becoming a lion you will annoy all the camels around you. Camels are peace-loving animals; they are always ready to compromise. They don't want to be disturbed, they don't want any new thing to happen in the world, because all new things are a disturbance. They are against the revolutionaries and the rebellious; and not about great things, mind you, not about Socrates and Christ, who are bringing great revolutions. The camels are afraid of such small things that you will be continually surprised.

Lions are not welcome. The society creates every kind of difficulty for the lions. The camels are afraid of these people. They disturb their convenience, they disturb their sleep, they create worry. They create a desire in the camels to become lions—that is the real problem.

The first, the state of the camel, is given by the society. The second state has to be attained by the individual. In attaining it, you become an individual, you become unique. You are no longer a conformist; you are no longer part of a tradition. The cocoon is dropped: you become a caterpillar, you start moving.

The state of the lion has these characteristics: independence, no-saying, disobedience, rebellion against the other, against authority, against dogma, against scripture, against the Church, against the political power, against the state. The lion is against everything! He wants to shatter everything and create the whole world anew, closer to the heart's desire. He has great dreams and utopias in his mind. He looks mad to the camels, because the camels live in the past and the lion starts living in the future.

A great gap arises. The lion heralds the future, and the future can come only if the past is destroyed. The new can enter into existence only if the old ceases to exist and creates space for the new. The old has to die for the new to be. So there is a constant fight between the lion and the camel, and the camels are the majority. The lion happens once in a while, the lion is an exception, and the exception only proves the rule.

Disbelief is his characteristic, doubt is his characteristic. Adam eats the fruit of the Tree of Knowledge—mind is born, the self becomes a defined phenomenon. The camel is nonegoistic, the lion is very egoistic. The camel knows nothing of the ego, the lion only knows the ego. That's why you will always find that revolutionaries, rebellious people—poets, painters, musicians—are all very egoistic. They are bohemians. They live their life, they do their thing. They don't care a bit about others. Let the others go to hell! They are no longer a part of any structure, they become free from the structures. The process of movement, the lion's roar, is bound to be egoistic. They need a strong ego to go into this.

Each individual has to be taught the ego before he will be able to drop it. Each individual has to come to a very crystallized ego; only then is the dropping of any help, otherwise not.

The first state, the camel, is unconscious. The second state, the lion, is subconscious—a little higher than the unconscious. A few glimpses of the conscious have started coming in. The sun is rising, and a few rays are entering the dark room where you are asleep. The unconscious is no longer entirely unconscious. Something is stirred in the unconscious; it has become subconscious. But remember, the change is not as great from the camel to the lion as it is going to be from the lion to the child.

The change is a kind of inversion. The camel starts standing on its head and becomes the lion. The camel says yes, the lion says no. The camel obeys, the lion disobeys. The camel is positive, the lion is negative. It can be understood; the camel has been saying yes so much, he must have been denying the no. The no accumulates and a point comes where the no wants to take revenge on the yes. The denied part wants to take revenge. Then the whole wheel turns; the camel turns upside down and becomes the lion.

The difference between the camel and the lion is great, but they exist on the same plane. The cocoon is static at one place; the caterpillar starts moving, but on the same earth. Movement is born, but the plane is the same. The first thing is given by the society: your being a camel is a gift of the society. Your being a lion will be a gift that you give to yourself. Unless you love yourself you will not be able to do it. Unless you want to become an individual, unique in your own right, unless you take the risk of going against the current, you will not be able to become a lion.

But if you understand the mechanism, in the very heart of the camel the lion is created. Again and again, in your saying yes and denying no, the no goes on accumulating. And one day comes when one is fed up with saying yes; just for a change one wants to say no. One is fed up with the positive, the taste of it becomes monotonous; just for a change one wants to taste no.

That's how the camel, for the first time, starts having dreams of the lion. And once you have tasted the no—the doubt, the disbelief—you can never be a camel again, because the lionhood brings such liberty, such freedom.

The majority is stuck at the camel stage, and the minority is stuck at the lion stage. The majority means the masses and the minority means the intelligentsia. The artist, the poet, the painter, the musician, the thinker, the philosopher, the revolutionary—they are stuck at the second stage. They are far better off than the camels, but the journey is not yet complete. They have not come home. The third stage is the child.

Listen attentively: the first stage is given by the society, the second is given by the individual to himself. The third is possible only if the caterpillar catches a glimpse of a butterfly; otherwise, it is not possible. How will the caterpillar ever think that he can fly on his own, that he can become a winged thing? It is not possible! It is impossible to think of. It will be absurd, illogical. The caterpillar knows how to move, but the idea that he could fly is just absurd.

I have heard about butterflies trying to tell caterpillars that they can fly, and they object. The caterpillars say, "No. It may be possible for you, but it is not possible for us. You are a butterfly, we are only caterpillars! We only know how to crawl." And one who knows only how to crawl, how can he imagine flying? That is a different dimension, an altogether different dimension—the vertical dimension.

From the camel to the lion, it is evolution. From the lion to the child, it is revolution. The first stage, the camel, was dependence; the second stage was independence. But in innocence one comes to know that neither is there dependence nor is there independence. Existence is interdependence; all are dependent on each other. It is all one.

The sense of the whole is born: no I, no thou. No fixation on yes or no. No obsession either to say yes always, or to say no always. More fluidity, more spontaneity; neither obedience nor disobedience but spontaneity. Responsibility is born. One responds to existence; does not react out of the past, and does not react out of the future.

The camel lives in the past, the lion lives in the future.

The child lives in the present, here and now.

The camel is pre-mind, the lion is mind, the child is post-mind, or no-mind.

The camel is pre-self, the lion is self, the child is post-self, or no-self.

The child simply *is*—ineffable, indefinable, a mystery, a wonder.

The camel has memory, the lion has knowledge, and the child has wisdom. The camel is either Christian, Hindu, or Mohammedan, theist; the lion is atheist; and the child is religious—neither theist nor atheist, neither Hindu nor Mohammedan nor Christian nor communist—just a simple religiousness, the quality of love and innocence.

Vertical and Horizontal: The journey into the depths of now

The mind comes out of the past; consciousness is never out of the past—consciousness comes out of this moment. The mind is time, and consciousness is eternity.

The mind moves from one moment to another on a horizontal plane. It is like a railway train: many compartments joined together, past and future like a train; many compartments joined together on a horizontal plane. Consciousness is vertical; it doesn't come from the past, it doesn't go into the future. This moment it falls vertically in the depth or it rises vertically into the height.

This is the meaning of Christ on the cross, and Christians have missed the meaning completely. The cross is nothing but a representation, a symbol, of two lines meeting: the vertical and the horizontal. Christ's hands are spread on the horizontal. His whole being, except the hands, is on the vertical. What is the meaning? The meaning is: action is in time; being is beyond time. The hands symbolize action. Jesus is crucified with his hands on the horizontal, in time.

Action is in time. Thinking is an act: it is action of mind. That, too, is in time. It will be good to know that hands are the outermost part of the brain. They are one, the mind and the hand; the head is joined to the hands. Your head has two hemispheres: the right hemisphere is joined to the left hand, and the left hemisphere is joined to the right hand. Your hands are the reaches of the mind into the world, the reaches of the mind into matter, because mind is also a subtle form of matter.

All action, physical or mental, is in time.

Your being is vertical. It moves in depth; it moves in height, not sideways.

When you judge a thing, for example, you become more and more identified with the horizontal, because how will you judge? For judgment, the past will be needed. Can you judge something without bringing the past in? How will you judge? From where will you get the criteria?

You say a particular face is beautiful. How do you judge? Do you know what beauty is? How do you judge this face to be beautiful? You have known many faces; you have heard many people talking about beautiful faces. You have read about them in novels, you have seen them in the movies; you have accumulated a notion, in the past, of what beauty is. It is a vague notion, you cannot define it. If somebody insists, you will feel puzzled and confused. It is a very vague notion, like a cloud. Then you say, "This face is beautiful." How do you know? You are bringing your past experience in, comparing this face with that vague notion of beauty that you have accumulated through experience.

If you don't bring the past in, then a totally different quality of beauty will happen. It will not be your judgment; it will not come from your mind. It will not be imposed; it will not be an interpretation. It will simply be a participation with this face here and now, a deep participation with this mystery, with this person here and now. In that moment the person is neither beautiful nor ugly; all judgments have disappeared. An unknown mystery is there, unnamed, unjudged—and only in that unjudged moment does love flower.

Love is not possible with the mind. With the mind sex is possible; with the mind action is possible, and sexuality is an act. Love is not an act; it is a state of being, it is vertical. When you look at a person and participate with no judgment—of either beautiful or ugly, or of good and bad, sinner or saint—when you don't judge but simply look into their eyes with no judgment, suddenly a meeting is there, a merging of energies. This merging is beautiful. This beauty is totally different from all the beauties that you have known. You have known the beauty of the form; this is the beauty of the formless. You have known the beauty of the body; this is the beauty of the soul. You have known the beauty of the periphery; this is the beauty of the center. This is everlasting.

If this happens with a person, the same becomes more and more possible, by and by, with things, also. You look at a flower with no judgment, and suddenly the heart of the flower is open for you; there is an invitation. When you don't judge, there is an invitation. When you judge, the flower also closes because in the judgment is the enemy. In the judgment is the critic, not the lover. In the judgment there is logic, not love. In the judgment there is superficiality, not depth. The flower simply closes. And when I say it simply closes, it is not a metaphor, it happens exactly as I say it happens.

You go near a tree; you touch the tree. If you touch with judgment, the tree is not available there. If you touch it without any judgment, just feel it with no mind at all, embrace it and sit by the side of it—suddenly a very ordinary tree has become the Bodhi tree. Infinite compassion is flowing from the tree towards you. You will be enveloped. The tree will share many secrets with you.

This is how even rocks can be penetrated to their very heart. When a buddha touches a rock, it is no longer a rock. It is alive; it has a heart throbbing in it. When you judge, even if you touch a person, it is a rock, already dead. Your touch dulls everything, because the touch carries the judgment, it is the touch of an enemy, not a friend.

If this is so with ordinary things, how much more will it be so when you come across higher stages of being and consciousness?

The mind is always either in the past or in the future. It cannot be in the present, it is absolutely impossible for the mind to be in the present. When you are in the present, the mind is there no more because mind means thinking. How can you think in the present? You can think about the past; it has already become part of the memory, the mind can work it out. You can think about the future; it is not yet there, the mind can dream about it. Mind can do two things: either it can move into the past, where there is space enough to move—the vast space of the past, you can go on and on and on. Or the mind can move into the future—again a vast space, no end to it; you can imagine and imagine and dream. But how can mind function in the present? The present has no space for the mind to make any movement.

The present is just a dividing line, that's all. It has no space. It divides the past and the future; just a dividing line. You can *be* in the present, but you cannot think; for thinking, space is needed. Thoughts need space, they are just like things. Remember it. Thoughts are subtle things, they are material; thoughts are not spiritual, because the dimension of the spiritual starts only when there are no thoughts. Thoughts are material things, very subtle, and every material thing needs space. You cannot be thinking in the present; the moment you start thinking, it is already the past.

You see the sun is rising; you see and you say, "What a beautiful sunrise!" It is already the past. When the sun is rising, there is not even space enough to say, "How beautiful!" because when you posit these two words "How beautiful!" the experience has already become past, the mind already knows it in the memory. But exactly when the sun is rising, exactly when the sun is on the rise, how can you think? What can you think? You can *be* with the rising sun, but you cannot think. For *you* there is enough space, but not for thoughts.

A beautiful flower in the garden and you say, "A beautiful rose"; now you are not with this rose this moment; it is already a memory. When the flower is there and you are there, both present to each other, how can you think? What can you think? How is thinking possible? There is no space for it. The space is so narrow—in fact, there is no space at all—that you and the flower cannot even exist as two, because there is not enough space for two, only one can exist.

That's why in a deep presence you are the flower and the flower has become you. You are also a thought, the flower is also a thought in the mind. When there is no thinking, who is the flower and who is the one who is observing? The observer becomes the observed. Suddenly boundaries are lost. Suddenly you have penetrated, penetrated into the flower, and the flower has penetrated into you. Suddenly you are not two, one exists.

If you start thinking, you have become two again. If you don't think, where is the duality? When you exist with the flower, not thinking, it is a dialogue, not a duologue but a dialogue. When you exist with your lover it is a dialogue, not a duologue, because the two are not there. Sitting by the side of your lover, holding the hand of your beloved, you simply exist. You don't think of the days past, gone; you don't think of the future reaching, coming—you are here, now. And it is so beautiful to be here and now, and so intense; no thought can penetrate this intensity. And narrow is the gate, narrow is the gate of the present. Not even two can enter into it together, only one. In the present, thinking is not possible, dreaming is not possible, because dreaming is nothing but thinking in pictures. Both are things, both are material.

When you are in the present without thinking, you are for the first time spiritual. A new dimension opens, that dimension is awareness. Because you have not known that dimension, Heraclitus will say you are asleep, you are not aware. Awareness means to be in the moment so totally that there is no movement toward the past, no movement toward the future—all movement stops. That doesn't mean that you become static. A new movement starts, a movement in depth.

There are two types of movement. And that is the meaning of Jesus' cross: it shows two movements, a crossroads. One movement is linear: you move in a line, from one thing to another, from one thought to another, from one dream to another dream; from A you move to B, from B you move to C, from C you move to D. This way you move—in a line, horizontal. This is the movement of time; this is the movement of one who is fast asleep. You can go like a shuttle, back and forth, the line is there. You can come from B to A, or you can go from A to B, the line is there. There is another movement which is in a totally different dimension. That movement is not horizontal, it is vertical. You don't go from A to B, from B to C; you go from A to a deeper A: from A1 to A2, A3, A4, in depth or in height.

When thinking stops, the new movement starts. Now you fall into depth, in an abysslike phenomenon. People who are meditating deeply, they come to that point sooner or later; then they become afraid because they feel as if an abyss has opened—bottomless, you feel dizzy, you become afraid. You would like to cling to the old movement because it was known; this feels like death. That is the meaning of Jesus' cross: it is a death. Going from the horizontal to the vertical is death; that is the real death. But it is death only from one side; on the other side it is resurrection. It is dying in order to be born; it is dying from one dimension to be born in another dimension. Horizontal you are Jesus, vertical you become Christ.

If you move from one thought to another, you remain in the world of time. If you move into the moment, not into thought, you move into eternity. You are not static—nothing is static in this world, nothing can be static—but this is a new movement, a movement without motivation.

Remember these words: On the horizontal line you move because of motivation. You have to achieve something—money, prestige, power, or God, but you have to achieve something; a motivation is there. A motivated movement means sleep.

An unmotivated movement means awareness; you move because to move is sheer joy, you move because movement is life, you move because life is energy and energy is movement. You move because energy is delight, not for anything else. There is no goal to it, you are not after some achievement. In fact you are not going anywhere, you are not going at all; you are simply delighting in the energy. There is no goal outside the movement; movement has its own intrinsic value, no extrinsic value. A Buddha also lives, a Heraclitus lives, I am here living, breathing—but a different type of movement—unmotivated.

Somebody was asking me a few days ago, "Why do you help people in meditation?"

I told him, "This is my delight. There is no why to it, I simply enjoy." Just like a person enjoys planting seeds in the garden, waiting for the flowers, when you flower, I enjoy. It is a gardening. When somebody flowers, it is a sheer delight. And I share. There is no goal to it. If you fail, I am not going to be frustrated. If you don't flower, that too is okay, because flowering cannot be forced. You cannot open a bud forcibly—you can, but then you kill it. It may look like a flowering; it is not a flowering.

The whole world moves, existence moves, into eternity; mind moves in time. Existence is moving into the depth and the height, and mind moves backwards and forwards. Mind moves horizontally: that is sleep. If you can move vertically, that is awareness.

Be in the moment. Bring your total being into the moment. Don't allow the past to interfere, and don't allow the future to come in. The past is no more, it is dead. And as Jesus says, "Let the dead bury their dead." The past is no more! Why are you worried about it? Why do you go on chewing it again and again and again? Are you mad? It is no more; it is just in your mind, it is just a memory. The future is not yet. What are you doing thinking about the future? That which is not yet, how can you think about it? What can you plan about it? Whatever you do about it is not going to happen, and then you will be frustrated, because the whole has its own plan. Why do you try to have your own plans against it?

Existence has its own plans, it is wiser than you; the whole has to be wiser than the part. Why are you pretending to be the whole? The whole has its own destiny, its own fulfillment. Why do you bother about it? And whatever you do will be a sin because you will be missing the moment, this moment. And if it becomes a habit—as it becomes; if you start missing, it becomes a habitual form—then when the future has come again you will be missing it because it will not be a future when it comes, it will be a present. Yesterday you were thinking about today because then it was tomorrow; now it is today and you are thinking about tomorrow, and when tomorrow comes it will become today—because anything that exists here and now, it cannot exist otherwise. And if you have a fixed mode of functioning, such that your mind always looks at tomorrow, then when will you live? Tomorrow never comes. Then you will go on missing, and this is sin. This is the meaning of the Hebrew root of "to sin." The moment the future enters, time enters. You have sinned against existence, you have missed. And this has become a fixed pattern: like a robot, you go on missing.

Learn a new mode of movement, so that you can move in eternity, not in time. Time is the world and eternity is the divine; horizontal is the mind, vertical is consciousness. They meet at a point certain—that is where Jesus is crucified. Both meet, the horizontal and the vertical, at a point, and that point is here and now.

From here and now you can go on two journeys: one journey in the world, in the future; the other journey into pure consciousness, into depth. Become more and more aware, become more and more alert and sensitive to the present.

How is it possible?—because you are so fast asleep that you can make that sensitivity to the present a dream, also. You can make that itself a thinking object, a thinking process. You can become so tense about it that just because of your tension you cannot be in the present. If you think too much about how to be in the present, this thinking won't help. If you sometimes move into the past, you will feel guilty—and you will—it has been such a long habit. Sometimes you will start thinking about the future—immediately you will feel guilty that you have committed a sin again.

Don't become guilty; understand the sin, but don't become guilty—and this is very, very delicate. If you become guilty you have missed the whole thing. Now, in a new way, the old pattern starts again: now you feel guilty because you have missed the present. Now you are thinking about the past, because *that* present is no longer present; it is past and you are feeling guilty about it—you are still missing!

So remember one thing: whenever you notice that you have gone to the past or into the future, don't create a problem out of it! Simply come to the present, not creating any problem. It's okay! Simply bring back your awareness. You will miss millions of times; it is not going to happen right now, immediately. It *can* happen, but it cannot happen because of your effort. It is such a long, long, fixed mode of behavior that you cannot change it right now. But not to worry, existence is not in a hurry; eternity can wait eternally. Don't create a tension about it.

Whenever you feel you have missed, come back, that's all. Don't feel guilty; that's a trick of the mind, now it is again playing a game. Don't repent: "I again forgot!" Just when you think of it, come back to whatever you are doing—taking your bath, come back; eating your food, come back; going for a walk, come back. The moment you feel you are not here and now, come back simply, innocently. Don't create guilt. If you become guilty, then you miss the point.

There is "sin" but there is no guilt, but that is difficult for you; if you feel there is something wrong, you become immediately guilty. The mind is very cunning. If you start feeling guilty the game has started again; it is being played on new ground but the game is old. People come to me, they say, "We go on forgetting." They are so sad when they say it: "We go on forgetting. We try, but we remember only for a few seconds. We remain alert, self-remembering, then again it is lost—what to do?"

Nothing can be done. It is not a question of doing at all. What can you do? The only thing that can be done is not to create guilt. Simply come back.

The more you come back—simply, remember, not with a very serious face, not with much effort but simply, innocently, not creating a problem out of it, because eternity has no problems. All problems exist on the horizontal plane; this problem will also exist on the horizontal plane. The vertical plane knows no problems, it is sheer delight; without any anxiety, without any anguish, without any worry, any guilt, nothing. Be simple and come back.

You will miss many times, that can be taken for granted. But don't worry about it, that is how it is. You will miss many times, but that is not the point. Don't pay much attention to the fact that you have missed many times, pay much attention to the fact that you have regained many times. Remember this. The emphasis should not be that you missed many times, it should be that you regained remembrance many times. Feel happy about it. That you miss sometimes, of course, is as it should be. You are human, you have lived on the horizontal plane for many lives, so it is natural. The beauty is that many times you came back. You have done the impossible; feel happy about it!

In twenty-four hours, twenty-four thousand times you will miss, but twenty-four thousand times you will regain! Now a new mode will start functioning. So many times you come back home, now a new dimension is breaking in, by and by. More and more you will be able to stay in awareness, less and less you will go back and forth. The span of going back and forth will be smaller and smaller. Less and less you will forget, more and more you will remember—you are entering the vertical. Suddenly one day, the horizontal disappears. An intensity comes to awareness and the horizontal disappears.

That is the meaning behind Shankara, Vedanta, and the Hindus calling this world illusory—because when awareness becomes perfect, this world, this world that you have created out of your mind, simply disappears. Another world is revealed to you.

AFTERWORD

The word "understand" is beautiful. When you are in meditation everything "stands under" you, you are far above it. That's the meaning of understanding. Everything is there far below you, so you can see . . . you have a bird's-eye view. You can see the whole from your altitude. Intellect cannot see it; it is on the same plane. Understanding happens only when the problem is on one plane and you are on a higher plane. If you are functioning on the same plane as the problem, understanding is not possible. You will only misunderstand. And that is one of the greatest problems to be encountered by every seeker.

Jesus says again and again to his disciples, "If you have ears, hear; if you have eyes, see." He was not talking to blind or deaf people, he was just talking to people like you. But why does he go on insisting?—for the simple reason that hearing is not listening, and seeing is not true seeing. You see one thing and you understand something else. Your mind immediately distorts it. Your mind is upside down, it makes a mess of everything. It is in confusion, and you look at things through that confusion, so the whole world looks confused.

Old Nugent loved his cat, Tommy, so much that he tried to teach it to talk.

"If I can get Tommy to converse with me," he reasoned, "I won't have to bother with ordinary humans at all."

First he tried a diet of canned salmon, then one of canaries. Tommy liked both, but he didn't learn to talk. Then one day Nugent had two extremely talkative parrots cooked in butter and served to Tommy with asparagus and french fries. Tommy licked the plate clean and then—wonder of wonders—suddenly turned to his master and shouted, "Look out!"

Nugent didn't move. The ceiling caved in and buried the old man under a mass of debris. Tommy shook his head and said, "Eight years he spends getting me to talk, and then the dummy doesn't listen!"

People have traveled thousands of miles to listen to a master and then ". . . the dummy doesn't listen." The mind cannot listen, it is impossible for the mind; it is not in a state of receptivity. The mind is aggressive, it jumps to conclusions so fast, so quickly that it misses the whole point. In fact, it has already concluded, it is simply waiting for its conclusion to be proved right.

Please don't try to understand; rather, try to meditate. Dance, sing, meditate, let the mind settle a little bit. Let the stream of the mind, which is full of dead leaves and dirt, settle a little. Let it become clean and clear, transparently clear; only then will you be able to understand what I am saying. Then it is so simple. I am not talking very complicated philosophy—it is not philosophy at all—I am simply indicating toward certain truths that I have experienced and you can experience any moment you decide to. But it has to be a journey.

And your totality is involved. Meditation is not of the body, not of the mind, not of the soul. Meditation simply means your body, your mind, your soul, all functioning in such a harmony, in such wholeness, humming so beautifully . . . that they are in a melody, they are one. Your whole being—body, mind, soul—is involved in meditation.

That's why my effort is to start every meditation with the body. That is something new. In the ancient days, people tried to start meditation directly in your innermost core. That is a difficult process. You don't know anything about your inner center; how can you start your journey from a place where you have never been? You can start your journey only where you already are. You are in the body; hence, my emphasis is on dancing, singing, breathing, so that you can start from the body. When the body starts becoming meditative. . . . And don't be puzzled by my use of the word "meditative" for the body. Yes, the body becomes meditative. When it is in a deep dance, when it is functioning perfectly, undividedly, as a whole, it has a meditative quality about it—a certain grace, a beauty.

Then move inward, then start watching the mind. Then the mind starts settling down. And when the mind has also settled, has become one with the body, then turn toward the center—a 180-degree turn—and a great peace will descend on you. It will pulsate from your soul to the body, from the body to the soul. In that pulsation you will be one.

So don't ask what part of oneself is involved in the understanding. Your totality is involved. And only when your totality is involved, there is understanding. Your body knows about it, your mind knows about it, your soul knows about it. Then you start functioning in unison, in unity.

Otherwise, the body says one thing, the mind says another, and the soul goes on in its own way, and you are always moving in different directions simultaneously. Your body is hungry, your mind is full of lust, and you are trying to be meditative!

That's why I am not in favor of fasting unless it is done purely for health purposes, as a diet for reducing weight, or maybe once in a while just for purification so the whole stomach is left alone for a day to rest, so the whole digestive system can sometimes get a holiday. Otherwise, it is continuously working and working and working—it too gets tired.

Now scientists say that even machines get tired. They call it metal fatigue, just like mental fatigue. Even metal needs rest, and your stomach is not made of metal, remember. It is made of very fragile material. It works for your whole life, so it is good sometimes to give it a holiday. Even God had to rest for a day—after six days' work he rested for one day. Even God gets tired.

So sometimes, just out of kindness to the poor stomach, who works for you continuously, fasting is okay. But I don't suggest that fasting is going to be helpful in meditation. When you are hungry, your body wants you to go to the fridge.

I am against repressing your sexuality, because if you repress sex, whenever you try to sit silently your mind will start fantasizing about sex. When you are occupied with other things the mind goes on fantasizing like an undercurrent, but when you are not doing anything it comes into the light. It starts demanding, it creates beautiful fantasies that you are surrounded by alluring men or women. How can you meditate?

In fact, the old traditions have created all kinds of barriers to meditation, and then they say, "Meditation is very difficult." Meditation is not difficult; meditation is a simple process, a natural process. But if you create unnecessary hindrances, then you make it something like a hurdle race. You create barriers, you put rocks in the way . . . you hang rocks around your neck, or you keep yourself chained, imprisoned, locked up from within with the key thrown out. Then of course it becomes more and more difficult, more and more impossible.

My effort is to make meditation a natural phenomenon. Give to the body what is the body's need, and give to the mind what is the mind's need. And then you will be surprised, they become very friendly. When you tell the body, "Now for one hour allow me to sit silently," the body says, "Okay. You have been doing so much for me, you have been so respectful to me, I can do at least this much for you." And when you say to the mind, "Please, keep yourself silent for a few minutes. Let me have a little rest," the mind will understand you. If you have not been repressing—if you have honored the mind, respected the mind, if you have not condemned it—then the mind will also become silent.

I am saying this from my own experience. Respect the body, respect the mind, so that they respect you. Create a friendliness. They are yours; don't be antagonistic. All the old traditions teach you to be antagonistic to the body and the mind; they create enmity, and through enmity you cannot move into meditation. Then the mind will disturb you more when you are meditating than at any other time. Then the body will become restless—more in meditation than at any other time. It will take revenge, it won't allow you to sit silently. It will create so many problems for you.

If you have tried to sit silently for a few minutes, you will know. Imaginary things will start happening. You will think that some ant is creeping on your leg, and when you look there is no ant. Strange! When you were sitting with closed eyes you felt absolutely that it was there, creeping, crawling, coming, and when you open your eyes there is no ant, nothing. It was just the body playing tricks with you. You have been playing tricks with the body, you have been deceiving the body in many ways, so now the body is deceiving you. When the body wants to go to sleep you force it to sit in a movie theater—the body says, "Okay. When the right opportunity arises I will see to it!" So when you sit in meditation the body starts creating problems for you. Suddenly you start feeling your back needs scratching . . . and you are surprised, because it never happens ordinarily.

One woman brought me a plastic hand with a battery attached to it, to scratch your back. I asked her, "Why have you brought this to me?"

She said, "You must be sitting in meditation. . . . Whenever I sit in meditation the only problem is that my back starts to itch. I feel so much like I have to scratch it, and I cannot reach it. So I have purchased this mechanical hand. This is very handy! You just switch it on and it can scratch anywhere."

I said, "I never sit in meditation. I don't need to sit because whatever I am doing, I am in meditation. If my back needs scratching I will scratch it meditatively."

Just take care of the body and the body will repay you tremendously. Take care of your mind and the mind will be helpful. Create a friendship with the body and mind, and meditation comes easily. Rather than trying to understand, because understanding is not possible before meditation, only misunderstanding.

There are not many hindrances to understanding, but only few. One is a repressed mind, because whatever you have repressed, whenever you will sit silently to meditate, that repressed idea, the repressed energy will be the first to overflow you and your mind. If it is sex, meditation will be forgotten and you will be having a pornographic session.

So first thing is: drop repressions—which is very simple because they are not natural, they have been told to you—that sex is sin. It is not. It is nature, and if nature is sin, then I can't think what can be virtue.

In fact, going against nature is sin. Just a simple understanding that whatever you are, existence has made you this way. You have to accept yourself in totality. This acceptance will remove the hindrance that can come from repression.

The second thing that comes as a hindrance is the ideas that have been impressed on your mind about God. The moment you use the word "meditation," immediately a Christian asks, "On what?" and a Hindu asks, "On what?" You think meditation needs an object because all these religions have been teaching just sheer nonsense. Meditation simply means that there are no objects in the mind and you are simply left alone with your consciousness, a mirror reflecting nothing. So if you are a Hindu you must be carrying in the unconscious some idea of God, Krishna, Rama, or some other idea, and the moment you close your eyes, "meditation" means to meditate *upon* something. Immediately you start meditating on Krishna or Christ and you have missed. Those Krishnas and those Christs are hindrances.

So you have to remember that meditation is not focusing your mind on something, it is emptying your mind of everything—your gods included—and coming to a state where you can say that both your hands are full of nothingness. That flowering of nothingness is the highest experience of life.

The third thing that can be a hindrance is to think in terms of meditation as if it is something you have to do in the morning for twenty minutes, or half an hour in the afternoon or in the night—just a small fraction of time and the remaining time you just remain the way you are. That's what all the religions are doing. One hour in church, an hour of prayer, an hour of meditation is enough.

But with one hour of meditation and twenty-three hours of non-meditation you cannot enter into a meditative consciousness. What you gain in one hour is wasted in twenty-three hours, and again you start from scratch. Every day you will do it, and you will remain the same.

So to me, meditation has to be something more like breathing. Not that you sit one hour, I'm not against sitting. What I am saying is that meditation should be something that goes with you the whole day just like a shadow, a peace, a silence, a relaxedness. Working, you are totally into it—so totally that there is no energy left for the mind to spin thoughts. And you will be surprised that your work, whatever it is, digging the ground or carrying the water from the well, or anything, has turned into a meditation.

Slowly, each act of your life can turn into a meditative act. Then there is a possibility to attain enlightenment. Then you can sit also, because that too is an act, but you are not specifically identifying sitting with meditation; just that sitting, too, is a part of your life. Walking you meditate, working you meditate, sometimes sitting silently you meditate, sometimes lying on your bed you meditate—meditation becomes your constant companion.

And this meditation that can become a constant companion is a very simple thing, I call it witnessing.

Just go on witnessing whatever is happening. Walking you witness, sitting you witness, eating you witness yourself eating, and you will be surprised that the more you witness things the better you can do them because you are nontense; their quality changes.

You will also note that the more meditative you become, every gesture of yours becomes soft, nonviolent, has a grace in it. And not only you will notice it, others will start noticing it. Even those who have nothing to do with meditation, who have never heard even the name meditation, will see that something has changed. The way you walk, the way you talk, there is a certain grace and a certain silence surrounding you and a certain peace. People will want to be with you because you will become a nourishment.

You must have known there are people in your life who are avoided because to be with them feels as if they are sucking you, as if they are pulling your energy and leaving you empty. And after they have left, you feel weak, you feel robbed.

Something just the opposite happens with the meditator. Being with the meditator you will feel nourished. You would like to meet the person once in a while, just to be with him or her. Not only will you start feeling changes, others will start feeling changes. All that is to be remembered is a simple word: witnessing.

About the Author

The Osho teachings defy categorization, covering everything from the individual quest for meaning to the most urgent social and political issues facing society today. His books are not written but are transcribed from audio and video recordings of extemporaneous talks given to international audiences over a period of thirty-five years. Osho has been described by the *Sunday Times* in London as one of the "1000 Makers of the 20th Century" and by American author Tom Robbins as "the most dangerous man since Jesus Christ."

About his own work Osho has said that he is helping to create the conditions for the birth of a new kind of human being. He has often characterized this new human being as "Zorba the Buddha"—capable of enjoying both the earthy pleasures of a Zorba the Greek and the silent serenity of a Gautam Buddha. Running like a thread through all aspects of Osho's work is a vision that encompasses both the timeless wisdom of the East and the highest potential of Western science and technology.

Osho is also known for his revolutionary contribution to the science of inner transformation, with an approach to meditation that acknowledges the accelerated pace of contemporary life. The unique "Osho Active Meditations" are designed to first release the accumulated stresses of body and mind, so that it is easier to experience the thought-free and relaxed state of meditation.

OSHO International Meditation Resort

The Osho International Meditation Resort is a place where people can have a direct personal experience of a new way of living with more alertness, relaxation, and fun. Located about 100 miles southeast of Mumbai in Pune, India, the resort offers a variety of programs to thousands of people who visit each year from more than 100 countries around the world.

Originally developed as a summer retreat for Maharajas and wealthy British colonialists, Pune is now a thriving modern city that is home to a number of universities and high-tech industries. The Meditation Resort spreads over forty acres in a tree-lined suburb known as Koregaon Park. The resort campus provides accommodation for a limited number of guests, and there is a plentiful variety of nearby hotels and private apartments available for stays of a few days up to several months.

Resort programs are all based in the Osho vision of a qualitatively new kind of human being who is able both to participate creatively in everyday life and to relax into silence and meditation. Most programs take place in modern, air-conditioned facilities and include a variety of individual sessions, courses, and workshops covering everything from creative arts to holistic health treatments, personal transformation and therapy, esoteric sciences, the "Zen" approach to sports and recreation, relationship issues, and significant life transitions for men and women. Individual sessions and group workshops are offered throughout the year, alongside a full daily schedule of meditations.

Outdoor cafés and restaurants within the resort grounds serve both traditional Indian fare and a choice of international dishes, all made with organically grown vegetables from the commune's own farm. The campus has its own private supply of safe, filtered water.

Visit www.osho.com/resort for more information, including travel tips, course schedules, and guest house bookings.

For more information

about Osho and his work, see:

www.osho.com

A comprehensive Web site in several languages that includes an on-line tour of the Meditation Resort and a calendar of its course offerings, a catalog of books and tapes, a list of Osho information centers worldwide, and selections from Osho's talks.

Or contact:

Osho International
New York
e-mail: *oshointernational@oshointernational.com*